THE HISTORY OF SRI LANKA

THE HISTORY OF SRI LANKA

Patrick Peebles

The Greenwood Histories of the Modern Nations
Frank W. Thackeray and John E. Findling, Series Editors

Greenwood Press
Westport, Connecticut • London

Library of Congress Cataloging-in-Publication Data

Peebles, Patrick.
The history of Sri Lanka / Patrick Peebles.
p. cm.—(Greenwood histories of the modern nations, ISSN 1096–2905)
Includes bibliographical references and index.
ISBN 0–313–33205–3 (alk. paper)
1. Sri Lanka—History. I. Title. II. Series.
DS489.5.P44 2006
954.93—dc22 2006012034

British Library Cataloguing in Publication Data is available.

Library of Congress Catalog Card Number: 2006012034
ISBN: 0–313–33205–3
ISSN: 1096–2905

First published in 2006

Greenwood Press, 88 Post Road West, Westport, CT 06881
An imprint of Greenwood Publishing Group, Inc.
www.greenwood.com

Printed in the United States of America

The paper used in this book complies with the Permanent Paper Standard issued by the National Information Standards Organization (Z39.48–1984).

10 9 8 7 6 5 4 3 2 1

For Mary

Contents

Maps

Series Foreword

The *Greenwood Histories of the Modern Nations* series is intended to provide students and interested laypeople with up-to-date, concise, and analytical histories of many of the nations of the contemporary world. Not since the 1960s has there been a systematic attempt to publish a series of national histories, and, as editors, we believe that this series will prove to be a valuable contribution to our understanding of other countries in our increasingly interdependent world.

Over thirty years ago, at the end of the 1960s, the Cold War was an accepted reality of global politics, the process of decolonization was still in progress, the idea of a unified Europe with a single currency was unheard of, the United States was mired in a war in Vietnam, and the economic boom of Asia was still years in the future. Richard Nixon was president of the United States, Mao Tse-tung (not yet Mao Zedong) ruled China, Leonid Brezhnev guided the Soviet Union, and Harold Wilson was prime minister of the United Kingdom. Authoritarian dictators still ruled most of Latin America, the Middle East was reeling in the wake of the Six-Day War, and Shah Reza Pahlavi was at the height of his power in Iran. Clearly, the past 30 years have been witness to a great deal of historical change, and it is to this change that this series is primarily addressed.

With the help of a distinguished advisory board, we have selected nations whose political, economic, and social affairs mark them as among the most important in the waning years of the twentieth century, and for each nation we have found an author who is recognized as a specialist in the history of that nation. These authors have worked most cooperatively with us and with Greenwood Press to produce volumes that reflect current research on their nations and that are interesting and informative to their prospective readers.

The importance of a series such as this cannot be underestimated. As a superpower whose influence is felt all over the world, the United States can claim a "special" relationship with almost every other nation. Yet many Americans know very little about the histories of the nations with which the United States relates. How did they get to be the way they are? What kind of political systems have evolved there? What kind of influence do they have in their own region? What are the dominant political, religious, and cultural forces that move their leaders? These and many other questions are answered in the volumes of this series.

The authors who have contributed to this series have written comprehensive histories of their nations, dating back to prehistoric times in some cases. Each of them, however, has devoted a significant portion of the book to events of the last thirty years, because the modern era has contributed the most to contemporary issues that have an impact on U.S. policy. Authors have made an effort to be as up-to-date as possible so that readers can benefit from the most recent scholarship and a narrative that includes very recent events.

In addition to the historical narrative, each volume in this series contains an introductory overview of the country's geography, political institutions, economic structure, and cultural attributes. This is designed to give readers a picture of the nation as it exists in the contemporary world. Each volume also contains additional chapters that add interesting and useful detail to the historical narrative. One chapter is a thorough chronology of important historical events, making it easy for readers to follow the flow of a particular nation's history. Another chapter features biographical sketches of the nation's most important figures in order to humanize some of the individuals who have contributed to the historical development of their nation. Each volume also contains a comprehensive bibliography, so that those readers whose interest has been sparked may find out more about the nation and its history. Finally, there is a carefully prepared topic and person index.

Readers of these volumes will find them fascinating to read and useful in understanding the contemporary world and the nations that comprise it. As series editors, it is our hope that this series will contribute to a heightened sense of global understanding as we embark on a new century.

Frank W. Thackeray and John E. Findling
Indiana University Southeast

Preface

Sri Lanka has received global attention in recent years for its civil war, program of economic liberalization, and the tsunami that devastated most of its coastline on December 26, 2004. It has a long and brilliant history, however, and these dramatic recent events should be understood in that context. History, however, has been a victim of the conflict between Sinhalese and Tamil Lankans that led to the outbreak of civil war in 1983. Both Sinhalese-Buddhist nationalists and Tamil separatists have constructed pasts for the island that support their vision of the future. One invents an unbroken island-wide Sinhalese-Buddhist history from the earliest known period; the other imagines that the presence of Tamil rulers in part of the island can be equated to a Tamil homeland. Both of these are distortions of what we know about the island's past. They demonstrate how important history is to understanding Sri Lanka today.

I have written what I believe to be a synthesis of the best available scholarship on the history of the island. I have attempted to describe the events in their own time and to avoid shaping the narrative to fit a particular view of the origins of today's ethnic relations. As one Lankan scholar said to me, this is the history of all Lankans, and there is much of which all Lankans have a right to be justly proud. There are also some events that should dismay all of us. In general I have tried to write a book that will serve as a useful introduction to the island's history and also stimulate those who already know much of what I have written. The space limitations have required me to omit much. I have tried to remove as much of my own biases as possible, but it is impossible to completely suppress opinions that have formed over more than 40 years of study of the island, beginning as a Peace Corps volunteer in 1962.

The scholarship on the history of Sri Lanka is uneven; some of it compares with the best historical writing anywhere, but large gaps exist. There simply have not been enough historians doing research on the subject, and some have been constrained by contemporary events. Much fine scholarship has been carried out in disciplines other than history; I have not been able to keep up with all of this, and I regret the omissions.

Without footnotes, the people to whom I am most indebted for their ideas and information are not given proper credit. The most important books are listed in the bibliography, but I would like to single out particularly the following past and present scholars: T. B. Abeyasinghe, S. Arasaratnam, P. Athukorale, S. Bandaranayake, T. Barron, A. Blackburn, J. Brow, R.A.E. Coningham, Chandra R. de Silva, Colvin R. de Silva, K. M. de Silva, S. U. Deraniyagala, Y. Gooneratne, H.A.I. Goonetileke, R.A.L.H. Goonawardana, D. Hellman-Rajanayagam, K. Indrapala, K. Jayawardena, A. P. Kannangara, W. D. Lakshman, K. Malalgoda, J. Manor, G. C. Mendis, E. Meyer, M. Moore, B. Morrison, G. Obeyesekere, R. Obeyesekere, B. Pfaffenberger, U. Phadnis, R. Pieris, J. M. Richardson, M. W. Roberts, J. D. Rogers, B. F. Ryan, V. Samaraweera, H. L. Seneviratne, W. I. Siriweera, C. G. Uragoda, J. Walters, L. A. Wickremeratne, A. J. Wilson, D. Winslow, W. H. Wiggins, and, of course, Robert Knox.

I would like to thank the people who have made it possible for me to share my fascination with Sri Lanka with students. Greenwood Press and particularly Steven Vetrano have been extraordinarily patient. Kristen Mallard skillfully drew the maps. My college (Deans James Durig, Bruce Bubacz, and Charles Wurrey) and department (Chair Louis Potts) have been very supportive. I have received a Faculty Research Grant from the University of Missouri-Kansas City and a research grant from the South Asia Center, University of Chicago. I have been helped immensely by the staffs of the British Library, University of California Memorial Library, University of Chicago Regenstein Library, and UMKC Nichols Library.

Acronyms

AMP	Accelerated Mahaweli Programme
BC Pact	Bandaranaike-Chelvanayakam Pact
B.C.E.	Before Common Era
BLP	Bolshevik Leninist Party
BTS	Buddhist Theosophical Society
CCS	Ceylon Civil Service
CIC	Ceylon Indian Congress
CNA	Ceylon National Association
CNC	Ceylon National Congress
CP	Communist Party of Sri Lanka
CRL	Ceylon Reform League
CWC	Ceylon Workers Congress
CWE	Cooperative Wholesale Establishment
DPLF	Democratic People's Liberation Front

DUNF	Democratic United National Front
EBP	Eksath Bhikkhu Peramuna (Monks' United Front)
EDB	Export Development Board
EIC	English East India Company
ENDLF	Eelam National Democratic Liberation Front
EPDP	Eelam People's Democratic Party
EPRLF	Eelam People's Revolutionary Liberation Front
EROS	Eelam Revolutionary Organizers [also incorrectly called Eelam Revolutionary Organisation of Students]
FTZ	Free Trade Zone
GA	Government Agent
GDP	Gross Domestic Product
HDI	Human Development Index
ICRC	International Committee of the Red Cross
IPKF	Indian Peace Keeping Force
ITAK	Illankai Tamil Arasu Kadchi
JHU	Jathika Hela Urumaya (National Heritage Party)
JSS	Jatika Sevaka Sangamaya
JVP	Janatha Vimukthi Peramuna (People's Liberation Front)
LSSP	Lanka Sama Samaja Paksha
MFA	Multi-Fibre Arrangement
MLC	Member of Legislative Council
MOU	Memorandum of Understanding
MP	Member of Parliament
NAM	Non-Aligned Movement
NLSSP	Nava Lanka Sama Samaja Party (New Lanka Equal Society Party)
NSA	National State Assembly
PA	People's Alliance

PC	Provincial Council
PPC	Political Parties Conference
PQLI	Physical Quality of Life Index
PROTEG	Protection of Tamils from Genocide
PTA	Prevention of Terrorism Act
P-TOMS	post-Tsunami Operational Management Structure
RAW	Research and Analysis Wing (India)
SC Pact	Senanayake-Chelvanayakam Pact
SCOPP	Secretariat for Coordinating the Peace Process
SLFP	Sri Lanka Freedom Party (Sri Lanka Nidahas Pakshaya)
SLMC	Sri Lanka Muslim Congress
SLMM	Sri Lanka Monitoring Mission
STF	Special Task Force
TELO	Tamil Eelam Liberation Organization
TNA	Tamil National Alliance
TNT	Tamil New Tigers
TRO	Tamil Rehabilitation Organization
TUF	Tamil United Front
TULF	Tamil United Liberation Front
UF	United Front
ULF	United Left Front
UN	United Nations
UNF	United National Front
UNICEF	United Nations International Children's Emergency Fund
UNP	United National Party (Eksath Jathika Pakshaya)
VOC	Dutch East India Company (Verreenidge Oost-Indische Compagnie)

Timeline of Historical Events

B.C.E.

c. 50,000 to 30,000	Prehistoric Period: primitive food-gathering
c. 30,000 to 1,000	Mesolithic Period: food-gathering
c. 1,000 to 300	Protohistoric Period: beginnings of agriculture and iron technology
c. 250–210	Traditional period of conversion of rulers to Buddhism by Ashoka's mission; founding of Mahāvihāra
103–89	Tamil rulers in power in Anurādhapura
89	Vaṭṭagāmaṇī Abhaya founds the Abhayagirivihāra

C.E.

67	Vasabha founds Lambakanna dynasty
150–250	Construction of monumental architecture
301–328	Tooth Relic brought to Sri Lanka
411–413	Fa-Hien visits Sri Lanka

429–455	Seven Dravidian kings rule at Anurādhapura
455	Dhātusena founds Moriya Dynasty
Fifth Century	Composition of *Mahāvamsa*
769	Poḷonnaruva becomes temporary capital
887	Lankan expedition sacks Madurai
947	Coḷas invade Sri Lanka
993	Coḷas invade Sri Lanka
1014–1017	Coḷas recapture regalia and treasure of the Paṇḍya kings; Mahinda V driven to Rohaṇa
1055	Vijayabāhu I conquers Rohaṇa
1070	Vijayabāhu I expells Coḷas from the island
1215	Māgha begins conquest of Rajaraṭa
1247	Chandrabhānu invades from Malay Peninsula
1284	Āriyachakravarti rules Jaffna Kingdom as vassal of Paṇḍyas
1344	Ibn Battuta arrives in Sri Lanka
1396	Bhuvanekabāhu makes Koṭṭē his capital
1408–1438	Chinese naval expeditions demand tribute, abduct Vira Alakeśvara to China
1505	Portuguese arrive in Sri Lanka (November 15)
1519	Çankili I rules in Jaffna
1521	Assassination of Vijayabāhu VI results in partition of Koṭṭē
1543	Çankili orders 600 Christians in Mannar killed
1560	Portuguese capture Nallur and built a fort on the island of Mannar
1565	Portuguese abandon Kotte and make Colombo the capital
1580	Dharmapala wills the whole island of Ceylon to Portugal
1581	Rajasinghe I succeeds to the throne of Sitavaka
1582	Rajasinghe I annexes Udarata (Kingdom of Kandy)
1594	Vimaladharma Suriya I builds the Dalada Maligawa and palace in Kandy

1597	Death of Dharmapala and accession of Portugal (May 27)
1602	First Dutch expedition arrives in Batticaloa (May 31)
1614	Portugal declares cinnamon trade a royal monopoly
1630	Portuguese invade Kandyan Kingdom
1638	Battle of Gannoruwa between Kandyans and Portuguese (March 28)
1658	Jaffna surrendered to Dutch (June 22)
1670–1675	Warfare between the Kandyan Kingdom and the Dutch
1716–1620	Kandyan Kingdom closes its border to the Dutch
1739	Accession of Śrīvijayarājasingha begins the Nāyakkar dynasty
1747–1782	Reign of Kirtiśrirājasingha
1762–1766	Warfare between the Kandyan Kingdom and the Dutch
1796	Colombo surrendered to British
1802	Sri Lanka ceded to Britain by Treaty of Amiens (March 27) and becomes the Crown Colony of Ceylon
1813	American Missionaries found the Batticotta Seminary
1815	Sir Robert Brownrigg invades Kandy (January) and signs Kandyan Convention (March 10)
1817–1818	Rebellion of the Kandyan Provinces brutally suppressed
1823	First coffee plantation at Sinhapitiya
1832	Colebrooke-Cameron Report; *rājakāriya* abolished
1833	Sri Lanka brought under a unified government for the first time and administered through five provinces
1844	Slavery abolished in Sri Lanka
1848	Martial law declared in Kandyan Provinces (October 10)
1858	Telegraph communication with India begins
1867	Opening of Colombo-Kandy Railroad
1873	Opening of Vidyodaya Pirivena at Peliyagoda
1875	Opening of Vidyalankara Pirivena at Kelaniya
1878–1883	Coffee blight destroys plantations; replaced with tea

1897	Waste Lands Ordinance enacted
1912	First Election to Legislative Council
1914	Railway and ferry service between India and Ceylon begins
1915	Martial law after Sinhalese-Muslim riots (June 2–August 21)
1924	Colombo radio station opened
1927–1928	Donoughmore Commission meets in Sri Lanka
1931	First elections to State Council
1936	Second elections to State Council
1938	Ratmalana airport opened; Radio Ceylon broadcasts in Sinhala
1939	Bank of Ceylon established; India bans emigration to Sri Lanka (September 1)
1942	Japan bombs Colombo (April 5) and Trincomalee Harbor (April 9); University of Ceylon replaces University College
1944–1945	Soulbury Commission meets
1946	Ceylon granted a new constitution (May 15)
1947	First election under Dominion Status (August 15); Cabinet takes office (September 26); Parliament opens (November 25)
1948	Independence (February 4); Ceylon Citizenship Act No. 18 of 1948 passed.
1949	Central Bank of Ceylon established (December 16)
1950	National Flag adopted (February 13); Sri Lanka becomes member of International Monetary Fund and World Bank (August 28)
1951	FP demands autonomy for Tamils of North and East; S.W.R.D. Bandaranaike founds SLFP
1952	Prime Minister D. S. Senanayake dies (March 22); UNP wins second Parliamentary elections (May 24)
1953	Prime Minister Dudley Senanayake resigns (October 12)
1954	Indo-Ceylon agreement signed (February 13); Buddha Jayanti commemorated (May 23); Sir Oliver Goonetilleke becomes first Lankan Governor-General (July 17)

1956	MEP under S.W.R.D. Bandaranaike elected (April 12); Parliament approves the Sinhalese Language Bill (June 15)
1957	Bandaranaike and Chelvanayakam Pact (July 26); Rice and Rubber Pact with China (September 19); Sri Lanka takes over the Trincomalee air and naval base (October 15) and Katunayake air base (November 1)
1958	Bus transportation nationalized (January 1); Bandaranaike abandons Bandaranaike-Chelvanayakam pact (April 9); Tamil Language (Special Provisions) Act passed
1959	Prime Minister Bandaranaike assassinated (September 26)
1960	Fourth general elections (March 19); Fourth Parliament Dissolved (April 23); SLFP wins Fifth General Election; Sirimavo Bandaranaike becomes world's first elected female PM (July 20); Sinhala made the only official language of the country (December 31)
1961	FP carries out civil disobedience campaign (April)
1962	Coup d'etat attempt discovered (January 27)
1963	Emergency rule ends after more than two years (April 30)
1964	Shastri-Sirimavo Pact provides for the expatriation of 525,000 people of Indian origin (October 30); 14 Members of Parliament resign (December 3)
1965	UNP wins Sixth General Election (March 22); PM Dudley Senanayake fails to implement agreement with FP
1966	Act passed to allow use of the Tamil language in the northern and eastern provinces (January 11); World Buddhist Congress in Colombo (July)
1967	Devaluation of the rupee (November 22)
1969	Universities closed after a student strike (December)
1970	Sixth Parliament dissolved (March 25); SLFP wins seventh general elections (May 27)
1971	Emergency declared (March 16); JVP insurrection suppressed (April)
1972	New constitution takes effect; Ceylon renamed Sri Lanka (May 22)

1974	University admission policies to increase Sinhalese representation in higher education
1975	LSSP expelled from the government (September 2)
1976	TULF adopts Vaddukottai Resolution (May 14); TNF reorganizes as LTTE; Nonaligned nations' conference held in Colombo (August–September)
1977	Emergency declared (February 15); UNP defeats SLFP and TULF sweeps northern seats (July 23); National State Assembly establishes a presidential form of government (September)
1978	PM J. R. Jayawardene becomes the first executive president (February 4); Tamil separatist organizations proscribed (May 19); National State Assembly renamed Parliament (August); New constitution promulgated (August 31)
1979	Prevention of Terrorism Act passed (July); Emergency declared in Jaffna (December 27)
1980	Sirimavo Bandaranaike expelled from Parliament (October 16)
1981	State of Emergency declared during communal violence (June)
1982	State of Emergency declared throughout the country (July 30); Jayewardene reelected President (October 20); Referendum extends Parliament six more years (December 22)
1983	Worst eruption of anti-Tamil violence since 1958 (July 25); TULF members lose their seats in Parliament when sixth amendment to constitution bans advocacy of separatism (August 4)
1984	All-Parties Conference meet throughout year
1985	Tamil groups propose diplomatic solution (February); Rajiv Gandhi and Jayewardene meet (June 3); Peace talks held in Thimphu, Bhutan (July 8); war escalates; Rajiv Gandhi says he would not accept a government military victory (December)
1986	Jayewardene promises autonomy for the Tamil north (June); Jayewardene announces new peace proposals (December 19)

1987	Terrorists kill nearly 300 Sinhalese (April 17–21); Invasion of Jaffna (May 26); first LTTE suicide bomber kills 30 soldiers in Jaffna peninsula (July 5); Prabhakaran meets with Rajiv Gandhi in Delhi (July); Jayawardene and Gandhi sign pact recognizing the Tamil language as a national official language (July 29); India, Sri Lanka, and LTTE announced a settlement (September 28); LTTE embarks on war against IPKF (October 5); thirteenth amendment to recognize Tamil as an official language and provide for provincial councils passed (November 12)
1988	Assassination of Vijaya Kumaratunga (February 16); IPKF launches Operation Checkmate (May); First Provincial Council elections held (November); Ranasinghe Premadasa elected President (December 19)
1989	UNP retains parliamentary majority (February 15); Premadasa asks for Indian withdrawal by July 29 (June 1); LTTE assassinates A. Amirthalingam (July 13); Cease-fire between LTTE and IPKF (September)
1990	Last Indian troops leave (March 21); Civil War resumes (June 10)
1991	LTTE kills Rajiv Gandhi (May 19)
1992	India proscribes LTTE (May); Land mine kills government generals in north (August)
1993	Lalith Athulathmudali shot to death (April 23); Bomb blast kills Premadasa (May 1); Ranil Wickremasinghe becomes Prime Minister (May 5)
1994	People's Alliance wins Parliamentary election (August); Bomb kills Gamini Dissanayake (October 23); Chandrika Bandaranaike Kumaratunga wins presidency (November 9)
1995	Civil War resumes (April 19); LTTE lose 400 cadres in raid on Weli Oya army camp (July 28); Government offensive recaptures Jaffna (October 17–December 5).
1996	LTTE bombs Central Bank in Colombo (January 31); LTTE overruns Mullaitivu military base (July 18).
1997	Government begins Operation Jaya Sikuru to open military supply route to Jaffna (May 13); truck bomb blast in Colombo Fort (October 14)

1998	LTTE bombs Temple of the Tooth (January 25); Government declares LTTE a banned organization (January 26); Operation Jaya Sikuru called off (December)
1999	Chandrika Bandaranaike Kumaratunga injured by bomb three days before reelection (December 18)
2000	LTTE captures Elephant Pass (April); PA returned to power (October 10)
2001	Suicide attack by LTTE destroys military and civilian aircraft (July 24); Kumaratunga dissolves Parliament hours before a no-confidence vote (October 10); Ranil Wickremesinghe wins parliamentary elections on a pledge to open talks with the Tiger rebels (December 5)
2002	Government and LTTE agree to permanent cease-fire (February 21); Prabhakaran holds first press conference in 12 years (April 10); First formal peace talks opened in Thailand (September 16–18)
2003	LTTE suspends peace talks after sixth round (April 21); President dismisses three key opposition party ministers (November)
2004	Kumaratunga dissolves Parliament and calls for elections on April 2 (February 7); "Colonel" Karuna separates from LTTE in Eastern Sri Lanka (March 3); Kumaratunga's UPFA wins 105 seats in Parliament (April 2) (UNF 82, TNA 22, JHU 9, SLMC 5, UCPF 1); Suicide bomb blast in Colombo (July 7)
2005	Assassination of Lakshman Kadirgamar (August 12); Election of President Mahinda Rajapakse (November 17)
2006	Government and LTTE meet in Geneva (February); European Union bans LTTE (May); increased violence threatens resumption of war

1

The Settings

Sri Lanka is a tropical island nation with a long history and an uncertain future. (Until 1972, it was known as Ceylon, and this book uses that name for the colonial era, 1505–1948.) In 2006 it was holding on to a fragile cease-fire in a 20-year civil war that has killed more than 65,000 people, and it faced the lingering effects of one of history's greatest natural disasters. A new government searched for a lasting peace, but the island drifted toward de facto partition: Sri Lanka remains a democracy that has experienced substantial economic growth since the liberalization of its economy in 1977, whereas the territory held by the separatist Liberation Tigers of Tamil Eelam (LTTE) is a dictatorship under its leader, Vellupillai Prabhakaran.

An advanced kingdom based on an elaborate network of irrigated rice cultivation flourished in the north-central plains of the island for a millennium. Its major contribution to civilization was the preservation of an early form of the teachings of the Buddha while Hinduism displaced Buddhism in India. This was the Theravāda (way of the elders) school, which continues today in Sri Lanka and Southeast Asia. The ancient kingdom went into decline a thousand years ago and disappeared through fragmentation, foreign conquest, and endemic malaria. A succession of weak successors faced European colonialism, beginning with the Portuguese in 1505 and culminating in the British conquest of the entire island in 1815. Since independence in 1948, it has remained a democracy but has been unable to create a stable and prosperous society, and in 1983 ethnic conflict flared into civil war.

THE GEOGRAPHICAL SETTING

The island is a 65,610-square-kilometer (25,332-square-mile) teardrop off the southeast tip of the Indian subcontinent. It is separated from the continent by the Palk Strait and Gulf of Mannar, but a chain of islands and sand bars known as Adam's Bridge links them. It is about 400 kilometers (273 miles) in length and about 220 kilometers (137 miles) at its widest point. The center of the island is mountainous; its highest point, Mount Pidurutalagala, rises to 2,524 meters (8,281 feet).

Geologically, weathering has deposited later soils onto the very old rock formations of the island. Its mineral resources are limited primarily to graphite and gemstones, including sapphires and rubies, although explorations are under way for oil deposits off its coasts. The soils of the island are diverse and relatively fertile, particularly the alluvial soils of the river basins, but have deteriorated where plantation monoculture has continued for long periods of time.

Just north of the equator, Sri Lanka has a tropical climate, warm and moist the year round. Its insularity and the mountainous interior do much to moderate its climate. There is little seasonal variation in temperatures. Lowland temperatures average 28 degrees C (82 degrees F) year round, with higher temperatures in the north-central plains. The temperature in the highlands varies with the elevation; towns at higher elevations have average high temperatures of 20 degrees C (68 degrees F) and lows of 10 degrees C (50 degrees F).

Two monsoon seasons bring seasonal variation to the climate. The southwest monsoon season brings rain to the heavily populated southern and western portions of the island from April to June, and the northeast monsoon season drenches most of the island from mid-October to mid-February. These rains divide the island into a Wet Zone and a Dry Zone. The Wet Zone, where rainfall levels can exceed 3,700 millimeters (146 inches) yearly in the Wet Zone, which also receives convectional rain throughout the year. The term "Dry Zone" is misleading because up to 1,500 millimeters (60 inches) of rain may fall during the monsoon season; it refers to the nine months of drought each year. Heavy rainfall brings forth lush tropical vegetation throughout much of the island and has made the magnificent irrigation system of the ancient civilization possible. As the ancient civilization declined, the centers of population moved to the Wet Zone, where rain-fed agriculture became the basis of the economy.

Altogether, there are more than a hundred rivers in Sri Lanka, many of them small. Twelve rivers contain about three-fourths of the total discharge. Half of this discharge passes through the Wet Zone and is of little use for irrigation. The one sizable river, the Mahaweli Ganga, descends from the central highlands to the east and turns north through the Eastern Dry Zone for 335 kilometers (210 miles) until it empties into Kottiar Bay. The Mahaweli Development Scheme has created a series of dams along the length of the river for irrigation and hydroelectric power.

Other notable Dry Zone rivers are the Aruvi Aru (Malwatu Oya) (164 kilometers/103 miles), which links the first capital of Sri Lanka, Anurādhapura, with the ancient trade emporium of Mantai; the Kalā Oya (148 kilometers/ 93 miles), which reaches the sea at Dutch Bay on the west coast; Yan Oya (142 kilometers/89 miles) flowing north between Anurādhapura and Trincomalee to the northeast coast; the Däduru Oya (142 kilometers/89 miles), which marks the approximate boundary between the Dry Zone and Wet Zone on the west coast; the Walawe Ganga (138 kilometers/86 miles), Mänik Ganga (114 kilometers/71 miles), and Kumbakkan Oya (116 kilometers/72 miles) in the southeast; and the Gal Oya (108 kilometers/68 miles) on the east coast, where the first major post-independence irrigation and hydroelectric project was carried out. All of these have been sources of irrigation water and have significant capacity for further development. The main rivers of the Wet Zone from north to south are the Maha Oya (134 kilometers/84 miles), Kälani Ganga (145 kilometers/91 miles), Kalu Ganga (129km/mi), and Gin Ganga (113 kilometers/ 71 miles).

Colombo is the only large city of Sri Lanka. The population within the city limits was 642,000 at the census of 2001. Three of the five next largest towns are in fact suburbs of Colombo: Dehiwala-Mt. Lavinia (210,000), Moratuwa (177,000), and Sri Jayawardenapura-Koṭṭē (116,000). Colombo has been a principal Indian Ocean seaport since colonial times, and its colonial heritage is reflected in the names of its districts. The oldest district of the city is the Fort, which originated as a Portuguese fortification in the sixteenth century. The Pettah (the Tamil word for the areas outside the fort) remains a district of small shops and sidewalk vendors. The exclusive residential quarter of Cinnamon Gardens was originally a plantation created in the eighteenth century.

Colombo was the political, administrative, and commercial center of the British colonial rulers, and it still has the appearance of colonial city, dotted with some new commercial buildings, apartment houses, and modern hotels. Its harbor was an important coaling station for the British Empire and has found new life as an efficient container depot. It is still the center of commercial activity, although most government offices have moved to Sri Jayawardenapura-Koṭṭē. In 1977 President Junius Richard Jayewardene decided to move the Parliament to land reclaimed from the swampland that surrounded Koṭṭē, which had been a capital until it was abandoned in 1565.

The other large towns in the southwest are Negombo (122,000), 30 kilometers (19 miles) north of Colombo, and Galle (91,000), 116 kilometers (72 miles) to the south. Jaffna in the north was the capital of Tamil kingdoms. It had a population of 118,000 at the census of 1981, but disruption caused by

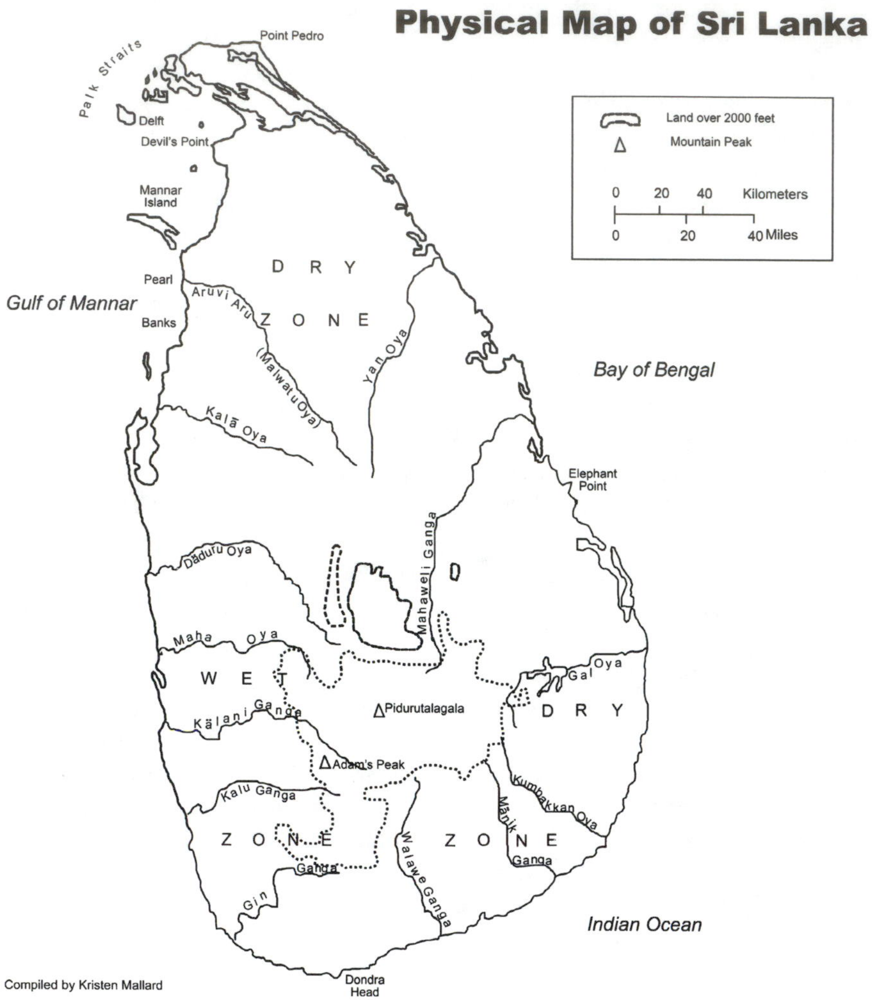

the civil war has reduced the population to an uncertain number. Kandy, the largest town in the interior of the island, has a population of 110,000.

THE POLITICAL SETTING

Sri Lanka is a democracy with high voter turnout but increasing frustration at corruption, electoral violence, and the inability of elected governments to solve the country's economic and political problems. Instability in the Sinhalese political leadership has resulted in frequent inconclusive elections in recent years. Minorities have been increasingly marginalized by policies that favor the Sinhalese majority and by restrictions on the Tamil-speaking population in the name of security.

The LTTE has created an authoritarian quasi-state in the northeast. It governs under permanent wartime conditions with heavy-handed propaganda, universal conscription (even of children and elderly people), and ruthless suppression of dissent. The leadership originated in the Jaffna peninsula, which is now under government control; this has created factionalism between themselves and leaders whose homes are in the eastern province. There is also friction between Prabhakaran's *karaiyar* caste and the majority *veḷḷāḷa* caste.

Universal adult franchise was granted in 1931, under which elections were held in 1931 and 1936. The State Council at this time had virtual self-government in many areas of domestic policy. At independence the Soulbury Constitution, negotiated by the British and conservative Sinhalese leaders, created a British-style parliamentary government. At independence the British handed power over to the English-educated Colombo elite, and a few Sinhalese *govigama* caste families have dominated politics.

New constitutions were written in 1972 and 1978. Under the latter, the cabinet form of government was replaced by a presidential system, with an elected president as head of state and government. It gives presidents near-dictatorial power, but creates a crisis when the president and prime minister (PM) are of different parties, as happened from 2001 to 2004. President Chandrika Bandaranaike Kumaratunga, elected in 1994 and reelected in 1999, proposed eliminating the executive presidency in yet another constitution but had not implemented it when her second term expired in 2005.

Colonial administration was highly centralized in government departments, and this continued after independence. The need to decentralize government has been discussed since 1931, but little had been achieved when civil war broke out in 1983. Despite the added urgency of the civil war, the government of Sri Lanka has not found a formula that could satisfactorily reunite the country. The Thirteenth Amendment to the 1978 Constitution introduced a system of Provincial Councils in 1987, but the central government has been unwilling to surrender power to these councils, and has in fact encroached on the constitutional rights of the councils given by the amendment.

Voters more often than not have voted the incumbent party out of office, but there is limited change in the political elite. In the Sri Lanka Freedom Party (SLFP), President Kumaratunga (president 1995–2005) is the daughter of Solomon West Ridgeway Dias Bandaranaike (PM from 1956 to his assassination in 1959) and Sirimavo Ratwatte Bandaranaike (PM 1960–1965, 1970–1977 and 1994–2000). Her brother Anura Bandaranaike has served as leader of the opposition. Chandrika's husband, Vijaya Kumaratunga, was a leading candidate for the presidency until his assassination in 1987. The United National Party (UNP, jokingly called the "Uncle-Nephew Party") was the creation of Don Stephen Senanayake (PM 1948–1952), succeeded by his son Dudley (PM

1952–53, 1965–1970) and their kinsman Sir John Kotelawala (PM 1952–1956) until power passed to J. R. Jayewardene (president 1977–1989) and his nephew Ranil Wickremasinghe (PM 1993–1994, 2001–2004). Much of Lankan politics can be seen as a competition among these families and their allies to win popular support at the expense of the other.

President Kumaratunga's Freedom Alliance, headed by the SLFP, gained control of Parliament in a coalition with the Sinhalese extremist party, the Janatha Vimukthi Peramuna (JVP) in 2004. The presidency passed in December 2005 to Mahinda Rajapakse, a leading member of the SLFP, who seemed to be committed to weakening the Bandaranaike family hold on the party.

THE HUMAN SETTING

It is generally believed that the ancient civilization supported a larger population through intensive agriculture than the island had until the twentieth century. The collapse of the ancient civilization left the former breadbasket, the Dry Zone, depopulated. Population grew steadily during the British colonial period, owing to high birth rates and immigration from south India. It grew more than 25.4 percent between 1931 and 1946, and even more rapidly after independence. Malaria eradication and improved health care in particular lowered mortality rates, while birth rates increased. Life expectancy rose from 42 years in 1946 to 73 years by 1991; this has produced a young and rapidly growing population. In recent years emigration and lower birth rates have slowed population growth down to only a little over 1 percent in the early twenty-first century.

In 2006 Sri Lanka had a population of more than 20 million people, although civil war has made it impossible to conduct a complete census since 1981. The incomplete census of 2001 enumerated 17.56 million and calculated that six percent of the population was not enumerated in the Northern and Eastern Provinces, for a total population on July 17, 2001, of 18.73 million. The precise population of the nation will be a matter of conjecture for many years, owing to the disruption caused by the civil war and the very large number of overseas Lankans, an uncertain number of whom will never return.

Sinhala is the mother tongue of three-fourths of the people of Sri Lanka; it is related to the Indo-European languages of north India. Most of the remainder of the population speak Tamil, from the Dravidian family of languages. A much larger Tamil-speaking population lives in south India. Centuries of interaction and assimilation have produced much linguistic borrowing from Tamil to Sinhala. There are also descendants of Malay immigrants who speak Malay and a significant number of Lankans of all communities whose first language is English.

English was the language of colonial administration for 150 years, and all of the local elites spoke English. The best schools were taught in English, particularly in the Jaffna peninsula, where American missionaries operated the best schools in Asia. Students were discouraged from learning Sinhala or Tamil in order to maintain a high standard of literacy and pronunciation in English. As a result, Sri Lanka's ruling elite at independence was highly Anglicized, and many could not read Sinhala or Tamil, or even speak either of those languages in an educated manner. The fact that a disproportionate number of this Anglicized elite, and therefore of educated professionals and government employees, were ethnically Tamil has contributed to ethnic tensions.

Sinhala and Tamil are both official languages, but the continuing civil war has resulted in a linguistic division. The devolution of power to the provinces has resulted in Sinhala being the language of government in the Sinhalese-majority provinces, whereas Tamil is the sole language in the north and east. Sri Lanka continues to be governed primarily by the English-speaking elite.

The people of Sri Lanka are grouped into a number of ethnic identities, which are rooted in the early history of the island but took their current form in the nineteenth and twentieth centuries. The small community of *väddā*s are popularly believed to be the descendants of the aboriginal population of the island. The Sinhalese and "Ceylon Tamils" (about 12.6 percent of the population) claim descent from Indian settlers more than 2,000 years ago. The "Ceylon Moors" (7.1 percent of the population) are Muslims who trace their origins to seafaring Arab merchants. Other ethnic communities were created during the colonial era: Tamil-speaking immigrants from south India were called "Indian Tamils" or "Indian Moors" (if Muslim) by the British. Muslims of recent Indian origin, primarily merchants, have assimilated to the larger Muslim community, but the descendants of Indians who immigrated as plantation laborers survive as an ethnic group known as "Plantation" or "Up-Country" Tamils (about 5.6 percent of the population); Malays descend from Southeast Asian immigrants during the colonial era; and Burghers are descendants of European settlers. The latter two groups number only a few tens of thousands.

Although ancient pedigrees are central to the current conflict between Sinhalese and Tamil Lankans, ethnic identities have changed throughout Sri Lanka's history. The example of the *väddā* s illustrates the complexity of ethnic identities in Sri Lanka. Most Lankans appear to believe that this group is racially distinct, but genetic studies have shown that they have no particular affinity to proto-Australoid populations elsewhere in Asia and little difference between themselves and other Lankans. Traditionally, they were hunters and gatherers living in caves in the Dry Zone, but they have been moved from their ancestral territories and settled in villages. The government of Sri Lanka considers that the number of *väddā*s have dwindled to a few hundred because they have changed culturally. A much larger number of people, perhaps tens of thousands, claim *väddā* identity.

The larger ethnic groups have equally complex identities. Entire Sinhalese and Tamil castes are believed to have their origins in the other linguistic group. Sinhalese literature includes many references to their south Indian as well as north Indian origins. The polarization of Sinhalese and Tamil communities became significant after the decline of the ancient civilization, when the Tamil-speaking north and east separated from the Sinhala-speaking south and central regions of the Island. In the nineteenth and twentieth century, many Sinhalese moved from the southwest and central parts of the island into the Dry Zone, and many Tamils left the north and east for other parts of the island, particularly Colombo. After the outbreak of civil war in 1983, many Tamils moved from Sinhalese-majority areas, either to Jaffna or overseas.

The ethnic composition of the island became rigid in the nineteenth century as the British administered the island in part through what they called "races," and they reinforced these identities in the decennial censuses that began in 1871. They distinguished between "Low Country" Sinhalese (about 60 percent), who had been under Portuguese and Dutch colonial rule, and "Kandyans" (about 40 percent), who lived in the territory of the Kingdom of Kandy conquered by the British in 1815. Eurasians who claimed descent from European colonists in Dutch service called themselves "Dutch Burghers" to distinguish themselves from "Portuguese Burghers," who were believed to be of Portuguese and African origins.

The British insisted on maintaining these separate ethnic identities. This retarded the assimilation of immigrant communities and the creation of a Lankan identity. When Indian Tamils, for example, attempted to register as Ceylon Tamils for the census of 1921 on the grounds that they were second- and third-generation Lankans with little connection to India, they were prevented from doing so. It is clear both from immigration statistics and from later census numbers, however, that many have adopted Ceylon Tamil—and to some extent, Sinhalese—identities.

There have been significant changes in the population composition since independence. Many Plantation Tamils were forced to emigrate to India after they were refused citizenship in Sri Lanka and India agreed to accept them. Some Plantation Tamils in Sri Lanka are considered citizens of India and are still appealing their citizenship status. Many Burghers have emigrated, particularly to Australia after that country changed its immigration laws to allow them.

Ethnic identities also continued to be negotiated; censuses no longer distinguish between Low Country Sinhalese and Kandyans or between Ceylon Moors and Indian Moors. The Indian Tamils objected to the label given them because they now have little connection to the home of their ancestors; however, now some do not want to lose their identity, which distinguishes them from other Tamil-speaking Lankans. As long as the civil war that has pitted Tamil separatists against Sinhalese nationalists continues, ethnic identity will continue to be a fundamental feature of life in Sri Lanka.

Castes are the hereditary, endogamous building blocks of Lankan society. They are a product of British colonial enforcement of what they considered to be ancient institutions. The majority castes, the *govigama* among the Sinhalese and *veḷḷāḷa* among the Tamils, are socially and politically dominant. Although no records have been kept, it is believed that each of these castes constitutes more than half of their populations. Both castes are internally segmented into caste grades. The caste structure is hierarchical, but because there is no Brahmin priestly caste among the Buddhists and no resident Brahmin caste among the Hindus, caste hierarchies are difficult to enforce. In all parts of Sri Lanka, castes with occupations that are considered polluting or provide services traditionally are considered lower than the castes they serve. Among both the Sinhalese and Tamils, other castes continue to face discrimination, and many are excluded from political power.

There are important regional differences in the caste structure. The independent *salāgama, karāva,* and *durāva* castes among the Low Country Sinhalese all took advantage of opportunities during the colonial era to rise in prosperity and social status. The *salāgama,* for example, were responsible for the production of cinnamon, the first major colonial export; those *salāgama*s who served the colonial rulers as administrators in the cinnamon industry became an elite grade within the caste. The most successful local entrepreneurs during the British colonial era were from the *karāva* caste. By the end of the nineteenth century, individuals in these castes were confident enough to challenge *govigama* supremacy, although their lack of numbers—together they are estimated to make up less than 10 percent of the Sinhalese population—made this an impossible task. All three castes are believed to be descendants of communities that immigrated from south India and established local dominance in the areas they settled.

The caste hierarchy is more rigid among the Tamils and Kandyans. The *veḷḷāḷa* s acquired a complete domination of Tamil society in the Dutch colonial era, and no castes have challenged the *veḷḷāḷa* caste as the *salāgama, karāva,* and *durāva* castes have done. In particular, the lower castes who served the *veḷḷāḷa*s as laborers were considered "slave castes" by the Dutch and improved their status only marginally during the nineteenth and twentieth centuries.

Kandyan society was feudal, and non-*govigama* castes were fixed in the caste hierarchy by service obligations to the *govigamas.* There were no equivalents to the *salāgama, karāva,* and *durāva* castes among the Kandyans before the British conquest in 1815. The *govigama* themselves are stratified, and the highest caste grade among the Kandyan *govigama,* the *radaḷa,* considered themselves to be socially superior to all other *govigama*s. The Plantation Tamils were recruited primarily from south Indian castes considered to be low in the social hierarchy, but some higher-caste immigrants worked on the plantations, particularly as foremen *(kangāni*s) and accountants *(kanakapiḷḷai*s).

The Sinhalese are predominantly Buddhist with a substantial Christian minority, particularly in the southwest. Most Tamils are Hindus, with a somewhat larger Christian minority. In the 1981 census, 69.3 of the population were Buddhist, 15.5 percent Hindu, 7.6 percent Muslim and 7.5 percent Christian.

THE ECONOMIC SETTING

Sri Lanka's economic policies have been a palimpsest of various approaches to growth and stability. The colonial economy that Sri Lanka inherited at independence was based on agriculture, either food for domestic consumption or the production of commercial crops for export. The UNP governments until 1956 made little change; in that year, the SLFP began to emphasize manufacturing for domestic consumption through state corporations. The UNP 1965–1970 encouraged the production of food crops. In 1970, a socialist United Front (UF) government nationalized land and industries, restricted foreign investment, and redistributed land to peasant cultivators. Then in 1977, the UNP turned to an export-oriented market economy, privatizing government corporations and encouraging foreign investment. These policies have continued through several changes in government.

Sri Lanka remains a poor country, but there have been visible improvements in some areas. Villagers increasingly live in permanent houses with running water and electricity rather than wattle-and-daub structures with woven palm-leaf roofs. People dress better and have access to television sets, refrigerators, telephones, bicycles, and other consumer goods. This is reflected in the so-called quality of life and Human Development Index (HDI) measures, on which Sri Lanka has been remarkably high for its income level.

Productivity has grown too slowly for the benefits to reach all her people, however. After sharp fluctuations in the early years of liberalization, growth has hovered around 5 or 6 percent per year. Those with the advantages of wealth, education, caste status, political influence, family connections, or residence in Colombo have had opportunities to prosper. The new entrepreneurial elite have had access to previously unimagined luxuries. However, some programs that sustained the poor, such as food subsidies and public services, have been curtailed. Since 1989, the government has implemented income redistribution programs called *janasaviya* by the UNP and *samurdhi* by the SLFP.

The economic future of the country is uncertain. Sri Lanka has fallen behind many countries, such as Thailand and South Korea, that were poorer than it was in 1948. The economy depends on massive amounts of foreign assistance, which has created equally massive budget deficits and foreign indebtedness. Aid donors have been sympathetic and willing to increase aid, but in recent years, promises of aid have been tied to progress toward a peaceful resolution of the civil war, which seems remote.

The leading sector has been the export of garments from Free Trade Zones (FTZ, also called Export Promotion Zones or Investment Promotion Zones).

It accounts for more than half of the nation's foreign exchange earnings. It depends on foreign investors who were attracted by generous tax and infrastructure concessions, some of the lowest wages in the world for its predominantly female workforce, and its export quota to the United States under the Multi-Fibre Arrangement (MFA). At the end of 2004, the MFA expired and many factories closed because they were not competitive. In 2005 the FTZ struggled to improve infrastructure and productivity in order to attract more investment. The second and third largest sources of foreign exchange, remittances from Lankans employed abroad and tourism, are uncertain.

THE CULTURAL SETTING

There is little that can be called uniquely Lankan culture in Sri Lanka today, but there has been a growth in the arts in both Sinhala and Tamil. A vigorous English literature is probably the best known artistic accomplishment.

After independence, Sinhalese literature reached a high level with the novels of Martin Wickramasinghe and the plays of E. R. Sarachchandra. They and the faculty of the University of Ceylon at Peradeniya successfully introduced Western literary forms to a generation of Lankan writers. The shift to Sinhala and Tamil in the university and decreased funding for higher education in the arts has weakened the connection with Western forms. Many of the outstanding bilingual teachers moved out of the country. The recent generation of Sinhala writers have been critical of these founders and have searched for indigenous literary forms.

Painting has flourished in Sri Lanka. British administrators and travelers tried to capture the beauty of the island in drawings and paintings. Modern art was led by Justin Pieris Deraniyagala (1903–1967) and George Keyt (1901–1993), both of whom adapted modern techniques to the Lankan environment. In 1943, photographer Lionel Wendt (1900–1944) brought them and other artists together in the 43 Group, in opposition to the sterility of officially supported art. Under their leadership, Sri Lanka became a center of modern art, which continues to thrive.

Architecture—with the important exception of the work of Geoffrey Bawa—tends to be bland and traditional. There are many survivals of Dutch and British colonial buildings, such as former president Chandrika Kumaratunga's 14,000-square-foot mansion, which is being turned into an upscale tourist destination. Her father built the home in the 1940s and was assassinated there in 1959. Bawa created numerous fine homes and hotels, the most famous of which is the spectacular eco-friendly Kandalama Hotel, considered one of the most beautiful hotels in the world. He also designed the parliament buildings at Sri Jayawardenapura-Koṭṭē.

Changes in society since 1977 have influenced the arts. On one hand, economic growth has provided resources for artistic production; on the other hand, the authoritarianism and political violence has generated dissent. Sarachchandra, late in his life, deplored the commercialization of art, but access to sponsors, audiences, galleries, and theaters have made it possible for creative young artists to thrive (and for more audiences to have access to drama, including Sarachchandra's plays through the new medium of television). The theme of protest in the arts is most visible in the theater, particularly the ideologically charged street theater.

Cricket has been played in Sri Lanka since 1832, and it has become the national sport Many Lankans have earned international recognition, and the national team brightened the otherwise dismal year of 1996 by winning the Cricket World Cup. Other popular sports are volleyball, soccer, bicycle racing, athletics, and various water sports.

THE CONTEMPORARY SETTING

On December 26, 2004, Sri Lanka was struck by one of history's greatest natural disasters, the tsunami that inundated three-fourths of the island's coastline and killed more than 35,000 people. Nearly a million people were made homeless. Recovery has been uneven. More than a year later, many people still lived in temporary housing. People living along the coast were not allowed to rebuild there, although permission was given for the restoration and refurbishing of tourist resorts. Much of the vast amount of aid promised was not used owing to corruption, inefficiency, and disputes between the government of Sri Lanka and the LTTE over its disbursement.

A fragile cease-fire was still holding in early 2006. The cease-fire has had beneficial effects: Death and destruction has declined, some refugees have been able to return to their homes, some land mines have been removed, and attempts have been made to return government-occupied Tamil regions to civilian control. The number and severity of cease-fire violations on both sides has increased, however. Neither side seems capable of either returning to all-out war or agreeing to the other's minimum conditions for peace, resulting in a stalemate.

Sinhalese-Buddhist nationalism has prevailed in most of the island: The police and military enforce Sinhalese domination, and minorities survive by acknowledging their subordinate status and adapting. Sinhalese have displaced Tamils in many areas in which Tamils and Burghers had flourished: business, government service, education, and the professions. The government-controlled areas in which the Sinhalese are a minority—the Jaffna peninsula and parts of the northwest and southeast—are essentially occupied by the Sinhalese military as foreign territory. The LTTE persecutes subjects in its territories who do question their power. The country is still attempting to find a solution in a unified Sri Lanka, but as long as the stalemate continues, the regions of the island will grow further apart.

2

Ancient Civilization to 1200

Anurādhapura in north-central Sri Lanka was the capital of a small but important kingdom for more than a millennium. Its major legacy to the world was the preservation of the teaching of the Buddha according to the *Theravāda* ("way of the elders") and is a focus of Sinhalese national pride; it attracted travelers, merchants, and pilgrims from as far away as Rome and China. Much is known of its early history of Sri Lanka because of a tradition of historiography that is unique in South Asia. The two narratives, *Dīpavamsa* (fourth century) and *Mahāvamsa* (fifth century) were written in Pāli, the language of Buddhist scholarship, and provide a chronology of the Sinhalese kingdom to about 300 C.E., and later texts continue the history to modern times. They present a narrow and incomplete picture of ancient Sri Lanka, however, and recent scholarship has furthered scholars' understanding greatly.

The *Mahāvamsa* constructs a history for Sri Lanka's past that is the foundation of many contemporary myths about its ancient history. It is a work of brilliant scholarship with few parallels, and it contains historical details that were centuries old and half a continent away at the time they were recorded—for example, facts about the career of the Indian Emperor Ashoka—which have been corroborated by modern research. It is based on the *Dīpavamsa* and earlier lost writings. Some evidence of these early texts is found in the commentaries of Buddhaghosa, about a century prior to the *Mahāvamsa*. However, these commentaries are a partisan account that emphasizes the Mahāvihara monastic order *(nikāya)*, the Theravāda school as practiced by that order, and the relationship of the community of monks *(sangha)* with the kings. There were at least a dozen monasteries in Anurādhapura; some of these looked to the Mahāvihara, but others did not. Although the *Mahāvamsa* may have been preserved as it was written in the fifth century C.E., the story it tells has been embellished and reinterpreted many times since then, and what passes as the "*Mahāvamsa* version" of Lankan history today is very much a product of these later accretions. Some Lankan Buddhists consider the *Mahāvamsa* to contain revealed truth and accept even the mythical sections.

The *Mahāvamsa* begins by establishing the magical connections of the Buddha with Sri Lanka and the direct connection of the island with the evolution of Theravāda Buddhism. It dates the life of Buddha to the sixth century B.C.E., more than 200 years earlier than recent scholarship suggests. In the fifth month after his enlightenment, the Buddha flew to Sri Lanka and appeared in the air above a great crowd of the Yakkhas (demons) who inhabited the island. He converted tens of millions of beings and freed the island from the control of the Yakkhas because it would become the place where his teachings would be preserved. Five years after his enlightenment, he returned to Nāgadīpa (island of the Nāgas, traditionally associated with the northern peninsula of the island) to prevent a war between two Nāga kings and to convert 800 million Nāgas to his teachings. Three years later, he returned a third time to consecrate a site at Kalyāṇī (near present-day Colombo) for the building of a temple, to leave his footprint on the Sumanakūṭa mountain (Adam's Peak), and to consecrate a third site, probably on the east coast. This is followed by a genealogical chapter and three councils at which Buddhists met to establish correct doctrine. Chapters 5–10 the founding of the Sinhalese state by Prince Vijāya, descended from a lion (*siha*, from which it derives the name *sihala* for the Sinhalese). Vijāya first married a daughter of the chief of the Yakkhas, and he and his men founded several cities and villages, including Anurādhapura. Later he abandoned his Yakkha wife to marry a princess from Madurai in south India, from which he brought brides for his followers and craftsmen from south India. After Vijāya's death, his nephew arrived from India to rule and established a dynasty based in Anurādhapura.

The remainder of the *Mahāvamsa* concentrates on two kings, Devānampiyatissa (250–210 B.C.E., Chapters 11–20) and Duṭṭhagāmani (161–137 B.C.E., Chapters 21–32). The four centuries after the death of Gamini are treated briefly, usually just listing the extent to which the kings promoted the Buddha's teachings and patronized the *sangha*.

PREHISTORY

New research in archaeology, paleoanthropology, and epigraphy has revised the history of early Sri Lanka. It is likely that anatomically modern humans migrated from Africa to South Asia about 60,000 years B.C.E. The first clear evidence of human settlement in Sri Lanka has been dated to 28,000 B.C.E. These are the earliest human remains found anywhere in South Asia. Compared with China or Europe, the Stone Age began early in South Asia and continued for a very long time. The Stone Age people of the island were physically related to early populations of India, Southeast Asia, and Australia and are generally classed under the name *proto-Australoid*. Those of Sri Lanka and Malaya were named Veddoid, after the *väddā* tribal population of Sri Lanka, in the belief that the modern hunter-gatherers were descendants of the early population.

South India and Sri Lanka were open to the spread of culture by sea. This increased after China and Rome provided markets for interregional sea trade but is also true of prehistoric times. Lothal, the Indus Valley port on the Gulf of Cambay, may have had local trade networks extending to the south. Some important trade items in the ancient world—pearls, ebony, and ivory in particular—may have originated in south India or Sri Lanka.

There was a land bridge between India and Sri Lanka for much of the Paleolithic era, and people and ideas crossed back and forth. In the late Stone Age, for example, the people of the coast of Tamilnadu and several locations in Sri Lanka used a specialized technique of stone flaking found nowhere else in India. The development of iron technology, rice cultivation, and the domestication of horses and cattle followed a parallel course in Sri Lanka and south India. Both seem to have been part of a widespread culture typified by their "megalithic burials," in which people were buried in pottery urns in pits lined with large stones; they have been found as far north as central India. Both Tamilnadu and Sri Lanka were relatively densely populated in the first millennium B.C.E.

There has been much speculation as to the ethnic identity of the Stone Age population, and it has become controversial in modern Sri Lanka. Sinhalese accounts minimize the contact with south India in favor of north India origins, whereas Tamil accounts take the cultural similarities between south India and Sri Lanka as evidence of Dravidian origins of Lankan culture. In fact, this culture probably preceded both Dravidian and Indo-Aryan influences. Both the Indus Valley culture (generally thought to be the parent of Dravidian culture) and the Aryan culture originated in the northwest of India and diffused slowly to the south. South India and Sri Lanka were at the end of this chain of diffusion, which may not have reached the region until late in the first millennium B.C.E.

The sand bar that connected India to Sri Lanka also prevented ships from passing through the middle of Palk Strait between them. Ships sailed instead through the narrow channel between Sri Lanka and Mannar Island. This led to the creation of a great trade emporium at Māntai (now known as Tiruketisvaram) near Mannar Island. References to Sri Lanka in Greek at the time of Alexander the Great (323 B.C.E.) show that the island was well-known in north India. The texts refer to travelers who had visited the island and use the name *Taprobane*, probably taking the name from Tambapaṇṇi used in the *Mahāvamsa*.

Māntai is near the mouth of the Aruvi Aru (also called Malwatu Oya), the river that led to the site of Sri Lanka's first urban settlement at Anurādhapura.

Ancient Sri Lanka

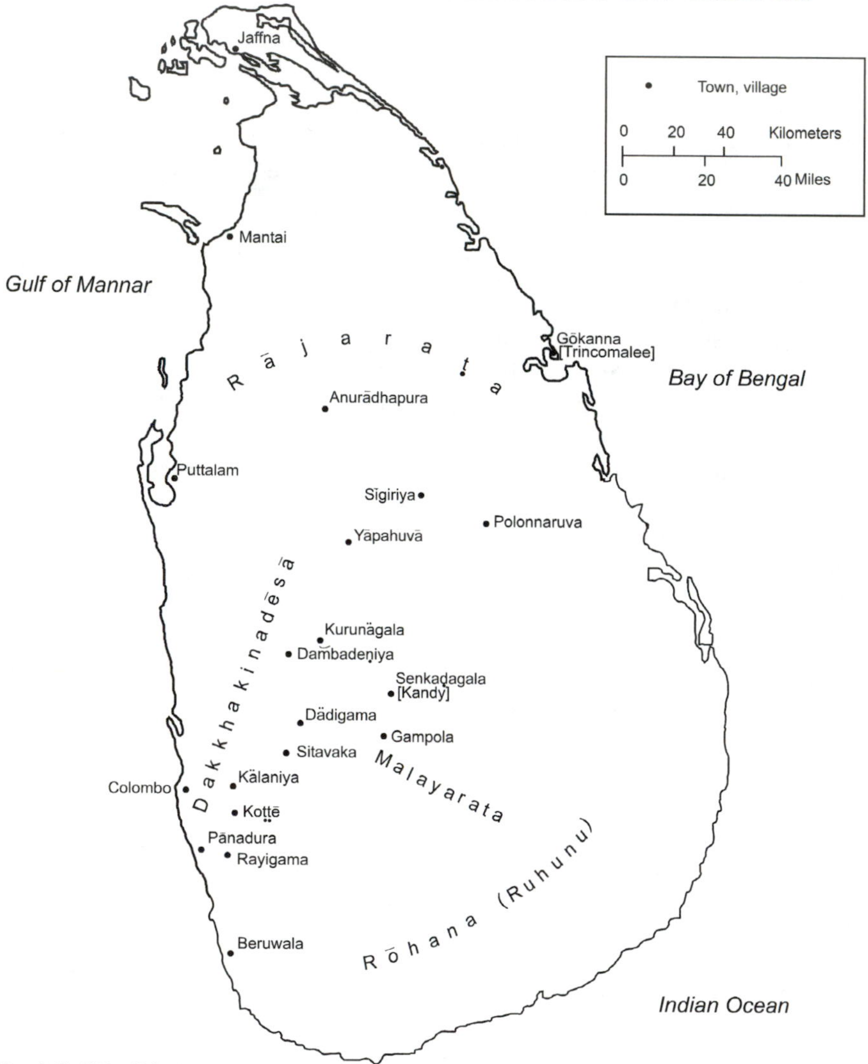

Compiled by Kristen Mallard

The earliest archaeological evidence uncovered at Anurādhapura suggests that there was a Stone Age settlement as early as 900 B.C.E. Rice cultivation, horses, cattle, and pottery appear at about the same time. Iron tools seem to have been used there at an early period and gradually spread throughout the island. Anurādhapura grew steadily and could be called a town by the seventh century B.C.E. It is the only urban settlement of the early Iron Age to have been excavated; it is believed that urban sites existed in the north (Kantarōḍ ai) and south (Tissamahārāma) of the island as well as Māntai.

HISTORICAL ANURĀDHAPURA

By the third century B.C.E., the northern Dry Zone was undergoing rapid change as early irrigation systems enabled an increase in rice production. The first written records appeared, and Anurādhapura, the largest city in South Asia outside of north India, emerged as a city-state under a monarchy. The turning point in the history of the island was the establishment of Buddhism and its patronage by the rulers at Anurādhapura. The great Indian emperor Ashoka sent one of his many foreign missions to Sri Lanka in about 250 B.C.E. According to the *Mahāvamsa*, Ashoka's mission to Sri Lanka followed diplomatic exchanges and the exchange of gifts, including bodily relics of the Buddha and "all that was needful for consecrating a king." It was led by his son Mahinda, who ordained monks (*bhikkhus*) who joined the Mahāvihara monastery established by Devānampiyatissa. Ashoka's daughter brought a branch of the bodhi tree under which the Buddha had attained enlightenment; it took root within the Mahāvihara monastery, where it became a shrine.

The Anurādhapura city-state extended its control over the succeeding centuries, as kingship passed between Devānampiyatissa's successors and various rulers identified as "Damiḷa" by the *Mahāvamsa.* In contemporary Sri Lanka, this has been interpreted as ethnic conflict between Sinhalese and Tamil (i.e. "Damiḷa") rulers. It is unlikely that either ethnic identity was formed at this time, and that the *Mahāvamsa* reflects conditions of the fifth century. This applies in particular to the epic tale of Duṭṭhagāmani in the midst of this period. He belonged to a branch of the royal family that consolidated control of Rohaṇa in the southeast of the island. Duṭṭhagāmani defeated thirty-two kings before defeating the Damiḷa Eḷāra, who had ruled at Anurādhapura for 44 years. After re-establishing Buddhist kingship and unifying the island, Duṭṭhagāmani patronized the Mahāvihara. The *Mahāvamsa* story seems to have drawn much of its inspiration from a conflict between the Sinhalese and Tamil rulers of Anurādhapura in the mid-fifth century, but it contains details that give us a suggestion of what some idea of politics in the early period might have been.

Whatever unity Duṭṭhagāmani may have brought to the island was short-lived. Civil war continued sporadically for two centuries. During this period

Vaṭṭagāmani Abhaya (103 and 89–77 B.C.E.) was deposed by a provincial revolt and by invasions from south India. Five Damiḷas from south India ruled in turn in Anurādhapura, until Vaṭṭagāmani defeated the last of them. The *Mahāvamsa* says that Vaṭṭagāmani then founded the monastic order that became the main rival to the Mahāvihāra, Abhayagirivihāra, because the Mahāvihara monks did not support his struggle to recapture Anurādhapura.

The major evidence for the early historic period is the corpus of more than 1300 inscriptions in the Brāhmī script, the ancestor of all indigenous South Asian scripts. The inscriptions are similar to those found in south India in script and in terminology but are much more numerous; their language remains controversial. Some Brāhmī-inscribed potsherds at Anurādhapura recently have been placed by radiocarbon dating to the period before the third century B.C.E., about 200 years older than any other known examples. Inscriptions are numerous in the Wet Zone from 250 B.C.E. to the first century B.C.E. but do not reoccur there until the tenth century C.E.

Many of the Lankan inscriptions record donations of rock shelters to the *sangha* and contain clues about life in ancient Sri Lanka. There are as many as 2,000 rock shelters on the slopes of hills throughout the island, created over several centuries. They are usually protected areas under the sides of boulders. Some shelters have no inscriptions, but experts maintain that they were occupied because of the presence of drip ledges cut to prevent rainwater from dripping inside. They indicate the spread of Buddhist practices throughout the island and the willingness of local populations to support Buddhist monks. The inscriptions name members of the royal family and official titles that appear in the *Mahāvamsa*, and also titles of local officials not mentioned in the texts.

The *Mahāvamsa* and other historical texts give little information about the administration and economy of the Anurādhapura kingdom. What historians have inferred from these texts and inscriptions refer to a period of more than a thousand years and may not accurately describe the evolution of the society over this long period of time. Power was concentrated in the hands of the kings, but regional and local authorities continued to survive; Anurādhapura often had little control south of the Kalā Oya and Mahaweli Ganga. Kings took more exalted titles as the centuries wore on, but there is little evidence of the rigid, authoritarian, and bureaucratic structure that is assumed for ancient "hydraulic" societies, in which irrigation was a major state enterprise. Succession to the throne seems to have usually passed to the senior surviving member of the royal family, usually a younger brother or paternal cousin of the king. In the late Anurādhapura period, succession seems to have passed regularly to the younger brothers of the king and then to the eldest surviving son of the eldest brother. The heir apparent was given a title to ensure his succession.

Stability was achieved by the founding of the Lambakanna dynasty by Vasabha (67–111 C.E.). Inscriptions suggest that no serious rivals challenged

Vasabha's authority throughout the island. His successors occasionally fought wars of succession and resisted raids from the rising kingdoms in south India, but the island seems to have been relatively peaceful and prosperous for nearly four centuries. The Lambakanna rulers constructed reservoirs and irrigation canals throughout the Dry Zone, which developed into one of the wonders of the ancient world.

The Chinese Buddhist pilgrim Fa-Hien lived two years in Sri Lanka around the years 411–413 . He calls the kingdom "Sinhala" and describes it as a peaceful and prosperous Buddhist kingdom with visiting merchants from as far away as Arabia and China. He describes the annual festival of the Tooth Relic *(daladā),* an object brought to Sri Lanka about a century earlier and believed by Lankan Buddhists to be the tooth of the Buddha, at Abhayagirivihāra.

The stability of the kingdom came to an end with an invasion from south India in 429. By this time south India had passed through a cultural revolution known as the Sangam Age, and the Paṇḍya kingdom at Madurai had become a regional power. Seven Damiḷa kings ruled in succession at Anurādhapura from 429 to 455. They appear from inscriptional evidence to have continued to support Buddhist institutions. A nobleman from Rohaṇa named Dhātusena organized resistance to them and defeated the last three of these kings, until finally founding his own Moriya dynasty at Anurādhapura. The Duṭṭhagāmani episode in the *Mahāvamsa* seems to commemorate his victory by attributing similar feats to the earlier king. Dhātusena (455–473) appears to have been a strong ruler, building new *vihāra*s and building the huge Kalāväva reservoir at Anurādhapura and a canal 54 miles long to fill it from the Kalā Oya. His sons fought over the succession; his elder son Kasyapa deposed him and eventually built the magnificent palace at Sīgiriya but was overthrown in turn by his half-brother Moggallana (491–508). Civil war and invasions from south India continued intermittently for nearly 200 years, interrupted by a few peaceful reigns. Rohaṇa appears to have been independent, and the warring factions became more dependent on mercenary troops from south India.

At the height of the Anurādhapura kingdom, an estimated 4 million to 7 million people lived in the northern Dry Zone, perhaps 90 percent of the population of the island. By the ninth century there was some settlement of the lower valleys of the mountainous interior and an increase of coconut cultivation along the eastern and southwestern coasts. Inscriptional evidence suggests that at this time the population centers of Sinhalese kingdom were moving to the southwest while Tamil settlements spread in the northern peninsula, the east coast, and in pockets within the kingdom. The area to the southwest of the core of the Anurādhapura kingdom was administered by the heir to the throne and came to be known as Māyāraṭa, in contrast to the Rājāraṭa, or king's division of the kingdom.

The last phase in the history of the Anurādhapura kingdom coincides with the rise of strong kingdoms in south India. From the seventh century onward, its international position declined from internal conflict, the shift of the Indian Ocean trade to new centers, and increased competition from south India.

South India had a larger population base than Sri Lanka, and the growth of aggressive kingdoms there posed a threat to the security of the Sinhalese kingdom. Mānavarma, a Sinhalese prince unable to succeed to the throne, joined the court of the Pallava king Narasinghavarman in the seventh century and helped him defeat the Chālukya kingdom to their north. In return, the Pallavas sent an army to help Mānavarma. After one unsuccessful attempt, Mānavarma took power in 684 and ruled until 718. The eighth century was relatively peaceful, aided by an alliance with the Pallavas against the Paṇḍyas. The latter sacked Anurādhapura during the reign of Sena I (831–851), and the Sinhalese were forced to pay a large indemnity. For the next century, the threat of invasion from the south India kingdoms was ever present, particularly as the imperialist Coḷas defeated the Pallavas and drove the Sinhalese and Paṇḍyas into a defensive alliance.

Religious differences between south India and Sri Lanka sharpened in this period. South Indian rulers became devout Saivite Hindus from the seventh century onward. When the Buddhist pilgrim Hiuen Tsang visited Kanchipuram in 640, it was still a center of Buddhism, but the Pallava king Mahendravarman I (600–630) had been converted to Saivism from Jainism and persecuted other religions.

Another sign of difficulty was the appearance of malaria, which eventually made the Dry Zone virtually uninhabitable until recent times. There is mention for the first time at the beginning of the tenth century the *upasagga* disease for which Kassapa IV (898–914) built hospitals and that forced Kassapa V (914–923) to recall an infected military expedition from Madurai. If, as is likely, this refers to malaria, it establishes a starting point for the depopulation of the Rājāraṭa, well before its conquest by south India. After the abandonment of the Dry Zone, it provided breeding places for the *anopheles culicifacies* mosquito in the stagnant reservoirs, creating a barrier between the modern Tamil and Sinhalese areas, where normal conditions are not favorable to malaria. The heavy rains of the southwest flush out potential breeding places, and the porous limestone of the Jaffna Peninsula does not allow many stagnant ponds to form. Thus, most of the population lived in areas where malaria was transmitted at a low level; the infection rate does not seem to have reached the levels of Africa or parts of India. However, Lankans did not acquire natural immunities to malaria and were subject to violent epidemics.

The Coḷas extended their empire at the expense of the Paṇḍyas and Sinhalese in the tenth century. Early in the century they occupied the Paṇḍyan capital at Madurai, and the king took refuge in Sri Lanka. The Coḷas retaliated for Sinhalese support for the Paṇḍyas with at least three major invasions in the tenth century. During the last of these in 993, Mahinda V (982–1029) abandoned Anurādhapura to the Coḷas. He was captured in Rohaṇa in 1017. The

Colas governed the heartland of the Anurādhapura as a province of the Coḷa Empire until 1070, when warfare elsewhere forced them to withdraw from the island.

POḶONNARUVA

The Coḷas moved the capital from Anurādhapura 100 kilometers (62 miles) southeast to Poḷonnaruva. In spite of the construction of monumental architecture and massive irrigation works in the eleventh and twelfth centuries, Poḷonnaruva appears not to have been a major population center. Unlike Anurādhapura, the ruins are close together, as they would be in a primarily ceremonial center. Moreover, the territory to the south and east of the capital is infertile and apparently was inhabited by Väddā hunter-gatherers then, as now.

Vijayabāhu I (1055–1110), who had united the south of the island in resistance to the Coḷas, was consecrated at Anurādhapura but made Poḷonnaruva his capital when he restored a Sinhalese monarchy. There the Sinhalese rulers attempted to emulate the greatness of the Anurādhapura kingdom but could not recapture the glory of the ancient city. After the death of Vijayabāhu I, the governors of Rohaṇa and Māyāraṭa became independent of Rājāraṭa, although acknowledging the supremacy of the Poḷonnaruva king. Parākramabāhu I (1153–1186), who originally ruled Māyāraṭa, subdued Rohaṇa after succeeding to the Poḷonnaruva throne and thereafter ruled the two regions directly rather than through governors. Sinhalese culture flourished under Parākramabāhu I. His successor Nissanka Malla (1187–1196), a ruler of Kalinga origin, also centralized control of the island, but thereafter unity of the island ended.

The Poḷonnaruva kingdom maintained an alliance with the Paṇḍyas against the Coḷas until the end of the twelfth century. Parākramabāhu waged war against the Paṇḍyas. Although the *Cūlavamsa,* a continuation of the *Mahāvamsa,* claims unbroken victories in south India, it is clear from south Indian records that the war ended in defeat and a Paṇḍyan invasion of Sri Lanka. Parākramabāhu I also raided the coasts of Burma. Parākramabāhu I and Nissanka Malla both invaded south India, allied with other enemies of the Coḷas.

The kingdom survived until about 1293, when it was abandoned after a series of foreign invasions and malaria epidemics. The Sinhalese capitals by then had shifted further south to the Wet Zone and abandoned the Dry Zone in the thirteenth century. The result was the "drift to the southwest" (the movement of the center of Sinhalese population from the north-central Dry Zone to the southwestern coast between 1000 and 1600), and a corresponding concentration of the Tamil-speaking population in the northern peninsula. There is little evidence of migration within Sri Lanka during this period, and the shift in the population seems to have been brought about primarily by natural increase of the population and migration from south India.

BUDDHISM

Buddhism arose in north India as a means of salvation taught as an alternative to Brahman doctrines and practices. The core of the Buddha's teaching is summarized in the Four Noble Truths: (1) Pain and suffering are inevitable parts of life; (2) They are caused by human desires and attachments; (3) People can overcome the desires and attachments that cause pain and suffering; and (4) The means to overcome these is the Eightfold Path. The last is a code of conduct that stresses moderation, contemplation, and serenity instead of the ascetic practices of Brahmins. Salvation consists of entering the state of *nibbāna* (Skt. *nirvāṇa*), which liberates one from the cycle of rebirth that is otherwise the fate of humanity. It was a course of behavior that could be pursued by anyone, and the many rock shelters occupied by Buddhists in ancient Sri Lanka are testimony to the great numbers of people who withdrew from society in order to follow the Eightfold Path.

Over time, monks formed into communities to transmit the Buddha's teachings. Initially they moved about living on food they begged, except during the rainy season, but monks became full-time residents of monasteries, supported by lay devotees. Monasteries ordained *bhikkhus*, and the principal monasteries in Sri Lanka became huge, reportedly 5,000 monks in the largest, Abhayagirivihāra.

Doctrinal differences arose in the absence of an ecclesiastical authority. According to the *Mahāvamsa*, three councils were held to resolve differences in doctrine; Lankan Buddhists followed the decisions of the third, called by Ashoka in the third century B.C.E. New traditions continued to develop in India, the most important being those summarized under the term Mahāyāna, or "greater vehicle." They referred to Theravāda as Hīnayāna, or "lesser vehicle," and claim that Mahāyāna had access to secret doctrines not understood by Theravāda Buddhists.

Anurādhapura became the center of Theravāda Buddhism, attracting pilgrims and scholars from as far as China. The Mahāvihāra considered itself the guardian of the authentic teachings of the Buddha, although they accepted some Mahāyāna concepts, such as that of the *bodhisattva*. A *bodhisattva* was a Buddha-to-be who remained in the world after enlightenment in order to help others follow the path to salvation. The Abhayagirivihāra seems to have been a center of ideas that were spreading in India, such as Māhayāna, and increasingly took root in Sri Lanka. Kings played a number of roles in relation to the Buddhist *sangha*. As patrons, they built religious monuments such as the gigantic domed *dāgäbas* at monasteries that housed relics of the Buddha. The largest of these, the Jetavana *dāgäba* built by Mahāsena had a diameter of 370 feet and was almost 400 feet high. Monasteries also provided the necessities of life for monks. At times they intervened in disputes on doctrine and monastic discipline within monasteries. *Bhikkhus* served as advisers to the kings.

Kings also became involved in the rivalries between monastic orders. Mahāsena (276–303) adopted Māhayāna Buddhist views, and when the Mahāvihāra objected to his consecration by a Māhayāna *bhikkhu* he prohibited laymen from supporting those Mahāvihāra monks who had left the capital in protest. The Abhayagirivihāra remained loyal to Mahāsena and was rewarded by the king. After the Mahāvihāra monks returned, Mahāsena allowed a third monastic order, the Jetavanavihāra, to build on land that had formerly belonged to the Mahāvihāra. These three orders provided the institutional framework for the monkhood up the end of the Anurādhapura kingdom.

Buddhism changed over time. In the later Anurādhapura period, developments in India such as Tantric Buddhism and devotionalism *(bhakti)* influenced Buddhism in Sri Lanka. Some monks attempted to return to the life of wandering mendicants. The Sinhalese kings gradually began to think of themselves as *bodhisattvas*. Kings also referred to themselves in terms previously reserved for religious figures, and some claimed descent from the Buddha's clan. These changes are not emphasized in the histories written by monks, who continued to emphasize Sinhalese Buddhism's adherence to the early textual tradition.

Buddhism lost its position as the state religion when the Coḷas occupied northern Sri Lanka from 993 to 1070, and it never returned to the position it had held. The abandonment of Anurādhapura meant the abandonment of the monastic complexes there also, and with it their proximity to the rulers. Saivism flourished under the Coḷas, and the *sangha* received little patronage. Vijayabāhu I restored the higher form of ordination *(upasampadā)* for monks and made the Buddha's Tooth Relic a symbol of his kingship. He and his successors continued to patronize Saivism also, however, and did not make Buddhism the state religion under Coḷa rule. The following two rulers, Vikramabāhu I (1111–1132) and Gajabāhu II (1132–1153) did not foster a close relationship between the king and *sangha*, and even confiscated *sangha* property. The monastic orders were weaker in the mid-twelfth century than they had ever been in the Anurādhapura kingdom. In 1164 Parākramabāhu convened a council of *bhikkhus* at which the monastic orders were merged under the name of Mahāvihāra and were put under the control of a *bhikkhu* appointed by the king. Nissanka Malla said that the ruler of Sri Lanka should be a Buddhist, but he also said that the ruler should be a Kshatriya, which could exclude Lankan Buddhists.

IRRIGATION SYSTEM

The kingdom supported a growing population, and this population increasingly depended on the central management of irrigation. Because early agricultural activity depended on unreliable monsoon rains, Lankans constructed canals, channels, water-storage tanks, and reservoirs to provide an elaborate irrigation system to counter the risks posed by periodic drought. The irrigation system enabled the kingdom to produce two large crops of rice each year, instead of one uncertain one.

The early development of Sri Lanka's irrigation works is uncertain. The *Dīpavamsa* and *Mahāvamsa* attribute the construction of large reservoirs to the legendary rulers who preceded Devānampiyatissa, but this reflects the importance of irrigation to their fifth- and sixth-century authors rather than reliable evidence. In the beginning, villagers must have built small dams and canals to irrigate their own fields; these are similar to those built in south India at the same time and continue to exist in both regions today.

Vasabha (67–111) seems to have been the first king to build irrigation works to supply water to these village "tanks," building large reservoirs and digging canals to bring water from the rivers of the wetter south to the dryer Malwatu Oya region. Texts refer to the construction of irrigation works as meritorious deeds by Buddhist kings, and inscriptions show that many other reservoirs and canals not recorded in the *Mahāvamsa* were built by kings and local authorities. By the time of Mahāsena (274–301), kings were constructing massive reservoirs, some of them drawing water from the Mahaweli Ganga.

The irrigation works were a source of wealth and power for the kingdom. They enabled a larger population to live more productive lives, and they were also a form of monumental architecture for the kings who built them. The demonstrated a high level of technological expertise and the ability to mobilize massive labor forces. Canals were engineered with only slight gradients over long distances—a skill beyond the capacity of the British engineers who attempted to restore them in the nineteenth century. A device known as a valve pit *(bisōkoṭuwa)* controlled the flow from increasingly large reservoirs with great precision.

The major construction of irrigation works seems to have ended in the seventh century, although their expansion and repair continued. They grew to become one of the largest irrigation networks in the ancient world and the most elaborate in South Asia. The system was declining from the thirteenth century if not before, about the time malaria became endemic in the Dry Zone.

SOCIETY

Caste was an Indian institution brought to the island at an early period. There are mentions of the Brahman priestly caste in the records, but with the influence of Buddhist ideas, their influence was negligible. Lankan kings, like Indian kings, claimed the status of the Kshatriya royal caste, but otherwise the four *varna* categories of Brahman, Kshatriya (rulers), Vaisya (merchants), and Sudra (laborers) had little relevance. There are also references to Untouchables, people outside the *varna* system called *caṇḍalā*. People seem to have been divided into hereditary, endogamous, and occupational castes *(jāti)*, and these would have been ranked into a hierarchy as they are today. They owed the king compulsory labor service (*rājakāriya*) based on caste obligations. This service probably provided the labor for the construction of irrigation works.

Many people held property rights in land, reservoirs, and irrigation water, but these varied considerably. The king had the right to collect a share of agricultural produce—one inscription sets the rate at a comparatively low one-sixth of the crop—and was considered to be the owner of uncultivated land, which facilitated public development of land. The king also charged a fee for the use of water from state-controlled irrigation works and taxed the fish caught in them. The king sometimes granted land to officials in return for service. The *sangha*, nobles, and officials were sometimes granted the revenues and service obligations of entire villages; inscriptions record that the kings purchased land for grants to monasteries. Cultivators had several forms of tenure. Some (called *pamunu* or *paraveni*) were hereditary and could be bought and sold.

The Anurādhapura kingdom engaged in a flourishing foreign trade that declined after the seventh century. Besides Māntai, there were ports on the east coast (Gokanna) and the northern peninsula (Jambukola). Much of the trade was in luxury goods—gems, pearls, and spices. In the fourth and fifth centuries, missions were sent as far as Byzantium and China. The discovery of hoards of Byzantine coins from the fourth to the seventh centuries suggests that trade with the Mediterranean continued for centuries. Sri Lanka sent embassies to China during the height of the Tang Dynasty, but these ended after 760.

The royal and priestly residences of wood in Anurādhapura have disappeared; only the ruins of brick and stone remain, and most of these are religious in inspiration. The Lohapāsāda at Anurādhapura was originally a nine-story building, of which only the large number of stone pillars that supported the upper floors survives. The most impressive monuments are the great *dāgäba*s. Many small *dāgäba*s were also built, often surrounded by concentric rows of stone pillars, which originally supported domed roofs. From the eighth century, temples displayed Buddha images in a large rectangular hall called a *geḍigē;* the finest example is the Lankātilaka at Poḷonnaruva built by Parākramabāhu I in the twelfth century.

Much fine sculpture survives. There are beautiful reliefs at Isurumuni, near Anurādhapura, that resemble those of the Pallavas of the seventh century. Staircases at Anurādhapura and Poḷonnaruva are beautifully carved with decorated pillars and carved stones called moonstones at the bottom of the staircase decorated with bands of animals and floral designs.

Early Buddhists represented the Buddha not by images but by relics, the Bo-tree, and the representations of objects such as the Buddha's footprints. The earliest image of the Buddha is a standing marble sculpture, probably imported from Amarāvati. The *Mahāvamsa* refers to earlier Buddha images, but there is no credible evidence of their existence. It and later histories also refer more plausibly to the casting of gold and bronze images from the third century onward, but the earliest surviving bronze images date from the sixth century. These images, which had to be consecrated before they could become objects of worship, most commonly depict the Buddha seated in a meditating posture. They were used as objects of meditation by monks. Standing bronze images of Buddha and standing *bodhisattva* figures have been dated to the late Anurādhapura period.

The Coḷas, who were masters of the medium, imported many bronze images. After their expulsion, there is a renaissance of Buddhist art influenced by south India art, perhaps by south Indian artisans who remained after the restoration of Sinhalese rule.

Literature for much of the Anurādhapura period was Buddhist, written in the Pāli language. The Buddhist scriptures were preserved in the island, first orally and then in writing. The three main monastic orders added their own commentaries, but only some of the Mahāvihāra texts survive. In the later Anurādhapura period, the production of Pāli literature declined and literary works in Sinhala appear.

3

Abandonment of the Dry Zone and the Kandyan Kingdom

The renaissance of Sri Lanka during the reign of Parākramabāhu I ended in administrative collapse, as court factionalism resulted in a succession of weak, short-lived rulers. Sinhalese rulers abandoned the Rājaraṭa in the thirteenth century, after new invasions, malaria, and perhaps climatic change brought about a precipitous decline in the population. Sinhalese political centers moved to the Wet Zone of southern Sri Lanka, and a Tamil kingdom established itself in the northern peninsula. Here the Lankans increased their contact with Indian Ocean trade, culminating in the first European presence in the sixteenth century. On the coasts people assimilated to the dominant cultures, with Muslim trading communities being the major exception. The island for the first time was divided into a Sinhala-speaking southeast and a Tamil-speaking northwest. A third region appeared when a Sinhalese kingdom survived in the central highlands while Europeans threatened the coasts. Warfare and famine in south India appear to have brought about additional migration to the island in this era.

Sinhalese accounts blame foreign invaders, particularly Māgha (1215–1255), for the decline of civilization in the Rājaraṭa, but this is an insufficient explanation. There had been invasions for centuries, and the civilization persisted. It is unlikely that an invader would consciously destroy such a great source of revenue. Parākramabāhu I created the most extensive and elaborate irrigation network the island had known, and its administration seems to have been more centralized than in previous centuries. Local institutions that maintained and repaired reservoirs and canals decayed. The political chaos after his death appears to have set into motion an irreversible decline. The weak rulers after Parākramabāhu I attempted ineffectually to repair irrigation works.

Other factors may have affected the irrigation system, including global climate change (the "medieval warm period," when world temperatures rose). The most significant factor was the appearance of malaria, which eventually made the Rājaraṭa virtually uninhabitable until recent times. The traditional heartland gradually returned to forests thinly occupied by a mixture of Sinhala-speaking and Tamil-speaking cultivators and by *väddā* hunter-gatherers, all subject to famine, disease, and drought. The island appears to have become less healthy in general following the decline of the ancient civilization. The death rate from malaria probably was equaled by the total of water-borne and food-borne diseases such as amoebic dysentery, typhoid fever, and cholera. Cholera and smallpox were not endemic in Sri Lanka but spread in epidemics from India.

The depredations of Māgha and his troops accelerated the decline. Most of what is known about Māgha comes from Sinhalese Buddhist sources, and they emphasize the destruction of temples and image-houses and the persecution of the *sangha*. They accuse him of destroying Buddhist texts and forcing people to adopt Hinduism, a rare instance of religious intolerance in the island. The army he brought from India appears to have pillaged the countryside during their conquest and then to have appropriated the revenues and much of the property of the Rājaraṭa for their support. He left no inscriptions or coins, adding to the impression that his conquest was an army of occupation. A *Damiḷa* king, Jayabāhu, ruled the northern Rājaraṭa in alliance with Māgha.

Militarily Māgha seems to have been more concerned with foreign threats than resistance from the Lankans. Although he had himself consecrated king in Poḷonnaruva and maintained his capital there, his forces were concentrated on the coasts. The Coḷas supported Māgha, but in the thirteenth century, the Paṇḍyas surpassed them as a regional power. As long as the Coḷas were a threat, the Paṇḍyas allied with the Poḷonnaruva kingdom, but as they declined, the Paṇḍyas became more aggressive. During most of Māgha's reign, however, the Paṇḍyas were preoccupied with the consolidation of their conquests to the north.

Chandrabhānu, a Buddhist ruler who had been dispossessed in the Malay peninsula, invaded the island in 1247. He wrested the northern peninsula from Māgha and settled his army there. The Paṇḍyas turned their attention to Sri Lanka again in 1251, 1258, and 1263. They may have been allied with the Sinhalese king Parākramabāhu II, who paid tribute to the Paṇḍyas. Māgha had died by time of the second Paṇḍyan invasion, which forced Chandrabhānu also to pay tribute. The third Paṇḍyan invasion deposed Chandrabhānu and placed his son on the throne and made northern Sri Lanka into a dependency of the Paṇḍyan empire. With the death of Māgha in 1255, Poḷonnaruva no longer was the capital; the centers of power moved to the southwest and the northern peninsula.

The Rājaraṭa fell into the hands of chieftains known as *vanniyā*. Little is known of their origins; the term may be related to the Sinhala word *vana*, meaning forest, but it was also used in south India to refer to semi-independent chieftains and to a military caste that is known to have settled in the island. These chieftains held local power in the Rājaraṭa in the thirteenth and fourteenth centuries, entering into feudal relations with the conqueror of the day. Both Sinhalese and Tamil *vanniyā* chieftains are known, although ethnic identity was certainly less important than it became in the Sinhalese and Tamil kingdoms that emerged outside the area. *Vanni* has come to mean the name for the Dry Zone as a whole.

SINHALESE KINGDOMS

While Māgha ruled in the Rājaraṭa, Sinhalese principalities arose in Māyāraṭa and Rohaṇa. Only some of these are recorded in the histories, and they treat those who extended their control over wider areas as kings. With the exception of Parākramabāhu VI (1411–1466), they were only the strongest among many competitors. Inscriptions show that Tamil rulers also established themselves in these regions. They built fortresses *(giri durga)* in locations where high rock formations gave the rulers a vantage point. One of these, Yāpahuva, still contains the remains of a fortress and palace. It proved to be vulnerable to attack from Māgha, however, and to be overly dependent on the dwindling supply of irrigation water.

A Sinhalese monarchy was restored by the short-lived dynasty that ruled at Daṁbadeṇiya, 121 kilometers (75 miles) southwest of Poḷonnaruva. It was founded by Vijayabāhu III (1232–36), whose origins are obscure. Some chronicles claim descent for him from early Anurādhapura kings, but others seem to suggest Indian (Kaliṅga) origins. He seems to have been a chieftain in the Vanni for some time, building a following. With no strong hereditary claim to the monarchy, he established himself as a patron of Buddhism to win support from the *sangha*. He recovered the Tooth Relic and Alms Bowl Relic, which Buddhist monks who had taken refuge in India had hidden from Māgha. He built a temple for the Relics, which had become potent symbols of the Sinhalese-Buddhist state, in a secure location in the interior of the island. The histories say he repaired monasteries, founded new *vihāra*s, reformed the *sangha*, and promoted learning.

Parākramabāhu II (1236–70) succeeded his father Vijayabāhu III while Māgha still ruled in Rājaraṭa. He is the hero of one section of the *Cūlavamsa*, which devotes eight chapters to his career, emphasizing his services to the *sangha*, his patronage of the arts and his conquest of non-Buddhist enemies. He extended his territorial control against the *vanni* chieftains. During his reign the island became known as a source of cinnamon. He appears to have become ill and turned the administration of the state to his son, who ruled as Vijayabāhu IV, in about 1262. Vijayabāhu built defensive fortresses around his kingdom and defeated an invasion from Chandrabhānu, who had raised an army in India and demanded to be given the two Relics, clearly hoping to use them to establish his legitimacy.

The death of Māgha and defeat of Chandrabhānu enabled Parākramabāhu II to extend his power into the Rājaraṭa. He strengthened the link between the Daṁbadeṇiya kingdom and ancient Sri Lanka by performing a consecration ritual in Poḷonnaruva in 1262. He restored villages to the *sangha* that Māgha had confiscated and enjoyed a period of relative peace. Although he does not seemed to have remained long in Poḷonnaruva—a hoard of buried Chinese coins with a latest date of 1265 may signal the end of its occupation—the histories say he repaired its buildings, returned the Tooth Relic, and held an ordination (*upasampadā*) ceremony for Buddhist monks. The long reign of Parākramabāhu II did not restore Poḷonnaruva to its previous glory, but it enabled his kingdom to claim a magnificent heritage, one appropriated by subsequent rulers.

Parākramabāhu II's successors held on to a weaker Daṁbadeṇiya dynasty for half a century after his death. His son Vijayabāhu IV was murdered after two years by the commander in chief of his army, who was overthrown in turn by Parākramabāhu II's second son Bhuvanekabāhu I (1272–1284). The latter recruited an army from the martial Rajputs of north India, a story confirmed by Rajput sources. Bhuvanekabāhu I attempted to rule from Yāpahuva, the last attempt to build a capital in the Dry Zone; he had governed from there since 1258. Bhuvanekabāhu I promoted trade, sending goodwill gifts to China and a trade mission to Egypt. Famine struck the region after his death in 1284, during which the Paṇḍyans invaded and carried off the Tooth Relic.

The Daṁbadeṇiya period was one of literary achievement in prose and poetry on Buddhist themes. The *Pūjāvaliya* (ca. 1266) is the earliest dated prose work in Sinhala. The *Saddharma Ratnavaliya* is a collection of stories based on Pāli originals. Parākramabāhu II himself was a noted poet. Sinhala histories from the thirteenth and fourteenth centuries, such as the *Pūjāvaliya* and the *Nikāya Sangraha* (ca. 1395), emphasize the *sangha* and its connection with the state. They are an attempt to show a continuous succession of Sinhalese kings, and represent their reigns as if they wielded the same authority as the ancient kings. They explicitly develop the theme of the destruction of the classical kingdom by Tamils and the efforts of rulers like Parākramabāhu II to restore unity to a fragmented Sinhalese society.

Bhuvanekabāhu I was the last Sinhalese ruler in the Dry Zone; his nephew Parākramabāhu III, who is considered to have been the legitimate king from

1287 to 1292, was a vassal of the Paṇḍyas, propped up in Poḷonnaruva. He persuaded the Paṇḍyans to return the Tooth Relic and probably survived until 1302. Poḷonnaruva by this time was reverting to jungle. According to legend he tried to blind his cousin, the heir apparent, but the latter fled, recruited an army, and built a capital in another of the fortified towns, Kurunägala, where he reigned as Bhuvanekabāhu II (1293–1302) . His son Parākramabāhu IV (1302–1326) presided over a literary revival before the dynasty ended a few years later. Sinhalese rulers became little more than warring chieftains, and the kingdom at Jaffna was the only strong kingdom in the latter fourteenth century.

Bhuvanekabāhu IV (1341–51) tried to establish himself in Daṁbadeṇiya but instead built his capital in the Kandyan hills at Gampola. His reign is notable for the construction of the important temples at Laṅkātilaka and Gadalādeniya, which show both the attempt to recapture the grandeur of Poḷonnaruva and also the religious and architectural influence of south India. Another ruler, Parākramabāhu V (1344–59) ruled less than 48 kilometers (30 miles) away in Dädigama. He may have been Bhuvanekabāhu IV's son, and he succeeded him at Gampola.

It is about this time that the great traveler Ibn Battuta visited the island and left a different perspective. He mentions a Muslim ruler at Kurunägala in 1344 who claimed to be the principal ruler of the island. Legend says that this ruler, Vathimi Raja, was the son of Bhuvanekabāhu I by the daughter of a Muslim chieftain.

THE JAFFNA KINGDOM

The Paṅḍyans dominated the north of Sri Lanka as they did the south in the second half of the thirteenth century under Jalavarman Sundara Paṅḍya (1251–72). Their fortunes declined in the early fourteenth century, however. The expansionist Muslim Khilji Dynasty in north India had defeated a rival kingdom to the Paṅḍyans, the Hoysalas, and the latter helped the Khilji general, Malik Kafur, to raid the Paṅḍyans in 1310 and loot their capital at Madurai (which probably stimulated migration to Sri Lanka). There followed a generation of Muslim rule, civil war, and the restoration of Hindu monarchies. The last Paṅḍyan ruler of Madurai was expelled in 1323, and the city was briefly the capital under a Muslim sultanate.

The upheaval enabled the Tamil rulers of northern Sri Lanka to establish their independence. The early history of this kingdom is uncertain. A Paṅḍyan general called Āryachakravarti, a title given to officials or provincial chieftains, led an invasion about the year 1284. He may have remained in northern Sri Lanka following the invasion, and he or a family member declared their independence as the Paṅḍyans declined. Sinhalese texts of the thirteenth and fourteenth centuries refer to the King of Jaffna by the same title.

A later Tamil text, the *Yālppāṇavaipavamālai,* identifies the founder of the Kingdom of Jaffna as Ceyavīra Ciṅkaiyāriyan, who was sent from Madurai with an army and built a capital and Siva temple at Nallur, where he was consecrated with Brahmin rituals. Later histories of the Jaffna kingdom suggest that the *veḷḷāḷa* caste played a central role in its creation. They state that the kings brought colonists from south India—Brahman priests, *veḷḷāḷa* administrators, and the eighteen *kuṭis,* or castes that were subordinate to the *veḷḷāḷa.* subordinates. *Veḷḷāḷa aṭikars,* or chieftains, advised the king.

The *Yālppāṇavaipavamālai* emphasizes that the kings had both Tamil and Sinhalese subjects, the latter sometimes rebellious. *Vanni* chieftains paid tribute to the Āryachakravartis, continuing the feudal relations they maintained with previous rulers. Varōtaya Ciṅkaiyāriyan (fl. 1310–1323) aided the Paṇḍyas during their last years and probably invaded the Daṁbadeṅiya kingdom. He appears to have taken control of the pearl fisheries that had been under the Paṇḍyas and took an increasing role in the Indian Ocean trade.

Ibn Battuta visited the Jaffna Kingdom in 1344. He landed at a port at which the king, possibly Varōtaya's successor Mārttānta Ciṅkaiyāriyan, was residing temporarily, perhaps Puttalam. The king had a large merchant fleet and was heavily involved in the export of cinnamon—which may have been the reason for his aggressive intentions toward the southwest coast. Mārttānta Ciṅkaiyāriyan appears to have levied tribute from Vikramabāhu III (1356–1374) of Gampola in 1359, collected customs duties in the Rājaraṭa, and established military bases along the west coast as far south as Colombo, taking advantage of dynastic disputes among the Sinhalese. They met sterner resistance, however, from the de facto ruler of the west coast, Nissanka Aḷagakkōnāra. Meanwhile, the founding of the Hindu kingdom of Vijayanagara in India in 1336 launched a new era for south India and Sri Lanka. By 1385 they claimed sovereignty over the Āryachakravartis and may have assisted them to invade the Sinhalese kingdom while Bhuvanekabāhu V was still at Gampola.

SOCIETY IN THE SOUTHWEST

Life in the new population centers of the southwest differed greatly from ancient society. Cultivators faced poorer soils, heavy but uncertain rainfall, and hilly terrain. The Sinhalese peasant learned to terrace steeply sloping fields and to plant tree crops and "dry grains" such as millet *(kurakkan)* where rice would not grow well; unirrigated rice culture was supplemented by shifting cultivation *(chēna).* Coconut cultivation was extended, and coconut became the main source of vegetable oil in place of sesame seed oil. Internal trade and the circulation of money decreased as productivity declined. Communication became difficult in the tropical rain forest; cities were reduced to local market towns.

The Indian Ocean trade flourished during this period, and Sri Lanka had become an important link in it by the fourteenth century. Cinnamon was the island's major export, along with other spices, areca nuts, gemstones, and elephants. Colombo and Galle (where the Chinese inscribed a trilingual inscription in 1411 in Chinese, Persian, and Tamil) were ports of external trade. Smaller ports engaged in coastal between India and Sri Lanka. The island imported rice, sugar, textiles, and spices.

The most important merchants were Muslims. Arab traders had come to the island from about the tenth century. Muslim settlements on the southwest coast of India had become the center of the Indian Ocean trade, and Muslim colonies at Colombo, Pānadura, Beruwala, and Hambantota connected the island to this trade.

Rulers no longer had the land revenue made possible by rice surpluses. Kings increasingly depended on universal compulsory service *(rājakāriya)* to cultivate royal land, pay officials, maintain public works, and supply trade goods. External trade became a royal monopoly and a major source of revenue. Kings dealt directly with seafaring merchants, which discouraged the development of local trade.

KOṬṬĒ AND THE PORTUGUESE

By the latter part of the fourteenth century, ministers of south Indian origin became the major power brokers in southwestern Sri Lanka. South Indian immigrants had come to the island in substantial numbers during the previous two centuries. One of them, Sēnalankādikāra, was adviser to Parākramabāhu V and Vikramabahu III, a nephew of Bhuvanekabāhu IV who ruled at Peradeniya. The Aḷagakkōnāra family was originally made up of merchants from Kerala who had settled in Rayigama near the coast ports. They had become so rich and powerful that Ibn Battuta mistakenly identified the Aḷagakkōnāras as the principal rulers in the island. Nissanka Aḷagakkōnāra, reportedly the tenth in succession as head of the family, married the sister of Parākramabāhu V and later succeeded Sēnalankādikāra as the chief adviser to Vikramabāhu III. He lived at Peradeniya with his patron and continued to advise his successor Bhuvanekubāhu V (1374–1408), who may have been a member of the same family.

Nissanka Aḷagakkōnāra repulsed an attack by Mārttānta Ciṅkaiyāriyan and built a fortress at Koṭṭē, just 13 kilometers (8 miles) from the trading post of Colombo. This location was chosen both for its proximity to the coast and the natural defenses provided by the surrounding marshes. He managed to expel the Jaffna representative from Colombo in 1368 and to resist a counterattack from the Āryachakravarti. Bhuvanekabāhu V was subruler at Koṭṭē after 1370 and moved his capital there in 1396. Under the name Alakeśvara, the Aḷagakkōnāra family continued to wield power rule from Rayigama but came to an untimely end in 1411.

The early Ming Dynasty sent seven great fleets into the Indian Ocean from 1405 to 1433. Admiral Zhenghe clashed with Alakeśvara during China's first expedition in early 1406 and withdrew. The second Chinese expedition avoided Sri Lanka, but the third attacked Koṭṭē and abducted the ruler's entire family. This opened the way for the greatest ruler of this era, Parākramabāhu VI (1412–1467), to seize power. He deposed the man placed on the throne by the Chinese and continued to pay tribute to the Chinese even after the naval expeditions ceased.

Parākramabāhu VI engaged in a series of wars that brought most of the island under his control. He counterattacked in India after an invasion from Vijayanagar in 1438, subjugated the *vanni* chieftains (many of whom appear to have been feudatories of Jaffna), and sent an expedition against the Vijayanagar client state in Jaffna in 1446. This expedition was led by a Tamil general, Sapumal Kumaraya (Senpaka Perumal in Tamil), who drove the king to India and ruled the kingdom for about 20 years under the overlordship of Koṭṭē. In 1463 Parākramabāhu VI faced a rebellion in the Kandyan highlands. The brief unity that he had created died with him; the Āryachakravartis returned to power in Jaffna, and the Sinhalese districts broke into civil war. Sapumal Kumaraya returned from Jaffna and overthrew Parākramabāhu VI's grandson to rule as Bhuvanekabāhu VI (1469–71).

Bhuvanekabāhu VI faced a revolt that may have been led by Sinhalese leaders against the non-Sinhalese character of his administration, although this is disputed by some scholars. In any case, the Kandyan highlands as well as northern Sri Lanka took the opportunity to establish their independence. Bhuvanekabāhu VI's successors claimed sovereignty over the entire island, but in fact held only its southwestern fringes. There they encountered a new threat with the arrival of Portuguese traders and conquerors.

The Portuguese first arrived in 1505. They intended to monopolize the trade between the Indian Ocean and Europe and to divert it to the sea route around the Cape of Good Hope. They displaced the Muslim merchants who had dominated trade previously and forced the Koṭṭē kings to sell cinnamon, areca nuts, and gems directly to them. Although undermanned and overextended, the Portuguese gradually asserted their domination of the coast, pushing the Sinhalese rulers inland.

For most of the sixteenth century the Portuguese were one of many contenders for trade and control of the coasts. Dom Lourenço de Almeida arrived in the disunited island in 1505 or 1506. A Portuguese delegation returned to the island in 1512, offering protection to the rulers in return for a trade monopoly. When they built a fort in Colombo in 1517, however, Vijayabāhu VI (1513–21) in league with the colony of Muslim traders unsuccessfully attempted to destroy it. The partition of Koṭṭē in 1521 gave the Portuguese an opportunity to strengthen themselves, ending with Bhuvanekabāhu VII as a puppet of the Portuguese. In 1524, they dismantled their fort because it was no longer needed.

After 1534, Roman Catholic missionaries, stimulated by the Counter-Reformation in Europe, began to convert large numbers of Lankans, particularly in the fishing communities of the west coast. The Council of Trent (1545–63) hardened Portuguese attitudes toward non-Catholics, and these were enforced from Goa from 1567 on. It declared all other religions to be intrinsically wrong and harmful, and demanded that the Portuguese spread the faith. It opposed forcible conversions but required its adherents to destroy other religions by demolishing their temples, expelling their religious leaders, destroying their religious texts, and refusing to allow pilgrimages, ritual bathing, or marriage ceremonies. Orphans were to be raised as Catholics, and non-Catholics were to be officially and legally discriminated against in business dealings and government service. Although the application of these edicts varied widely, they enforced a degree of religious intolerance heretofore unknown in the island.

The assassination of Vijayabāhu VI in 1521 resulted in the partition of the kingdom among his three sons. Bhuvanekabāhu VII (1521–51) reigned at Koṭṭē, but his youngest brother Māyadunnē created a kingdom between the highlands and the coast known as the kingdom of Sītāvaka. The brothers clashed over policy toward the Portuguese. Bhuvanekabāhu VII expelled Muslim traders and granted the Portuguese generous trade concessions. Māyadunnē sided with the Muslims and opposed the alliance with the Portuguese. The Portuguese repeatedly intervened to prevent Māyadunnē (who was allied with the Zamorin of Calicut on the west coast of India) from defeating Koṭṭē. Bhuvanekabāhu VII also sent an embassy to Portugal to secure the succession for his daughter's young son Dharmapāla (1551–97), with his son-in-law Vīdiyā Bandāra as regent. Vīdiyā Bandāra resisted the Portuguese attempt to make Koṭṭē a client state and was imprisoned, despite his conversion to Catholicism. He escaped in 1553 and led a revolt in alliance with Māyadunnē. The latter, however, joined with the Portuguese to defeat Vīdiyā Bandāra when he proved too successful.

Dharmapāla was educated by the Franciscans and converted to Christianity in 1557. This, and his confiscation of lands owned by the *sangha* and *devālēs*, alienated many of his subjects, and he lost territory to Sītāvaka while the Portuguese took over his administration. Eventually, the Portuguese abandoned Koṭṭē and brought Dharmapāla into their fort. Māyādunnē's son Rājasingha succeeded him in 1581 and continued the pressure on the Portuguese until his death in 1593, after which the kingdom of Sītāvaka disintegrated. The Portuguese then reclaimed the original extent of the Koṭṭē Kingdom and took formal possession when Dharmapāla died in 1597. They claimed that Dharmapāla had donated his kingdom to the king of Portugal.

The Jaffna Kingdom under Pararājasēkaran (1478–1519) was independent after the decline of Vijayanagar, but was much reduced in size and strength.

It occupied a strategic location on the Gulf of Mannar, however, and became a target for intervention. The Portuguese took over the pearl fisheries of the Gulf and converted many people to Christianity. Pararājasēkaran's son Çankili (1519–1561) challenged the Portuguese by raising a stronger army and confiscating the cargoes of ship wrecked on his coasts. When threatened by a Portuguese fleet in 1543, Çankili agreed to pay tribute and compensation. The following year, however, he angered the Portuguese by putting to death Christian converts. The Portuguese launched an attack on the kingdom in 1580, and Çankili sued for peace. They took the crown prince as a hostage, which started a civil war among rival claimants for the throne. In 1570 the Portuguese were able to install their own candidate and exerted an increasing influence on the kingdom.

The Portuguese invaded the Jaffna peninsula in 1591 and made Ethirimanna Ciṅkam king with a promise to promote Christianity. The *aṭikars* had weakened in the political upheavals of the previous generation; the Christian converts among them looked to the Portuguese for advancement, but the majority remained Hindu and opposed the spread of Christianity. Ethirimanna Ciṅkam was caught between the two and maintained a precarious balance between his foreign overlords and his administrators until his death in 1615. His nephew, Çankili Kumara, seized power but faced a revolt of his Christian subjects. The Nayak of Tanjore sent troops to crush the rebellion, but in June 1619 the Portuguese annexed the kingdom outright.

The only surviving Lankan kingdom after 1621 was the kingdom of Kandy in the interior highlands of the island. The interior had become a political center when a capital was built at Gampola in the mid-fourteenth century. When the capital moved to Koṭṭē by the end of the century, the region remained the home of members of the royal family. The Koṭṭē rulers could not control the region during the civil wars that followed the death of Parākramabāhu VI in 1467. Sēnāsammata Vikramabāhu (1469–1510), who may have been a grandson of Parākramabāhu VI, built a capital at Senkaḍagala (Kandy) sometime before 1474. Although Vikramabāhu used the titles of an independent sovereign in his documents, Koṭṭē did not allow him the full rights of a king. He paid tribute to Koṭṭē, including sending his subjects to perform compulsory service, and twice military expeditions were sent to reinforce their subordinate status. Neither Vikramabāhu nor his son, Jayavīra Bandāra (1511–51), was able to exert their political independence from Koṭṭē, but the feeling of a distinct cultural identity seems to have grown in the *udaraṭa.*

Kandy became involved in the political rivalry that followed creation of the Sītāvaka kingdom. Jayavīra approached the Portuguese for military aid against Māyadunnē in return for tribute in the 1540s, but this arrived too late to fend off an invasion from Sītāvaka. Karaliyadde Bandāra (1552–1581) entered into an alliance with Koṭṭē and the Portuguese against Sītāvaka, but to no avail. Sītāvaka invaded Kandy three more times, and in 1581 Rājasingha conquered the kingdom, aided by rebellious nobles led by Weerasundara Bandāra.

The kingdom of Kandy ceased to exist for a decade. Opposition to Rājasingha grew, however, as he converted to Saivite Hinduism over the objection of his subjects and raised taxes to pay for his wars against the Portuguese. He suspected Weerasundara Bandāra of treason and had him put to death. Weerasundara's son, Konnappu Bandāra, escaped to the Portuguese. When the Kandyan territories revolted in 1590, Konnapu Bandāra seized power. He converted to Buddhism and expelled the Portuguese missionaries from Kandy, ruling under the name Vimaladharmasūriya I (1591–1604). In 1595, he produced the symbol of Sinhalese Buddhist kingship, the Tooth Relic, which he said had been hidden in a temple (and not destroyed in 1560 as the Portuguese claimed), and placed it in a temple in Kandy.

The Portuguese attempted to bring Kandy under their control as they had Koṭṭē and Jaffna, claiming that Kandy was included in the donation of Dharmapāla. Kandy proved to be much more difficult to conquer, however. The mountainous interior was crossed with rivers that became impassable during the monsoon season. Foreign armies had to move in single file, harassed by the guerrilla tactics of the Kandyans. The Kandyans retreated behind these natural defenses in the seventeenth and eighteenth centuries as the colonial powers on the coasts became stronger.

Senarat (1604–35), who married Vimaladharmasūriya's widow, signed a treaty with the Portuguese in 1617, recognizing their rule on the coasts, paying tribute, and agreeing not to admit their enemies to the interior, in return for Portuguese recognition of their weak state. It was a tenuous peace, as the Portuguese annexed the east coast ports of Trincomalee and Batticaloa, which had been part of the Kandyan Kingdom. Senarat's son Rājasingha in return raided Portuguese territory in the southwest and routed them in the battle of Randenivela in 1630. Another treaty was signed in 1663, but as Rājasingha II (1635–87), he set about to expel the Portuguese. This he did at a great cost; he promised to give the Dutch East India Company (VOC, Verreenidge Oost-Indische Compagnie) a monopoly of the spice trade and to pay the costs they incurred for driving out the Portuguese.

The Dutch initially returned to Rājasingha the fortresses the Portuguese had built in Trincomalee and Batticaloa, but after they expelled the Portuguese in 1658, the VOC refused to return the conquered areas to the king. They retained the cinnamon-producing areas on they grounds that they needed it to recover the costs of warfare—which they priced at a level the king could never repay—and they kept the territories of the old kingdom of Jaffna in the north. The VOC took advantage of a rebellion against the king in 1665 to more than double their territory, including the ports of Trincomalee and Batticaloa. The cinnamon-producing lands, all of the coasts, and a sizable population were now under foreign domination. They declared all major imports except rice to be their monopoly, which forced up prices in the Kandyan kingdom. Rājasingha II raided Dutch-occupied territories and managed to disrupt trade in the period 1670–75, but he never recovered the lost territory.

Rājasingha II kept a number of Europeans captive. The most notable of these was Robert Knox (1641–1720), who was taken prisoner by the Kandyans in 1660; he was able to travel throughout the interior the island but was not allowed to leave until he escaped in 1679. After his return to England, he published an account of his experiences, *An Historical Relation of Ceylon* (1681), which became one of the great travel books of the period. It is now clear that the printed text of Knox's book was embellished by his editors in London, particularly in regard to Rājasingha, who is portrayed as a cruel tyrant.

The Kandyan Kingdom was theoretically centralized but appears to have been politically decentralized, with the chieftains in a feudal relation with the King, for whom they provided a militia in return for relative independence. The two highest officials in the king's administration were two *adigārs*, each responsible for one-half of the kingdom (and for preventing each other from becoming too powerful). The Kandyan chieftains governed hereditary territories. The nine districts close to the capital were known as *raṭas*, administered by *raṭērālas*, and appear to have been under close supervision. The larger, more distant, and less populated districts were *disāvane*s. There were as many as 18 *disāvane*s, though this number had been reduced to 9 by the time of the British conquest. They were governed by *disāvas*, who had considerable autonomy. All these chiefs formed a council at court to advise the king. The *vanni* continued to be quasi-independent, under the control of *Vanniyārs*, who paid tribute to the king. Local occupations, service obligations, taxes, and social hierarchies were based on caste.

The officials were chosen from the *radaḷa*, the highest grade of the largest and highest caste, the *govigama*. The majority of *govigama* were cultivators; members of other castes also cultivated the land but had occupational specialties as well. Knox emphasizes that skilled artisans such as smiths were independent and not subservient to their clients.

Vimaladharmasūriya II (1687–1707) succeeded his father and attempted without success to regain control of the ports and end the VOC trade monopoly. The Dutch, for their part, wanted to renegotiate the 1638 treaty to reflect the political situation. There resulted a long stalemate, during which the Kandyan Kingdom suffered a great loss of revenue from the VOC control of trade. The Kandyan kings generally isolated themselves from the coasts and attempted to move their subjects away from the Dutch borders on the southwest and to allow the jungle to create a barrier, except at well-guarded gates.

Vimaladharmasūriya's son Narendrasingha (1707–1739) likewise was unable to influence the VOC. Some Dutch governors considered invading the kingdom and imposing a treaty more favorable to them, but this was rejected by the VOC headquarters in Batavia. In 1708 Narendrasingha built the Temple of the Tooth Relic, which still stands. When Narendrasingha died without an heir, the VOC anticipated political instability that they could exploit. Instead, there was a peaceful transition to a non-Sinhalese dynasty.

In the absence of other royal families in Sri Lanka, Vimaladharmasūriya II and Narendrasingha both chose their queens from the Nāyakkar community of Madurai in south India. The Nāyakkars were originally from the Telugu-speaking *vaduga* caste but had migrated to the south as a result of Muslim invasions. When he became ill in 1732, Narendrasingha adopted the youngest brother of his Nāyakkar queens as his son and heir, and he ascended the throne as Śrīvijyarājasingha (1739–1747) without objection. Dutch governors, who feared that south Indian connections would strengthen the kingdom, hoped to exploit the rivalry between Nāyakkar and Sinhalese "factions" at the court; this in turn gave rise to a myth that there was such a rivalry, which was not the case.

The Nāyakkar rulers proved to be great patrons of religion. Śrīvijyarājasingha's tutor, Välivița Saraṇaṃkara (1698–1778) started a reform movement within the *sangha* that required monks to live up to the Buddhist ideals of piety, devotion, moderation, and scholarship. In the early seventeenth century, the higher ordination of *bhikkhus* died out because there no longer were five senior *bhikkhus* who could ordain new ones. The Buddhist monks were *gaṇinnānses*, who lived in temples but were not celibate and had limited knowledge of Buddhist scholarship. After several unsuccessful attempts, *bhikkhus* from Ayutthia (Siam) arrived in 1753 to ordain Sinhalese *bhikkhus* at a consecrated site. A hierarchy of the *sangha* was created, with Saraṇaṃkara at the top as the chief monk *(sangharāja)*. Monasteries were trained in Buddhist texts, building on Saraṇaṃkara's extensive scholarship in Sinhala, Pāli, and Sanskrit.

Kirtiśvīrājasingha, the second Nāyakkar king, forced undisciplined monks out of the *sangha* and in 1765 restricted the ordination to the monastic orders at Malvatta and Asgiriya. These monks became the Siyām Nikāya (Siamese fraternity), which restricted membership to the higher grades of the *govigama* caste. He repaired temples and endowed them with land grants. He also attempted to rebuild Anurādhapura and Poḷonnaruwa but succeeded only in building a wall at Anurādhapura to protect it from further damage.

Kirtiśvīrājasingha built a temple to the Hindu deity Vishnu in Kandy in 1748 to replace the shrine of a local deity. He placed the four Hindu temples of Kandy at the head of the annual feudal ritual, the *Äsala perahära*. Under the influence of the Thai monks, this event, which still takes place in August, was reorganized from a procession of Hindu deities to one centered on the Tooth Relic.

In 1761 the ongoing conflict with the VOC broke into warfare. The Kandyans had raided the southwest coast in support of a rebellion against the Dutch and captured two forts. In retaliation, the Dutch invaded Kandy in 1762 but were driven back in 1763. Kirtiśvīrājasingha turned for aid to the British, whose power in the Indian Ocean was steadily increasing. His kinsmen in Madras started talks with the English East India Company (EIC), but they were unwilling to make any concessions to the Kandyans. Angered by the Kandyan negotiations with the EIC, the VOC invaded again in 1765 and sacked Kandy. Although the Dutch troops in Kandy were decimated by starvation and disease, the kingdom faced famine conditions and was forced to sign a new treaty in 1766. For the remainder of its history, the Kandyan Kingdom was completely landlocked and had no control over its foreign trade, even for essential commodities such as salt and foodstuffs.

4

Portuguese, Dutch, and British Colonialism

The Kandyan Kingdom survived until 1815, becoming progressively weaker as European control of the coasts extended around the island and took on a permanent form. The Portuguese established their control over Koṭṭē by 1600, only to face a stronger foe as Dutch trading ships began to appear in the Indian Ocean in the late sixteenth century. The Dutch East India Company (VOC) began its conquest of the island in 1638; 20 years later, the VOC expelled the Portuguese and absorbed the Tamil kingdom in the north. The VOC declined in the second half of the eighteenth century and was replaced by the English East India Company (EIC) in 1796. Ceylon became the Crown Colony of Ceylon under the British Parliament in 1801, and they annexed the interior in 1815. After some experimentation, the British administration took its mature form with the implementation of the Colebrooke-Cameron Reforms in 1833.

PORTUGUESE COLONIALISM

When the Koṭṭē king Dharmapāla died 1597, the Portuguese faced many obstacles to administering the colony, which was their largest possession in Asia. They were undermanned, the Dutch and French threatened their coasts, and the unification of Portugal with Spain reduced their support at home. Nevertheless, they exerted a strong cultural influence on the territories they controlled.

The captain-general was subordinate to the Viceroy in Goa but took on the aura of a king in his administration; Portuguese gentlemen *(fidalgos)* replaced the higher officials of the kingdom. This new layer of rulers was more oppressive than the kings had been. They adopted the local administrative hierarchy and increased the number of local officials in order to control the population and exploit the export trade. The most numerous of these were the *mudaliyārs* (a term that has come to mean a man eligible for appointment to one of these offices under the Portuguese, Dutch, or British). *Mudaliyārs* at that time held territorial offices with revenue, judicial, and military functions. They had subordinate officials known as *muhandirams* and *āracci,* and they commanded a militia *(lascarins).* They were subordinate to the *disāva,* a Portuguese officer who had assumed a Sinhala title. The Portuguese created new officials called *vidāna,* who were in charge of either a department *(badda)* or a district *(kōralē).*

The Koṭṭē kings used *rājakāriya* to supply trade goods, but the Portuguese wanted to increase their trade beyond that allowed by customary service obligations. During the sixteenth century their demand for cinnamon increased steadily. They made cinnamon a strict government monopoly and regulated its collection. In its last years in Ceylon, the Portuguese state made immense profits from the cinnamon monopoly.

The Portuguese manipulated Sinhalese land tenurial arrangements to increase the supply of cinnamon and to provide revenue and services for their administration. They appropriated royal lands *(gabaḍgama),* which had provided the revenue for the court, and temple lands *(vihārāgama* and *devālāgama),* which were distributed among their officials and followers. Landholders were required to provide commercial crops from their private holdings *(pravēni)* as a land tax in kind.

Sixty years of direct Portuguese rule in the southwest brought two generations of Sinhalese officials through a transition from minor officials of a sovereign state to agents of a foreign commercial administration. The people complained about the concentration of power in the hands of Sinhalese officials and the use of *rājakāriya* for nontraditional labor. Under the Portuguese, headmen and landholders had to cultivate, pick, and transport their crops, which the Sinhalese believed were menial tasks that should be reserved for the lowest-status coolies, or unskilled laborers. Village headmen were required to cook and provide other personal services for officials and Portuguese soldiers. The *mudaliyārs* were becoming the colonial elite, which persisted into the twentieth century.

Efforts to convert the island to Roman Catholicism changed Lankan society. Converts were rewarded while Buddhists and Hindus were persecuted, their lands expropriated, and their temples destroyed. Catholic communities grew in the southwest and the north and survived despite being persecuted in turn by the Dutch. The presence of Sinhalese Christians was troubling for Sinhalese

Buddhists, who had come to believe that their religious and cultural identities were inseparable.

The Portuguese introduced the term *caste* to refer to the social units of the island. The economic activities of the Portuguese produced dramatic changes for the castes of the coasts. The *salāgama* caste traces its origins to weavers from south India brought by Vijayabāhu III in the thirteenth century. The king of Koṭṭē had required some of them to peel and collect cinnamon, and the Portuguese greatly increased the numbers required to do so. These "cinnamon peelers" *(kuruňdukāra)* became a grade of the *salāgama* caste subordinate to their commanders *(hēvāpanna)*. The *salāgama*s rose in importance as the caste primarily responsible for the collection of cinnamon. The *karāva* caste members were disproportionately Christian and lived in close proximity to Portuguese centers. Their experience in dealing with the Portuguese led eventually to their emergence as artisans and entrepreneurs. The elite among these two castes accumulated wealth and land, and began to challenge the predominance of the *govigama* elite. When the Portuguese honored this new elite with *mudaliyār* appointment and other titles, some *govigamas* accused them of recruiting officials of "lesser quality" or "inferior birth."

Portuguese rule in Jaffna was fairly short-lived (1619–1658) but had a great impact on the economy and society. The Portuguese, and the Dutch after them, encouraged small holders to grow tobacco, and this brought prosperity to the peninsula. Cultivation was highly labor-intensive; irrigation water was drawn from wells and composting was mandatory in the infertile soil. This hardened the caste hierarchy in Jaffna, because the *veḷḷāḷas* owned the wells and the land; labor was performed by Untouchable castes, which were their hereditary dependents *(aṭimai)*. Over time the status of the *aṭimai* castes fell and that of the *veḷḷāḷa*s rose. As the latter prospered from the sale of tobacco and the rising price of land, they became patrons of temples and hired Brahmins from India to serve in them. They were also able to demand the service and artisan *(kutimai)* castes to perform their traditional secular and ritual occupations for the *veḷḷāḷa* families to which they were attached. These castes included the five artisan castes (Goldsmiths, Blacksmiths, Carpenters, Temple Carvers, and Coppersmiths) and the other professional castes (Potters, Masons, Washermen, Barbers, and Drummers). The *karaiyar* of the Jaffna Peninsula challenged the *veḷḷāḷas,* as their Sinhalese counterparts the *karāva* did—but with less success.

DUTCH COLONIAL ADMINISTRATION

The Dutch colonial empire in the seventeenth century was the most efficient the world had seen. The VOC was a joint-stock corporation based in Batavia on the island of Java. It controlled the Asian trade with Europe, outstripping the Portuguese and leaving the EIC with only scraps of trade.

The first Dutch expedition arrived in Ceylon on May 31, 1602, at Batticaloa, where they made contact with the Kandyan Kingdom. Kandy signed a treaty with the Dutch in 1638, and together they gradually deposed the Portuguese. Instead of leaving as they had promised, however, the Dutch occupied the ports of Galle and Negombo on the specious grounds that Kandy had not paid them what was owed for dispelling the Portuguese.

The Dutch were unable to conquer the interior because they were more concerned with the threat to their seaborne empire from the English and the French. The Dutch ruled a larger territory of the island than the Portuguese had and thus divided it into three provinces: The governor was based in Colombo, and commanders administered the other two from Jaffna and Galle. They required more subordinate officials. They gave the *mudaliyār*s grants of land and organized those attached to the central administration (*vāsala,* or "gate" *mudaliyārs*), as interpreters and translators to high officials. The *mudaliyārs* had to profess Christianity, which required a nominal conversion from Catholicism to the Dutch Reformed Church for those who had served the Portuguese.

The VOC attempted to repopulate and bring back into cultivation areas devastated by warfare. This increased their reliance on the Sinhalese officials to enforce the demand for *rājakāriya.* They developed taxes and trade monopolies to provide local revenue to run the colony. (Trade profits were not available for this purpose.) Rice, arrack (a liquor distilled from palm nectar), the seasonal fish catch, and other economic activities were taxed. The rights of tax collection and of engaging in the trade monopolies were auctioned out to tax farmers or "renters." They tried unsuccessfully to collect a tax on tree crops, as well as on paddy.

The Dutch encouraged the cultivation of export crops such as pepper and cardamom, but the low fixed prices they paid gave cultivators little incentive. High taxes and the oppressive nature of the demand for *rājakāriya* —including its fraudulent use by Dutch officials—appear to have caused a decline in agriculture. Eventually, the Dutch resorted to growing cinnamon on plantations.

The Dutch also created opportunities for social mobility through new professions in schools and the church. They opened schools for the local population at every church. New posts as interpreters, translators, and clerks were created with the title of *mudaliyār.* Genealogical records in the Dutch *tombos,* or registers, suggest that many of the prominent Sinhalese families at the time of the British conquest can trace their origins to a founder during the early eighteenth century, when the role of the *mudaliyār* was expanding. Governor Gustav Willem Baron Van Imhoff (beginning 1737) reacted against abuses of power by the chiefs.

Governor Imhoff also established a printing press in 1737 and had movable type created for Sinhala and Tamil. It was used primarily to publish government documents and Protestant tracts. The British colonial government used this press in their early years.

The VOC introduced European courts to their subjects. They codified the customary laws of the Tamils of Jaffna in the *Tesavalamai* in 1706, and they introduced Muslim laws that had been codified in Java. Roman-Dutch law was applied to the Low Country Sinhalese, owing to the variety of local customs. By the time the British replaced the Dutch, few traces of traditional law survived in their territory.

DUTCH REACTION 1737–1769

By the middle decades of the eighteenth century, the influence in the hands of the *mudaliyārs* became a concern to the Dutch. The massive registration of land and population in *tombos* was directed at reducing their reliance on headmen. Governors reduced the land grants attached to higher offices and resumed some personal grants at the death of the grantee. The bureaucracy was reorganized. The offices of *mudaliyār* and *korāla* began to be combined in the same person. Appointments were made to the subordinate office of *muhandiram* rather than to additional *mudaliyārs*. By 1770, the *mudaliyārs* lost all vestiges of military power but continued to be indispensable to Dutch colonial administration.

When Governor Jan Schreuder (1757–61) tried to tax their land grants, the *mudaliyārs* rose in rebellion, which precipitated a war with Kandy. Schreuder confiscated the property of the rebellious *mudaliyārs* and banished their leaders. Most of the banished men were eventually reprieved by Batavia; all of the leading families in this period appear to have recovered from such setbacks and even to have prospered. Jacob Burnand, who served both the Dutch and the British, wrote that the *mudaliyārs* had become "Lords in their Provinces" by the middle of the eighteenth century, and that Dutch efforts to control corruption among them only made them more secretive.

Most of the rebels were given new appointments. In 1767, for example, the Dutch gave Louis Perera, who had been banished to the Cape Colony, the office of *kūruvērāla,* or supervisor of the elephant department, and his son Abraham was made his assistant the following year. By 1790 Abraham had succeeded his father with the expanded title of *kūruvē mudaliyār,* and he entered British service as the head of the most prominent family of the Western Province, after his in-laws, the deSaram family.

Prosperity in Ceylon in the declining years of Dutch rule enhanced the returns from other civil functions of the *mudaliyār*s—particularly tax collection. Dutch administrators turned to the *mudaliyār*s to carry out a wide variety of local administrative tasks rather than develop an extensive bureaucracy. By 1796 they were firmly in control of the lower levels of Dutch colonial administration, and they reaped social benefits from it.

A colonial elite emerged among the Low Country Sinhalese well before the British accession. Their status was not simply due to Dutch patronage, but to the ways they used the power and prestige attached to their offices to raise their status in Sinhalese society. Wealth and authority were converted to social status by accumulation of the symbols of power, acquisition of landed estates, the establishment of group status for their kinsmen, and, above all, the enforcement of *rājakāriya*.

DUTCH BURGHERS

Another influential community existed by the end of the Dutch period known as "Dutch Burghers." The Dutch attempted unsuccessfully to settle colonies of Dutch citizens, or Burghers. These Burghers alone had the privilege to keep shops and were given liberal grants of land, the right of free trade, and preference for appointment to office. Marriage between a Burgher and a local Christian woman (often Indo-Portuguese) was permitted, and a community of mixed descent emerged. The daughters of these marriages were expected to marry Dutchmen.

By the eighteenth century, a culturally European community of Portuguese, Dutch, Sinhalese, and Tamil origins had developed. They dressed in European style, attended the Dutch Reformed Church, and spoke Dutch or Portuguese. They intermarried among themselves and with newcomers in the VOC service. They began to think of themselves as Dutch Burghers if they could demonstrate European ancestry through the male line, were fair-skinned, adhered to the Dutch Reformed Church, and spoke (and often read and wrote) Dutch.

A second community of mixed origins evolved over time: the Portuguese Burghers (called later Mechanics). They had a supposed (but not certain) European ancestry, were dark skinned, practiced Catholicism, and spoke Creole Portuguese (which continued to be used in Ceylon as a colloquial language until the end of nineteenth century).

At the time of the British conquest in 1796, there were about 900 families of Dutch Burghers residing in Ceylon, concentrated in Colombo, Galle, Matara, and Jaffna. Their numbers expanded by the VOC's employees of European origin who chose to remain in the island. They quickly adopted English and were recruited to serve in the British colonial administration.

JAFFNA

The Dutch defined the status of the *aṭimai* untouchable castes, particularly the agricultural laborers, as "slavery," which deepened *veḷḷāḷa* domination of them. These castes had not been slaves as the term was used by eighteenth-century Europeans; they had rights and privileges, such as the right to desert a cruel master. The result was the growth of a slave-based export economy, in which Jaffna produced intensively cultivated Palmyra products (toddy, jaggery, and fronds), onions, gourds, chillies, turmeric, ginger, pumpkins, and eggplants in addition to tobacco. Rice was imported. The Dutch profited from this import and export trade and made no attempt to curtail the social abuses it encouraged.

POPULATION

The population of the island may have been at its lowest level in a millennium in the mid-seventeenth century. Living conditions improved in the eighteenth century, particularly during the last 30 years of Dutch control, when the cultivation of cash crops and coastal trade increased. It is unlikely that the population of the Kandyan kingdom increased, as most of the population was concentrated in a small area between the malarial zones to the north and east and the inhospitable (to the Sinhalese) mountains. The Dutch attempted to register the entire population under their control in the period 1742–1759. The *mudaliyārs* resisted the registration because their knowledge of land tenures was a key to their value to the Europeans; a population register would also have limited their opportunity to exact *rājakāriya* for personal use. Despite this resistance, the register was completed in 1760 and was revised haphazardly in the period 1766–1771. In 1789 the colonial governor estimated the population in his own territories at 817,000, which is probably a tally of the figures in the 1771 registers.

BRITISH CONQUEST

During Dutch rule the EIC was allowed to trade in Lankan ports. In the second half of the eighteenth century, the EIC had conquered a territorial empire in India and became the dominant commercial power in the Indian Ocean. From the early 1760s the British sent spy missions to Kandy and attempted to establish commercial relations. The EIC captured Trincomalee and held it briefly in 1782; they sent an ambassador to Kandy, but the new king Rajadhirājasingha (1782–98) was unable to reach an agreement. The VOC was entering a severe decline at this time and lost the entire island to the EIC in 1796.

After France occupied the Netherlands, the British government dispatched an expeditionary force against Ceylon, and the Dutch capitulated early in 1796. Brig. General P. F. de Meuron transferred the allegiance of his mercenary Swiss regiment from the Dutch to the British, and Lord Hobart, Governor of Madras, appointed him commander of the troops and the chief authority of Ceylon. In 1798 the British made the entire island, except the kingdom of Kandy, a crown colony. The 1802 Treaty of Amiens, which terminated the second phase of the Napoleonic Wars, formally ceded the Island to Great

Britain. The kingdom of Kandy was also occupied briefly in 1803 and annexed to the crown colony in 1815. The British controlled the entire island for another 133 years and greatly influenced Ceylon.

The EIC governed the island from 1796 to 1801 as an appendage of its empire in India, administered from Madras. The heavy-handed exploitation of the colony's revenue by Madras officials and the subordinates they brought with them produced a rebellion by Sinhalese villagers that lasted nearly a year from March 1797 to early 1798.

Parliament appointed a civilian governor, Lord Frederick North, an eager but inexperienced son of a prime minister, to replace de Meuron in October 1798. The island was under the dual control of Parliament and the EIC until it became the first Crown Colony on January 1, 1802, administered through the Colonial Office.

North energetically set about creating government departments and appointing officials, but his lack of experience and financial difficulties prevented much success. He tried to reduce the independence of the *mudaliyārs* but found that they were indispensable to the administration. The Secretary of State explicitly required North to restore the authority of the *mudaliyārs* and to enforce *rājakāriya*. The British did not want to give up the benefits of *rājakāriya,* which, under the Dutch, had been the primary means of providing essential services to the administration.

British innovations from 1796 to 1802 have shaped Ceylon and Sri Lanka to the present. Although they later developed a more nuanced construction of Lankan society, their starting point was the model of South Asian society developed during two centuries of contact with India. In general, they chose to identify people with social categories and to control those people through their use of those categories. They considered the Sinhalese, Tamils, Burghers, "Moors," and others to be distinct "races," and governed each separately. (Kandyans, after the conquest of the interior, were also treated as a separate race.) Each race was divided into ranked subcategories. The British considered these castes, or caste-like units, to be the building blocks of Lankan society. Furthermore, castes were further divided internally into ranked grades, and the highest grades of the highest caste—the "first-class" *govigamas* and *veḷḷāḷas*—were chosen as collaborators in colonial rule. As they did in India, the British viewed the structure they created as a "caste system" among the Sinhalese and the Tamils. It was to them not only a rigid system but one that had been fixed in time.

North's successors were military officers who transitioned the administration into permanency. To them, Ceylon was a strategic outpost for the growing British empire. They continued to enforce Roman-Dutch Law and the *Tesavalamai,* and they created a new Code of Muslim Law. They created a series of courts: a supreme court of British judges with criminal jurisdiction over the whole island and civil jurisdiction over Colombo and all the Europeans.

Courts of the justice of the peace had civil jurisdiction elsewhere. Trial by jury was established in 1812; initially juries were created on a caste and class basis.

Burghers and sons of *mudaliyārs* attended the Colombo Seminary; after 1828, all *mudaliyārs* were required to know English. The government provided little other opportunity for education, and even the sons of non-*govigama mudaliyārs* faced discrimination, as the *govigama* boys refused to sit with boys of other castes.

Caste had been a fluid category in Lankan history; the social categories mentioned in Sinhala inscriptions have little similarity to those in colonial times. New social groups such as the *salāgama, kārava,* and *durāva* made their appearance among the Sinhalese as the political centers moved from the Dry Zone to the southwest, where immigrants from south India were absorbed into the culture. South Indians recruited by the Portuguese as soldiers merged into Low Country castes. The *salāgama* caste absorbed other cinnamon peeling castes, and fishing castes came to be identified with the *karāva* caste. South Indian migrants who accompanied the Kandyan kings assimilated to the culture.

A similar process took place as the north and east coasts became Tamil-speaking regions. The *veḷḷāḷa* caste seems to have been created from the amalgamation of immigrants from several groups of relatively high status. It is not even clear how many Tamil castes existed—there were dozens of groups that may or may not have been castes.

British policy froze the traditional social structure by turning these fluid relationships into a rigid system and enforced status distinctions. Although caste was not discussed publicly as it was in India, the hegemonic character of colonial rule forced Lankans to accept the British construction in order to survive in the colonial society.

Among the reforms implemented by the governors before 1833 was the abolition (for the first time but not the last) of slavery. Slaveholding by Europeans and Westernized Lankans, in which a person was the chattel property of another person, was easily dealt with and was abolished in 1821. In Jaffna, however, the condition of the *aṭimai* castes proved to be more difficult to resolve. They had been unfree laborers dependent on *veḷḷāḷas*, but the Dutch had treated them as chattel slaves. Simply abolishing slavery did not change their status and in fact worsened their condition as they remained dependent on the *veḷḷāḷas*.

There was an attempt to develop commercial crops. Governor Edward Barnes (1824–1831) started a coffee plantation and waived land taxes on plantations and duties on some export crops to encourage cultivation. In 1820 the government abolished the export duty on coffee, and in 1824 coffee land was exempted from the land tax. Europeans were permitted to buy agricultural land and then encouraged to do so by extremely low sale prices. The duties on the import of agricultural implements were repealed, and even before the abolition of *rājakāriya,* coffee laborers were exempted from its service obligation. Government officials were prohibited from engaging in trade.

The *mudaliyārs*, the former employees of the Dutch Company, and Muslim renters and traders took advantage of opportunities. Some of the descendants of the *mudaliyārs* who made their fortunes in the early years of British rule have remained influential today. Don Solomon Dias Bandaranaike was *mudaliyār* of two *paṭṭus* of Siyane Kōralē East near the Kandyan border. He was awarded with a gold medal and substantial land grants for his service against the Kandyans in 1803, but the prosperity of the family can be attributed to the building of the Colombo-Kandy road through his *kōralē* rather than on its original course further south. Don Solomon marshaled the labor through *rājakāriya* for the construction of this road, which increased the value of the lands he and his family acquired near it. His son and grandson succeeded him in this post, and the latter, Sir Solomon Dias Bandaranaike, held the highest post of in the *mudaliyār* system, Maha Mudaliyar, for 32 years, from 1895 to 1927. Sir Solomon's son, S.W.R.D. Bandaranaike, was prime minister, and his daughter, Chandrika Bandaranaike Kumaratunga, was elected president in 1994.

The most notorious of the early *mudaliyārs* was Adrian Jayewardene, better known as "*tambi mudaliyār*," the ancestor of President Junius Richard Jayewardene and Prime Minister Ranil Wickremasínghe. *Tambi* is the Tamil word for younger brother, and for that reason it is sometimes claimed that his ancestors were Muslims or Tamil Christians. He probably was the son of a *goyigama lascarin*, and the nickname was probably given to him by the British troops from south India who captured him in 1795. Shifting loyalty to the British, he rose rapidly as a scout and spy for the troops during the unsettled first decade of their rule. The family's fortune originated from his appropriation of nearly 2,612 acres in Chilaw District that was controlled by a *mudaliyār* who had deserted to Kandy in 1803. Although never accepted into the highest ranks of the *mudaliyārs*, his descendants became prominent lawyers.

KANDYAN REBELLION

The British invaded Kandy in 1803 but were overcome by diesease and fatigue. They withdrew when soldiers deserted in increasing numbers. In 1815 the British and Kandyan chieftains deposed the king and signed the Kandyan Convention on March 2, 1815. This recognized British sovereignty in the island in return for preserving the laws of the country, including the king's duty to protect and maintain Buddhism, the monasic orders, and their temples

Two years after the annexation of the Kandyan Kingdom, it erupted into a rebellion to drive out the British and return the monarchy to power. The rebellion seemed at first to succeed, but the British—with the aid of loyal chieftains, Low Country Sinhalese, and reinforcements from India—crushed the rebellion in 1818. They ruthlessly suppressed all resistance and destroyed the rebellious districts. About 1,000 British troops and 10,000 Kandyans died.

The remaining resistance ended when the "pretender" who proclaimed himself king in July 1817 turned out to have no claim to the throne, and the British captured the Tooth Relic.

The British reacted to the rebellion with severe measures. They dismissed many chiefs, reduced their privileges, and applied differential taxes to districts, punishing those that had rebelled with higher rates. A proclamation of November 21, 1818, reduced the chiefs from feudal lords to bureaucrats, appointed by the government and paid a fixed salary. They began to withdraw the protection promised to Buddhism by the Kandyan Convention. Religions other than Buddhism were recognized, and the government neglected the maintenance of the *sangha* and temples.

In the Convention of 1815 the English agreed to retain the laws, institutions, and customs of the Kandyan kingdom. After the rebellion, however, the Proclamation of 1818 became the basis of the Kandyan administrative system. Until 1833, British officers administered the Kandyan districts through a board of commissioners, consisting of the commander of the troops in Kandy, a judicial officer, and a revenue officer. Higher chieftains were replaced by British officials, aided by Low Country Sinhalese subordinates. The *disāvas* and *ratē mahamayas* were supervised by this board and, like the low-country *mudaliyārs*, enlisted the deference they were given by the people in the service of the foreign rulers.

By the 1820s, Ceylon was no longer primarily a military outpost, but it had no clearly defined role in the empire. It was also continually spending more than it collected in taxes, due in part to the EIC's restrictions on trade with the subcontinent and in part to the Government of Ceylon's inability to maintain the profitability of the trade monopolies in cinnamon, pearls, and other commodities. As a result, dramatic reforms were implemented after 1833.

COLEBROOKE-CAMERON REFORMS

A Royal Commission headed by W.M.G. Colebrooke arrived in 1829 to recommend reforms in the administration of the colony. A year later, Charles Hay Cameron joined him to examine the judicial system. Their recommendations were very progressive, marking in some ways the high point of British colonial administration in Ceylon.

Colebrooke collected a vast amount of information from all sources while in Ceylon, which remains a huge and largely untapped repository of information on the period. Colebrooke received hundreds of petitions from Lankans, but much of the British viewpoint on Low Country Sinhalese society in this period came from one man, Abraham de Saram Wijesekere, son of Maha Mudaliyar Johannes de Saram. He entered British service in July, 1804, and was awarded a gold medal in 1819 for service in the Kandyan rebellion. As spokesmen for the *goyigama mudaliyārs*, he presented the replies of the *mudaliyārs* to the Colebrooke-Cameron Commission. More importantly, he supplied the Collector of Colombo with a detailed list of caste ranking, and another to Governor Horton in 1832.

Colebrooke recommended opening the civil service to Lankans, recruited by competitive examination. He opposed the hereditary privileges of the *mudaliyārs* and the system of *rājakāriya* that was the basis of their local power. Economically, he wanted to open up the colony to private investment, free trade, and the free movement of wage labor. Cameron's Charter of Justice was intended to prevent the governors from abusing their executive powers.

Colebrooke urged the growth of schools to diffuse the knowledge of the English language and recommend the formation of a school commission. At the time there were about 12,000 students in a school-age population about 250,000 throughout the island. Fewer than 800 students were studying in the English medium. He wanted to shift the emphasis from proselytization, as it had been under the Dutch, to training to serve in the colonial administration, but he recognized the financial advantage of leaving schools in the hands of the Christian clergy. The colony eventually provided a rigorous education in English for a relatively small number of elite youth, and a vernacular education for a much larger population. In English, Sinhala, and Tamil, education was unequally distributed by religion, language, region, and caste.

Some of their recommendations were implemented. A legislative council was created in 1833 as Colebrooke recommended, with nine official members and six unofficial members. Although it gave Lankans a limited opportunity to comment on government business, it contained inherent weaknesses. The unofficial members were appointed by the governor, usually three Europeans, one Sinhalese, one Tamil, and one Burgher. The latter were chosen from a few elite families but were considered to represent their communities, the beginnings of the notion of communal representation that later divided the country. The Burghers were recognized, unlike Kandyans or Muslims (who were included later in the nineteenth century), but this was a double-edged sword; it called attention to the fact that the British considered them racially distinct from Europeans.

CHRISTIANITY IN CEYLON

After 300 years of Portuguese and Dutch promotion of Christianity in Jaffna and the southwest coast of Ceylon, these regions had both Roman Catholic and Dutch reformed Protestant communities. Both governments made profession of Christianity a prerequisite of government employment and vigorously sought conversions. Early British estimates misinterpreted this and overestimated both the number of Christians and the likelihood that the entire island would be converted to Christianity. However, when the British made it known that they did not require conversion to their form of Christianity, many Lankan Protestants changed their professed religion to Hinduism or Buddhism.

English evangelists had for years failed to gain the admittance of English missionaries into the territories of the EIC but found a receptive field in Ceylon. Governor Thomas Maitland allowed four ministers of the London Missionary Society—who had opened missions in Colombo, Matara, Galle, and Jaffna in 1805—to continue but resisted further increase. Governor Robert Brownrigg, however, was an evangelist who allowed the Church of England Missionary Society (1811), Baptists (1812), Wesleyan Methodists (1814), and even the American Board of Commissioners for Foreign Missions (1813) to establish missions in the island. The Americans, who came to Ceylon after they were refused admission into India, were exiled to Jaffna, where they established a large and active mission. The missionary societies emphasized education as a means to conversion.

Brownrigg's successors wanted only Anglican missionaries in Ceylon. They were given permission to operate a printing press, but the more active Americans and Wesleyans were obstructed. The Church Missionary Society obtained free land for churches and schools. In all, favoritism for the Anglicans was thought of as a positive encouragement to missionary activity and the conversion of the island to Christianity.

The efforts of American missionaries played a large part in the future of Jaffna. The American Board of Commissioners for Foreign Missions was founded in June 1810. After the EIC resisted the board's attempts to establish missions there, they settled on Ceylon and were sent to the north.

CONCLUSION

The suppression of the Kandyan Rebellion unified the entire island under a single government for the first time in its history. In doing so, the British simultaneously divided the country by ruling through categories of Lankans that they considered natural groups among the population. The Low Country Sinhalese, Kandyans, Tamils, and "Moors," or Muslims, were distinct races to the British, and each was treated differently. The British encouraged British subjects, particularly Indian merchants and laborers, to settle in the country, but in the course of the nineteenth century they focused their attentions on the Sinhalese and on the "Ceylonese" Tamils and Muslims; other groups were marginalized. Colonialism introduced beliefs about racial superiority and identity, which resulted in two opposed nationalisms (Sinhala and Tamil) and laid the foundations for the present ethnic conflict between the two groups.

In 1833, Ceylon was still a colonial dependency in which rulers from England controlled a non-European population. Europeans were not allowed to

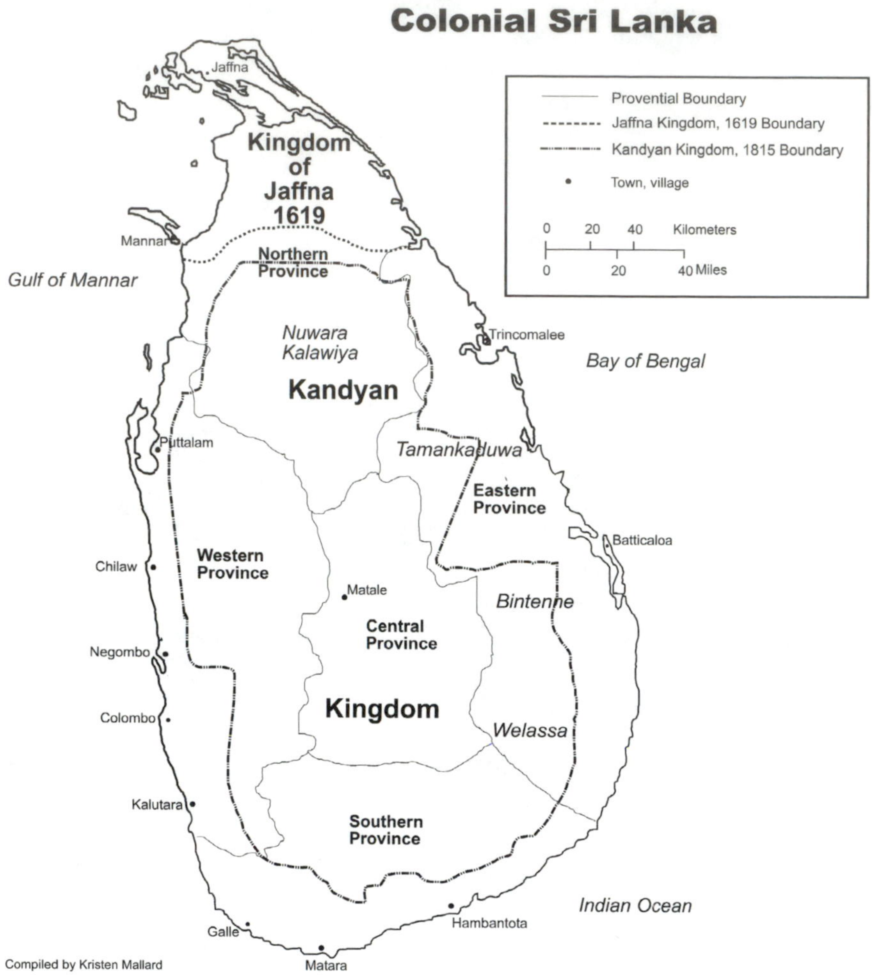

settle in the country without permission. On one hand, they were reluctant to disrupt the social structure intentionally, but on the other hand, they enforced what they believed to be the real social institutions. They divided the country by rigid ethnic categories and governed through them, which facilitated governance but created immense problems for the future. The barrier between the Tamil and Sinhalese people has been the most difficult to overcome, but class and caste divisions in society also solidified. Even the abolition of slavery did little to improve the status of those who were members of what were considered slave castes. Likewise, the enforcement of *rājakāriya* for nontraditional uses until 1833 increased the power of dominant families and increased the burden on the poorest segments of the population.

5

A Colonial Society

British colonial Ceylon transformed itself from a military outpost to a hybrid society in which the government tried to balance the interests of the plantation economy with the need to govern a large indigenous population. The Colebrooke-Cameron reforms opened the way for the emergence of a dualistic export economy, but the colony evolved in ways not anticipated by the reformers. Coffee plantations spread across the mountainous interior. The British rewarded their allies among the people with land grants, titles, and administrative offices in which they had a free hand to wield their power. Local elites maintained order and were expected to assimilate to the rulers' culture, which created an Anglicized elite that was increasingly distant from the people. By the time the coffee plantation industry collapsed after 1878, it had provided substantial revenue. The government used this revenue to build roads and railroads, to improve irrigation works and the harbors, to transform overseas communications though steamships and telegraphs, and to establish schools and churches.

COLONIAL ADMINISTRATION

Many of Colebrooke's recommendations were never implemented or weakened over time. The colonial government was concerned primarily with maintaining order and with providing adequate revenue to make the colony self-sufficient. The former was achieved by an autocratic governor, a civil service that was almost entirely British, and the active participation of local elites. The latter was provided by the coffee plantation industry, which also created a British constituency for the colony.

The Colonial Office considered governors and other higher officials to be interchangeable, and they were transferred from colony to colony for five-year terms. A Legislative Council of nine official and six "unofficials" advised the governors. Half of the unofficial members were to be Lankan, and Governor Horton made them racial by appointing one Sinhalese, one Tamil and one Dutch Burgher. This was considered progressive in 1833, but the Legislative Council remained a purely advisory body until the twentieth century and became increasingly anachronistic as other British colonies introduced a degree of self-government. The addition of Kandyan and Muslim members in 1889 only emphasized its ceremonial character.

The most influential officials were the members of the elite Ceylon Civil Service (CCS). The CCS got its start with the officials brought from England with Governor North. The Colonial Office continued to send new recruits until by 1831 there were 38 men in the CCS. They were a highly paid, but not particularly capable, group; Governor Horton said that 11 of the CCS officers were "decidedly incompetent" and 9 were "barely competent." Their salaries cost the government more than all the clerks, magistrates, and local staff who served under them combined.

When the British Treasury reduced the salaries of the CCS in 1833, by as much as 60 percent for some of the junior posts, morale deteriorated. Many turned to coffee planting to supplement their incomes, until this was prohibited in 1844. The lower salaries would have been sufficient if the CCS had been opened to competition from the local population, as Colebrooke had recommended, but the colony continued to recruit Englishmen. They were attracted by the prospect of high salaries and early retirement at a generous pension.

Governors did appoint some local CCS officers, but these were drawn from the small European and Burgher communities until 1845. In that year, two Lankans, who had been doing the work of civil servants as District Judges, Simon Casie Chetty and Frederick de Livera, were added to the CCS. From 1845 to 1846, five more Lankans were added to the CCS, all of them serving in judicial offices. Over time it became more difficult for Lankans to secure positions in the CCS. In 1868, there were 74 British and 10 Lankans in the CCS. Competitive examinations were introduced for candidates aged 20–23 in 1870. Few Lankans succeeded, especially after 1880 when the examination was held London only. In 1891, a subordinate division of the CCS was created to provide opportunities for sons of elite families.

The British classed the population into ethnic categories and controlled each group through what they considered traditional elites. The traditional administrators (*mudaliyārs* among the Low Country Sinhalese, Tamil *maniagars* and Kandyan *rate mahatmayas*) were recruited from the leading families of the *govigama* and *veḷḷāḷa* castes and became almost hereditary, although by mid-century, elite families from other castes were also selected. They were collectively known as the Native Department and were supplemented by large numbers of men who were awarded honorary titles; they had no salaries or administrative duties but shared in the prestige and local power of the Native Department.

The Native Department served as local representatives of the Government Agents (GAs) and Assistant Government Agents (AGAs) for nominal salaries but enormous opportunities to use their power and prestige for their personal gain. In addition, the CCS depended on Sinhala and Tamil interpreters and translators to carry on business.

The administration took some interest in village conditions, but this was based on distorted expectations of what a Lankan village should look like. Drawing on speculation about autonomous, self-sufficient "village communities" in South Asian history, nineteenth-century legislation presumed that the ideal village should have its own headman, village council, and occupational specialists, centered around a temple, irrigation reservoir (tank), and a paddy field.

In reality, much of rural Ceylon consisted of small, dispersed hamlets, often populated by members of a single caste. These were not isolated but integrated into networks of temples and markets. Furthermore, the British paid little attention to the means used by local elites to maintain social control. Elites combined hereditary authority, the might of British colonial administration, and violence carried out by local gangs to dominate local society. These were used to prevent riots and suppress crime, but they also appear to have been used to intimidate rivals, restrain lower castes, and engage in extralegal activities for personal profit.

The British set about to restore what they believed to have been ancient village institutions. They created village officials (unpaid police and irrigation headmen who reported to the *mudaliyārs*), village councils (*gamasabhāva*), and village tribunals. Ordinance 9 of 1856 created Village Councils, which informally settled cases involving irrigation, fisheries, and paddy cultivation. They were made permanent with enlarged responsibilities in 1867. Ordinance 26 of 1871 established Village Tribunals to hear minor cases. They were voluntary and made summary judgments from which there was no appeal. The intention was to revive the cooperation within a village that presumably existed historically, but they remained in the control of local notables.

Rice was the primary grain crop, but in much of the country it was not the staple one. Many cultivators grew "dry grains," such as millet, where irrigation water was not available. Slash-and-burn or *chēna* cultivation was an integral part of peasant life: Villagers cut down forests and burned them to provide nutrients for grain or vegetable cultivation. When productivity fell, a new area was cleared and farmed. Land was rotated until there was enough growth to repeat the process on the first plot. *Chēna* cultivation increased in the nineteenth century. The British initially encouraged it to remove the forest that the Kandyan kings had used as a barrier between the kingdom and the coasts; however, they began to discourage it after the coffee plantations opened. The forest was declared crown property in 1840, and the British attempted to suppress the *chēna* cultivation as a wasteful practice. In fact, *chēna* often provided a necessary supplement to rice and tree crop cultivation, and some administrators were reluctant to prevent it. Between the plantations and *chēnas,* much of the forest cover of the highlands was destroyed in the nineteenth century.

The middle decades of the nineteenth century were crucial ones for the formation of modern Sri Lanka. Besides the growth of the coffee industry, the most significant changes were the integration of the Kandyan territories into the remainder of the colony, the uneven spread of education (which created an entrenched Anglicized elite), and the revival of Buddhism and Hinduism.

PLANTATION ECONOMY

The creation of an export economy was a conscious policy of the colonial government that resulted in the coffee plantation industry, which flourished from 1840 to 1883. Europeans also invested in sugar, cotton, indigo, and coconut cultivation for export, but coffee monoculture succeeded for a variety of reasons. The British exported coffee produced by peasant cultivators, as the VOC had done, but they also expended extraordinary efforts to create a plantation industry. Roads were built to connect lands suitable for plantation agriculture with the Colombo harbor. Experimental coffee plantations were opened, and the Botanical Gardens at Peradeniya produced seeds for planters.

Cinnamon had been the most valuable export and the chief source of revenue until the early nineteenth century. The Dutch produced it more cheaply on their plantations in Java, however, and exports fell, especially as the British continued to levy high export duties. Cassia also became an inexpensive competitor. Cinnamon became a minor crop, as it is today, and the plantations were sold to private investors.

Three external changes in the 1830s created the conditions which made planting popular and lucrative in Ceylon: (1) consumption of coffee in Europe increased rapidly; (2) abolition of slavery in the British West Indies interrupted supplies; and (3) Lankan coffee became cheaper after import duties in Britain were reduced. As Ceylon's favorable position became obvious, investors and planters rushed to the island.

There was a steady growth of plantation agriculture from 1836 until 1840, primarily from local investment. The "coffee mania," typified by the mad rush of civil servants into plantation investment, lasted from 1840 to 1846. From 1842 to 1846 the cultivated area quadrupled, from less than 15,000 acres to nearly 60,000 acres. The rise in the sale price of land from 5 shillings to 20 shillings in 1844, combined with the inability of the Survey Department to keep up with the demand for land, put an end to the first phase of plantation expansion. Financial difficulties in England shut off the flow of capital in 1847, by which time approximately 300,000 acres of Crown Land were sold as coffee lands.

One Lankan who purchased land on the same scale as the Europeans in the early coffee boom was Warsusahännädigē Joronis de Soysa. He first purchased the royal coffee garden at Hanguranketa in 1837. This garden, in which the king had grown coffee trees for their flowers, covered more than 480 acres and cost de Soysa £411. Eventually, he owned about 870 acres in public land alone during the first boom in coffee exports.

Under the Crown Land Encroachment Ordinance No. 12 of 1840, the government claimed all land to which no one had clear title, including much of the suitable land for coffee in the hill country. The civil servants who sold the land were themselves large speculators in coffee lands, and some used their positions to appropriate the best land. Civil servants neglected their duties to attend to their own plantations. The ordinance also recognized prescriptive rights, which enabled many villagers to acquire title to lands they had occupied for 10 years or more. This, combined with other methods of granting title to villagers, created a land market.

The abolition of *rājakāriya* did not produce a labor market for the plantations as the British unrealistically expected. They blamed the "lazy natives," but the problem lay in the plantation industry itself. The planters imposed the structure of the Caribbean slave plantations, which required a controlled, residential labor force. Kandyan villagers worked for hire in the clearing of jungle for plantations, but few Lankans were willing to put up with the miserable life of a plantation laborer. Fortunately for the coffee planters, a labor force was available in the poor laborers from south India, who for centuries had migrated to the island in search of employment. Gangs of laborers under their foremen (*kangāni*s) found their way to the plantations and hired out as residential workers. The government, which earlier opposed the exploitation of Indian laborers in the British empire, welcomed the workers with open arms.

Working conditions on the plantations initially proved unbearable even for the immigrant laborers; they suffered high mortality rates and were often unpaid by the inexperienced and improvident first wave of planters. Despite the passing of draconian labor laws to coerce workers to remain on the plantations, labor shortages began to appear. Immigration declined from 1844 to 1846, and it became impossible to harvest the bumper crops. *Kangāni*s demanded larger fees to retain their workers.

After India began to allow the recruitment of its laborers in 1847, planters sent large numbers of *kangāni*s to south India to recruit workers. They left after the end of the coffee harvest and brought gangs of laborers following the paddy harvest there. Many laborers returned to India after a few years, but the residential population grew steadily. Perhaps a third of the labor force left a plantation every year, some to India, others to find employment elsewhere in Ceylon.

In the 1870s a leaf fungus infected the plantations, and production declined rapidly. After experiments with cinchona and coconut, tea proved successful, and the planting districts were soon replanted. The plantation industry had led to extensive development of the infrastructure of the island. The government built more than 2,000 miles of roads, a railway line from Colombo to the planting districts by way of Kandy, and improvements in the harbor at Colombo.

Lankans took advantage of the policies used to give clear title to land to British planters to acquire land themselves. More than half of the two million acres of Crown Land alienated by the government in the nineteenth century were purchased by Lankans. Some wealthy investors acquired large expanses of land in order to live as a landed aristocracy. Much of their land was devoted to the cultivation of coconuts for export. Coir, copra, and coconut oil were processed and exported by European firms.

Many peasants also acquired title to small plots of land—although others also lost land when the government refused to recognize title to *chēna* land. Rice cultivation lagged; an island that had one of the finest systems of irrigation in the ancient world was barely able to keep pace with the growth in the rural population, and yields did not increase significantly. Malaria prevented the reclamation of the ancient Dry Zone, but there was little incentive to increase paddy cultivation: Rice was taxed heavily until 1892; little was done to improve irrigation; planters preferred to import cheaper Indian rice to feed their laborers; and the unpaid rural headmen did little to encourage development.

KANDYAN PROVINCES

Kandyan territory was gradually integrated into the administration created in the coastal provinces. A network of roads increased communication between the interior and the southwest coast. In 1833, most of the territory of the Kandyan Kingdom was attached to four coastal provinces, named by compass points, leaving only the Central Province. Later separate provinces were created from the old Kandyan territory: Northwestern Province (1845), North Central Province (1873), Sabaragamuva (1886), and Uva (1889). These nine provinces were arbitrary divisions of a centralized government.

The British remained suspicious of the Kandyans as they constructed an identity for the Kandyans that treated them as racially distinct from the Low Country Sinhalese. Whereas the Low Country Sinhalese were considered docile and obsequious, even effeminate, the Kandyans were described as independent, martial, and implacably hostile to the British. The characterizations had little foundation in reality, but Kandyans had reasons to be disillusioned with the British: Coffee plantations appropriated land they considered theirs, a new population of laborers of Indian origin inhabited the plantations, and Lankans from other parts of the colony serviced the plantation industry and the colonial government. Government-licensed arrack taverns appeared throughout the territory, and alcoholism became a problem. The new courts opened up opportunities to exploit each other through malicious litigation. Irrigation reservoirs were left unrepaired. Buddhist temples and monasteries were allowed to deteriorate from the lack of government supervision.

In 1835, disgruntled Kandyan chiefs were accused of treason, although anonymous palm-leaf documents of dubious authenticity supplied by an informer were the only evidence of a conspiracy. The chiefs were found not guilty by the Sinhalese majority on the jury, but the government deposed the *adigar* in favor of their informant. "Pretenders" to the Kandyan throne appeared in 1842. The police reported that these men were Low Country Sinhalese who had been collecting money from the villagers on the pretext of restoring the monarchy, intending to abscond with the money. The fact that the scam could succeed was evidence that Kandyan resentment persisted.

An incident in 1848 had different consequences. The governor was an inexperienced young aristocrat, George Byng, Seventh Viscount Torrington. He attempted to balance the budget with regressive and punitive taxes. The taxes included a Road Ordinance that forced villagers to build roads for the plantations, which seemed to be a return to *rājakāriya*. When the people protested, officials scolded chiefs and headmen, expecting them to control any opposition. In the Central Province, however, villagers proclaimed two men to be "Kings of Kandy," and large crowds demonstrated. Governor Torrington panicked; thinking there was a rebellion, he took extreme steps over the objections of his own officials. Troops shot protesters, issued proclamations, confiscated property, and shot alleged rebels after brief courts-martial. No Kandyan chief or priest was involved, no European lives were lost, and very little property was damaged. Torrington continued to enforce martial law long after the protests ended, and civil tribunals were created to convict some of the captives for high treason. A Buddhist monk named Kuddapolla Unnanse was tried and convicted by a court-martial for failing to volunteer information that might have led to the arrest of a rebel. The Queen's Advocate begged the governor to pardon the monk, but Torrington refused to do so and the monk was shot in his robes.

Torrington was recalled along with his chief advisers. The episode showed that the government was an autocracy of the governor, but that resistance could bring intervention from the Colonial Office. It also showed that the

British needed to pay more attention to their Lankan subjects. After Torrington, the colonial office appointed experienced administrators as governors.

EDUCATION

Sri Lanka has always valued education. Traditionally, temples offered lessons to small groups of villagers—something that is documented primarily by the many disparaging remarks about them by missionary and government educators. Education according to the British, in contrast, took place in schools with a Western curriculum, and these were encouraged by the government in order to produce an educated workforce, and, in particular, an inexpensive English-speaking staff for the lower levels of the bureaucracy. English education became the key to success, and the demand outstripped the available opportunities throughout the nineteenth century.

A Central School Commission met from 1834 to 1867. Five English-medium schools were opened in 1832, and by 1848, the colony had 60 English schools with 2,714 pupils. The Commission was most notable for the bickering that went on among the government, the Anglican establishment, nonconformist denominations, and the missionary organizations. There were three types of schools according to method of financing: government schools, which did not levy fees; aided schools, which levied fees and received a subsidy from the government; and private schools, which levied fees and were not subsidized. Before 1861 few missions received subsidies other than those in Jaffna. In that year the Schools Commission offered grants to any mission schools, but with stringent restrictions on religious content of the curricula. This limited grants to those very few schools willing to surrender most of their power to proselytize during school hours.

After 1869, grant-in-aid schools were allowed to require religious teaching as long as three hours daily were devoted to secular education. This made grants-in-aid more attractive to missionaries. The new conditions set off a competition among missions to open as many schools as possible, resulting in a proliferation of schools in areas where the demand was high. The government restricted grants to schools placed in close proximity to existing schools, a policy that was bitterly opposed by the Roman Catholic hierarchy, who were unable to open denominational schools in some Catholic areas where Protestant mission schools existed. Expenditure on education declined when revenue from the coffee industry fell in the 1880s.

Along with the rapid expansion of elementary education in the vernaculars, a group of elite schools provided an intensive English-language curriculum, particularly St. Thomas College at Mt. Lavinia and the Colombo Academy (renamed Royal College in 1881). The elite schools were modeled after English public schools; students were socialized to adopt English habits, dress, manners, and customs. Corporal punishment helped to exorcize most traces of a Sinhala or Tamil accent. English-medium schools were given more generous grants than Sinhala- or Tamil-medium *(swabasha)* schools. The grants were based on the number of students passing their examinations at a high level, however, which inhibited the spread of English education to other classes.

The best schools in the island—some say the best schools in Asia—were in the Jaffna peninsula. American missionaries supported education as means to convert students; the people of Jaffna responded enthusiastically to the opportunity. Jaffna Tamils used education to move into the English-speaking occupations in government, the private sector, and the professions. Many Tamils migrated to the southern and central regions for employment, leading to Sinhalese protests that the British favored Tamils over the majority Sinhalese.

The pinnacle of Jaffna education in the first half of the century was the Batticotta *(Vaṭṭukottai)* Seminary, which provided a University-level education for its graduates. Two of its graduates took the examinations at the newly founded University of Madras in 1857 and received the first degrees awarded by that institution. One of these, Charles Winslow Thamotherampillai, became a noted author and critic of missionary proselytization.

The majority of indigenous schools were not eligible for grants at first because they did not offer the Western subjects that were considered secular. After 1880, however, the government began to aid Buddhist and Hindu schools. Buddhists also opened Vidyodaya (1873) and Vidyalankara (1876) Piriveṇ(as seminaries for educating *bhikkhus*) to produce Pāli and Sanskrit scholars. Hindus in Jaffna opened schools in competition with missionary schools, and educated more students than they did.

Sri Lanka today is shaped very much by the school system created in the nineteenth century. Education was primarily in the hands of Christian missionaries. The schools reinforced linguistic, religious, class, caste, and ethnic divisions. The gap in prestige and income between the English-educated and the *swabasha*-educated was immense. The elite became a class of people with a highly literary education but little scientific or technical knowledge. Their extensive vocabulary, literary allusions, and distinctive accent marked the product of an elite education and became a weapon to use to keep those less facile with English rhetoric from breaking into elite circles. Sinhala-educated Lankans referred to the power that an education in English gave the elite as the *kaḍuva* (sword).

Newspapers were an important part of colonial life since the 1830s as rare opportunity for public debate within a colonial dictatorship. Governor Horton started a newspaper in 1832, but the Colonial Office disapproved. In 1834, the merchants of Colombo started the *Observer and Commercial Advertiser,* which survives today as the *Sunday Observer.* It became the first daily paper in Ceylon in 1873. The *Observer* tended to criticize the government and came to represent the interests of the planters. The progovernment *Ceylon Herald* appeared in 1838 and became the *Ceylon Times* in 1846 until renamed the *Times of Ceylon* in 1882. Other important English language newspapers were the *Examiner* (1846), the *Independent* (1888), the *Morning Leader* (1907) and the *Daily News* (1918).

The earliest nineteenth-century Sinhala and Tamil serial publications were Protestant missionary tracts, beginning with the *māsikatäägga,* which appeared in 1832 in Sinhala and the *utayatarakai,* published in Tamil by American missionaries in 1841. The first successful Sinhala newspaper was the *lakmiṇipahana* in 1862, followed by the *lakrivikiraõa,* the *lakmiṇipahana,* and the *aruṇōdaya* in 1863. Many other newspapers followed. Some of these had religious affiliations, such as the Catholic *jnānārthapradīpaya* (1866) and the Buddhist Theosophical Society's *sarasavisandaräsa* (1880). The first Sinhala daily newspaper was the *dinapatapravṛtti,* published by the playwright Don Bastian in 1896. In Tamil the *satiyavedapathukavalan* (1876) was a Catholic newspaper, and Hindus published the *indhusatanam* in 1888.

RELIGION

The government was explicitly Christian until the disestablishment of the Church of England in 1881. The British, especially in their early years, favored Christians—Sinhalese, Tamil, and Burghers—in government employment. The Church of England hierarchy was paid by colonial revenues, and missionary societies sent their own representatives. There were about 100 ordained Protestant ministers in Ceylon in 1848, including several Lankans. In addition, most missions included the missionaries' families and converts who served in missionary societies without ordination.

The British government had agreed by the Kandyan Convention to administer the property and service obligations of Buddhist monasteries and temples. Under pressure from missionaries, the government withdrew from this obligation in 1847. It was disastrous to the Buddhist institutions because the government created no legal alternative. The monks had no experience in administering them, and Kandyan headmen and the families of *bhikkhus* exploited the situation. The government appointed a commission in 1856, but its report was not implemented. Another ordinance was drafted in 1877 to vest the administration of Buddhist temple and monastic property in three commissioners. When the Colonial Office objected to giving the commissioners so much power, the government delayed further reforms until 1889.

British policies toward Buddhism eventually brought *bhikkhus* into public opposition. They had debated among themselves over matters of ritual, monastic discipline, the organization of the *sangha,* and Sinhala and Pāli linguistic issues. Ecclesiastical controversies sharpened the lines between the Siyām Nikāya and new *nikāyas* (fraternities) in competition with the Siyām Nikāya. These were led by Low Country Sinhalese and were open to non-*govigama* castes. The number of *bhikkhus* increased in the nineteenth century: About half of all *bhikkhus* belonged to the Siyām Nikāya; a third to a number of fraternities collectively known as the Amarapura Nikāya; and a sixth to the Ramañña Nikāya, which was founded in 1862. The Ramañña Nikāya claimed to follow more authentic, reformed practices. Literary controversies were aired in the newspapers and pamphlets. These controversies brought erudite *bhikkhus* into public debate and into contact with lay scholars.

Beginning in the 1860s, *bhikkhu*s began to respond to missionary attacks on Buddhism. In tracts and pamphlets, missionaries proclaimed the superiority of Christianity and challenged Buddhists to defend their teaching. *Bhikkhu* Hikkaḍuvē Sumaṅgala (1827–1911) and the ex-*bhikkhu* Baṭuvantuḍāvē Devarakṣita (1819–1892) published scholarly responses and advocated reforms that would strengthen Buddhism. The best-known opponent of Christianity was *bhikkhu* Mohoṭṭivattē Guṇānanda (1823–1890). He founded the first voluntary association for Buddhists, established a printing press, and challenged Christian ministers in public debates. Combining arguments drawn from European writings with oratorical brilliance, he won over large crowds in a series of debates.

The revival of Hinduism in Jaffna owes much to the efforts of Ārumuga Nāvalar (1822–1879). Born into a high-status *veḷḷāḷa* family, he was, as many Buddhist nationalists were, educated in Christian schools. He studied Tamil with tutors, and became a Tamil scholar and English teacher in 1841. He translated the Bible into Tamil, but he reacted against missionary proselytization and in 1848 opened the first of many Hindu schools in competition with mission schools. His printing press published anti-missionary literature along with scholarly books on Saivite Hinduism. He discouraged practices such as animal sacrifice that missionaries had criticized and he instilled pride among the Jaffna Hindus in the *Saiva Siddhanta* textual tradition. He opposed social reform, however, and his commitment to preserving the power and status of the *veḷḷāḷa* caste weakened his appeal.

EMERGENCE OF A COLONIAL ELITE

The biggest beneficiaries of British colonialism were those who spoke English. This gave an immediate advantage to the Dutch Burghers, who by mid-century dominated the legal, medical, and clerical professions. During the course of the nineteenth century, English-educated Sinhalese and Tamil men began to outnumber them in both the private sector and government service, as the colony required continually larger numbers of local collaborators. The cultural homogeneity of this elite temporarily obscured the divisions within the society.

In addition to their greater numbers, the Low Country Sinhalese had other advantages. The Sinhalese districts on the southwest coasts were the center of British administration and economy, and when the Kandyan kingdom was conquered, Low Country Sinhalese flocked to the Kandyan hills as traders, planters, and government employees. The main roads and railroads passed through Sinhalese districts, and Colombo became a great port for products exported by Sinhalese entrepreneurs such as coffee, coconuts, rubber, and graphite. In spite of this initial advantage, Sinhalese entrepreneurs lagged behind Tamils in commerce. In addition to the Jaffna Tamils, who had greater access to English education, traders and moneylenders from India dominated Colombo's commerce.

The legal profession in particular was an important opportunity for educated Lankans. After 1801 advocates (barristers) and proctors (solicitors) were admitted by Supreme Court Judges. In 1858 a Board of Examiners was created to admit lawyers; a Council of Legal Education provided lectures for advocates from 1874, and in 1889 proctors were required to follow lectures and pass examinations. Finally, a Law College was opened in 1895.

The new elite usually lived in Colombo and mixed socially across ethnic lines. Their homes, clothing, recreation, and cuisine all emulated that of the British. Many built manors *(valavva),* where they blended the lifestyle of families of traditional high social rank with that of wealthy plantation owners. Whether they arrived at elite status through the Native Department, landowning, or entrepreneurship, the new elite educated their sons and to a lesser extent their daughters in English and increasingly adopted English as their home language.

One consequence of the emergence of an Anglicized elite was the depletion of the pool of capable recruits to the Native Department and a deterioration in the quality of their performance. The numbers of applicants continued to grow, often stating a hereditary claim to an office, but the most talented members of their families took up other careers. The lawyer and scholar James Alwis (1823–1878) is one notable example along with the three brothers J. C. Dias (the first Lankan proctor of the Supreme Court), the reverend S. W. Dias, and Harry Dias (the first Sinhalese barrister, knight and Supreme Court Justice). Among Tamil elites, Ponnambalam Arunachalam (1853–1924) won a government scholarship and attended Cambridge. He was the first Lankan to pass the entrance examination to the CCS and became one of the most outstanding civil servants, although prevented by racial discrimination from promotion to the highest administrative posts. Members of the Native Department also tended to be less well educated because many candidates began serving as volunteers at young age in hopes of an appointment.

In the coffee era the government recognized the emergence of new elites among the Sinhalese outside the *govigama* families who had dominated *mudaliyār* appointments. The newly wealthy *karāva* families, in particular, educated their sons in the elite schools, and they began to acquire a disproportionate share of appointments to the *mudaliyār* system and an increasing number of honorary *mudaliyār* appointments. The Gate Mudaliyarship awarded to the *karāva* Jeronis de Soysa in 1852 did not break down caste barriers—there had been non-*govigama mudaliyārs* before him—but it opened up the ranks of government honors to persons outside government service. As the numbers of honorary ranks awarded grew, more and more of them came to be awarded on the basis of public service. This was interpreted by some as a return for philanthropy.

The wealth of the *karāvas* led them to challenge the *govigamas* for social supremacy. They never acknowledged that *govigama* preeminence in numbers and government patronage represented a superiority of that caste. They invoked the Indian Varna system—familiar to the British rules but never salient in Ceylon—to argue for a ritual superiority of their caste. Drawing on dubious literary evidence, they argued that the *karāvas* were Kshatriyas, or the ruling caste, and thus superior to the *govigamas*, who could only be Sudras, or commoners, in the Varna system. Few people outside the *karāva* caste have accepted this argument, but it and comparable arguments by the elite of the *salāgama* caste illustrate the divisions that lie beneath the surface of the elite.

A disproportionate number of the elite were Jaffna Tamils; Sinhalese Buddhist nationalists today claim that this was the result of "divide and rule" policies by the British, favoring the Tamil *veḷḷāḷas* over the Sinhalese. In fact, Jaffna's elite were the product of the American missionary effort, Christian denominational schools, and a lack of opportunity in the north, which put a premium on educational achievement. However, British policies did promote ethnic competition by emphasizing differences between ethnic groups. For example, both Sinhalese and Tamils began to take seriously the absurd British notion that the "Dravidian" Tamils and "Aryan" Sinhalese were racially distinct, simply because the two languages belonged to different linguistic families.

Opportunities for Lankans to succeed were limited by the colonial economy. The main import and export trade was dominated by the British and Indians, and Indians monopolized much of the retail trade. British bankers and South Indian bankers from the *chettiar* merchant caste between them controlled the finances of the colony, making it difficult for Lankans to get business loans.

POLITICAL CHANGE

During the expansion of the coffee plantation industry, planters demanded greater government expenditure on roads and on the recruitment, transport, and medical needs of the labor force. The one political incident in this period took place in 1865 over the cost of the garrison of troops stationed there. The troops were there to serve the British Empire, and they were overstaffed: The salaries alone of the engineers, for example, cost more than the work they did was worth. Ceylon's contribution to their costs had been steadily increased until by 1864 the colony paid the entire cost of the garrison—at a time when the colonies of white settlement refused to pay any Imperial military expenses. In that year, the unofficial members of the Legislative Council resigned in protest, but most soon returned.

English and Dutch Burgher members of the Legislative Council protested against the lack of participation in government, as European descendants elsewhere in the British Empire were granted a degree of self-government. A Ceylon League was founded just after Governor Hercules Robinson arrived in the colony in 1865. It was a brief alliance of British planters and Lankan elites, but Robinson split the two factions by the simple expedient of using the increased revenue from the coffee industry for the benefit of planters—he built roads and the railroads, repealed the export duty on coffee, and strengthened planter control over their laborers—and planters' interest in constitutional reform waned.

The only concession to the Lankan elite was the creation of Municipal Councils in Colombo, Kandy, and Galle to regulate urban construction and provide public services. In Colombo, a small voter list elected nine Councillors in January 1866, six of them Burghers, and the governor nominated five officials. Even this was later modified, when Governor Arthur Gordon, apparently thinking this was too democratic, placed the council under an official as chairman and raised the number of governor-nominated officials to nine, creating an official majority. A town hall was built in the Pettah in 1873. Nevertheless, Municipal Councils provided the only opportunity for political experience for Lankan elites until the creation of an educated Ceylonese seat in the Legislative Council in 1912.

6

A Plantation Economy

The colony entered a period of unprecedented prosperity in the 1860s and 1870s as the coffee plantation economy brought wealth to the planters and a steadily increasing revenue to the government. Most Lankans lived better than they ever had previously; a few families accumulated large fortunes and lived lives of unprecedented luxury. After the colony survived the collapse of coffee, the tea plantation industry created ever greater wealth. The plantation economy—along with the spread of education in English, increased circulation of newspapers, the extension of roads and railways, and the growth of the postal system—created a superficial unification of the island.

Lankans began to resent the extent to which the society was dominated by foreigners, and divisions within the society became greater. Because the Anglicized elite were drawn from many ethnic groups, the illusion of ethnic harmony was created. They expected to take a larger role in governance at the same time that the social and economic gap widened between them and the people they professed to represent. Although roads and railroads increased the contact between Tamil-majority and Sinhalese-majority regions and between the Kandyan and Low Country Sinhalese districts, the British tended to maintain the separation of ethnic communities in their administration. Sinhalese Buddhist leaders, in particular, felt that the majority community's legitimate interests were being neglected.

EXPORT ECONOMY

Coffee planters considered themselves the benefactors of the colony, publishing numerous self-congratulatory memoirs of their achievements. They called their plantations "estates" and lived in luxury. They lobbied for expenditure on their behalf—assistance with the recruitment and medical care of laborers in addition to improvements in the colony's infrastructure—but opposed other development of the colony. In the 1860s they also agitated for an increased self-government, but when Lankans became politically active, they tended to side with the government against the reformers.

Some Lankans participated in the coffee industry. Lankans worked in various capacities on the plantations, and a large percentage of coffee exports was produced by village cultivators. (It is impossible to estimate the amount of coffee produced by villagers because plantations sold coffee that they purchased from villagers, and some of the coffee sold by villagers was pilfered from plantations.) Until the coming of the railroad, Lankan carters delivered the coffee to the ports and rice to the plantations. Educated Lankans provided professional services as lawyers, accountants, and brokers. Towns with a mixed population grew in the planting districts. Tavern-keepers sold arrack to the laborers, and shopkeepers sold a variety of supplies to the plantations and the laborers. In the latter case, the most successful merchants were Muslims from south India known as "Coast Moors."

The plantation economy brought about demographic changes. The population grew steadily and was accompanied by migration; Tamils moved from the north to Colombo, Low Country Sinhalese settled in the Kandyan regions, and cultivators began to reclaim the Dry Zone. Plantation laborers and merchants emigrated from India. The first modern census of the colony was taken in March 1871 and enumerated 2.4 million people. Corrected for underenumeration, the population was probably more than 2.8 million. The population may have doubled in the course of the nineteenth century, and it continued to increase in the late nineteenth century.

It is difficult to estimate the extent of immigration; the notoriously unreliable statistics on passenger traffic between India and Ceylon have confused the issue. The Colonial *Blue Book* in 1847 estimated 42,491 immigrants (called "aliens and resident strangers") on the island (29,547 of them in the Central Province, most of them plantation laborers). According to the 1871 census more than 8 percent of the population (193,777), were born in India. About 55 percent of the people born in India were plantation laborers, the remainder merchants and urban laborers. At the height of the coffee economy, there may have been 200,000 plantation laborers of Indian origin.

Unlike earlier south Indian immigrants, plantation laborers neither assimilated into one of the older communities nor retained their Indian identity. Although they were not separated from other Tamil-speaking Lankans as

"Indian Tamils" until the census of 1911, the government began treating them as a separate community in the 1840s. British construction of a separate identity prevented assimilation and created a new uniquely Lankan community. Today, the descendants of south Indians who immigrated to work as plantation laborers are known as "Plantation Tamils" (or "Estate Tamils").

Plantation labor in Ceylon was free, compared to the system of indenture that developed elsewhere in the British Empire. They were confined to the plantation, however, by draconian labor legislation and by autocratic coffee planters who were allowed by custom, but not by law, to rule the plantations through physical force. Unlike indentured laborers, their term of servitude continued indefinitely.

Plantation Tamils were socially homogeneous in the coffee era. The great majority were agricultural laborers earning low wages on the plantations, picking coffee beans and performing other unskilled tasks. A few of the laborers were traditional occupational specialists—priests, washers, barbers—but for the most part the only distinct group were the *kangāni*s, who often were of higher caste status than the laborers. *Kangāni*s were incorporated into plantation management as labor recruiters and supervisors of work crews. A laborer would begin his or her career in debt to the *kangāni* and would remain under his control until the debt was repaid.

Living conditions on plantations were virtually identical: laborers lived in makeshift huts or uniformly constructed "lines" of rooms ten feet wide and twelve feet long, with a six-foot veranda. The food was monotonous and nutritionally deficient; their diet consisted of large quantities of rice with small amounts of chilies, dried fish, and vegetables. Medical facilities on the plantations and within reasonable distance were rudimentary, although the high death rates following the arrival of refugees from the south Indian famine of 1876–1877 produced some changes. There was more less equal immigration of male and female plantation laborers after 1870.

The plantation economy provided the bulk of the island's revenue. In addition to export duties on coffee and import duties on the rice they fed their laborers, much of the substantial profit of the railroads was generated by the plantations from the transportation of plantation laborers and the import of rice to feed them, as well as the shipment of coffee. When the colonial government invested these revenues in development, it repaid the colony many times over. The extension of railways enabled more planting districts to open, lowered transportation costs, encouraged growth in towns, and increased revenue. Improvement of the Colombo harbor made it "the great coaling station of the East," as Governor Hercules Robinson called it in 1870. Colombo had only an open roadstead until the growth of coffee exports and the opening of the Suez Canal increased traffic, and the British began construction of a 4,212-foot breakwater sheltering more than 500 acres. The port encouraged the export of other products such as graphite and coconut products, and it provided employment and income for dock workers, marine engineers, coal and liquid fuel importers, and freight handlers and brokers as well as traders. In 1906 it became the largest artificial harbor in Asia, 643 acres in size.

Unfortunately, the government seldom saw past the needs of the plantations. A few Orientalists dabbled in the study of Sri Lanka's history and culture, but little was done to preserve the island's heritage. The response to Lankan demands for education was halfhearted, leaving the bulk of education to private (usually mission) schools under a system of grants-in-aid. Some revenue was spent on irrigation, but most of that went toward the restoration of ancient irrigation works that were valued less for their productivity than as a demonstration of imperial power.

The plantation economy discouraged the development of local enterprise. Much of the profit was remitted to Britain, and the planters chose to recruit laborers in south India rather than locally. Planters preferred to import any goods they needed. This included rice to feed the laborers, consumer goods from candles to ice, and producer goods such as machinery and tea chests. Some of the cheap rice they imported from India and Burma and issued to laborers was traded for vegetables, spices, millet, and arrack, which depressed prices of domestic rice and made the country more dependent on imports.

This created a "dual economy" in which the plantations appeared to be a modern, capitalist sector, and the domestic economy was based on traditional subsistence agriculture. The two sectors were separated more by colonial policy than economic organization, however. The modern sector of the domestic economy was restrained by a conscious policy of the planters and their government. Government institutions and British firms provided such services as financing, marketing, shipping, and insurance. Much of the non-British trade and finance was in the hands of Indians.

There were few areas for indigenous capitalist development: the gem trade, the distillation and sale of arrack, the growing, processing and export of coconut products, and the graphite industry. Lankans who succeeded in business tended to invest their wealth in their sons' overseas education in order to move them into the Anglicized elite.

FROM COFFEE TO TEA

The coffee plantation economy reached its peak in the late 1870s. It then faced a coffee blight and increased competition from Brazilian coffee. Tea soon replaced coffee as the staple export crop; the transition created hardship for many and permanent dislocation for others. Banks and moneylenders failed, although the government bailed out the leading English bank. Many individually owned plantations failed and their owners returned to England, ending the era of the planter who owned and operated an estate. Tea plantations were generally owned by absentee owners, often large corporations like Lipton's, and managed by superintendents.

The plantation laborers were the most vulnerable, many of them remaining on the plantations at reduced pay or leaving the plantations for other occupations, but village cultivators were also caught in a trap. As the amount of money in circulation increased, the government required cultivators to pay their land taxes in cash, but many were unable to do so when coffee declined. Their land was seized and sold to pay taxes; the tax on paddy was belatedly abolished in 1892.

The tea economy became much more of a dual economy than the coffee economy: The plantations were larger, the labor force more homogeneously south Indian in origin, and more of the profits were alienated to British owners. Living conditions on the plantations improved, but plantation laborers continued to be the poorest Lankans. It allowed for much less local participation than the coffee industry. Not only were there few small-scale producers, but there was less demand for local contractors. The replacement of the privately owned cart transportation by the government-owned railway is a dramatic example of the decline of local enterprise.

THE ANGLICIZED ELITE

English-educated Lankans flourished in the late nineteenth and early twentieth centuries. They made careers in government service; the professions, especially law; and services to the plantation industry. The Anglicized elite understandably expected to share in the governance of the island. They were loyal, and they were better educated and wealthier than the British citizens who dominated the colony. Unlike the British, they had a permanent interest in the future of the island. To the British, however, the more the local elite became like proper Victorian gentlemen and then Edwardian dandies, the less suitable they became as rulers. By virtue of their elite education and luxurious lifestyles, many of them had less contact with ordinary Lankans than British administrators.

The ultimate career for an English-educated Lankan was the CCS. A handful of Lankans, most of them from families with aristocratic pretensions, were nominated for the CCS. During the economic crisis of the 1880s, a retrenchment committee of the Legislative Council discussed increased recruitment of Lankans as a means to reduce costs; the secretary of state endorsed the principle, but the governor failed to act on the suggestion. The competitive examination for entrance to the CCS was not held in Colombo again until 1920, after which the number of Lankan civil servants increased rapidly.

Education increasingly was in the hands of religious institutions. As late as 1870 more students attended government schools than private schools, but new conditions for grants-in-aid unleashed a competition among missionary societies for schools. Financial difficulties restricted government school building after 1882, and by 1900 more than two-thirds of the students and almost three-fourths of the schools were aided. In 1896 there were 848 aided schools, only 12 of them Buddhist and 5 Hindu. Of the 87 English-language schools in 1896, 62 were Protestant and 25 Roman Catholic. The much larger number of temple schools (many with only a handful of students) were unaided. Still education was not widespread: Only 1 in 34 school-age children attended school, and in Kandyan districts and among girls—especially Muslim girls—it was much less.

From 1870 a scholarship was awarded every year to one student to study in England. Initially it was confined to the Colombo Academy. In 1880 it was opened to everyone who sat for the Senior Cambridge. A second scholarship was awarded from 1905.

In 1833 Ceylon was an advanced colony because it included Sinhalese, Tamil, and Burgher nominated members on the Legislative Council. By the time a Muslim and a Kandyan member were added in 1889, it was politically backward. The Lankans had no influence on policy and were chosen on an ethnic basis from a small pool of wealthy upper-class candidates.

The elite joined voluntary organizations and became more active in civil society. The most notable of these, because of its name, was the Ceylon National Association. It was essentially an organization of new elites other than the *govigama* mudaliyārs. The Westernized *govigama* elites had created the Ceylon Agricultural Society in the 1860s to lobby with the government as the British Planters' Association (est. 1854) did. C. H. de Soysa, son of Joronis Soysa, and others founded the Ceylon Agricultural Association in 1882. It adopted the name Ceylon National Association in September 1888, echoing the name of the Indian National Congress, over the opposition of de Soysa. The organization lobbied with Governor Gordon for more representation of Lankans in government service, but it was in fact apolitical; the "National" referred to the fact that it was open to all social classes. Gordon sneered that this mixture of Tamils, non-*govigama* Sinhalese, and nonelite *govigamas* was "a grotesque clique."

Lankan elites built mansions in Colombo, which was the center of all activity. All government departments and courts were based there, most roads and railroads led there, and virtually all the newspapers were published there. What had been cinnamon plantations in the Dutch era became "Cinnamon Gardens," the most exclusive residential area of the city. The Lankan elite joined in social clubs and professional organizations that cut across ethnic lines in which they shared a second-class status below the British colonial rulers.

BUDDHIST REVIVAL

The Buddhist revival took a different turn in 1880 with the arrival in the colony of American Theosophist Henry Steele Olcott, who had read about the Buddhist-Christian debates. He founded the Buddhist Theosophical Society

(BTS), which opened Buddhist schools, most importantly Ananda College in 1883. Olcott also published a short summary of the doctrines of Buddhism for popular consumption modeled after the Christian Catechism. He also popularized what is now recognized as the Buddhist flag, consisting of horizontal and vertical blue, yellow, crimson, white and orange stripes, representing the rays that are believed to have emanated from the Buddha's body.

Buddhists also campaigned to restore the ancient capital of Anurādhapura as a sacred site. The sites that came to be known as the eight sacred places *(aṭamāstana)* had continued to draw pilgrims during the nineteenth century despite their deterioration and endemic malaria. The British visited Anurādhapura (and Polonnaruwa) in 1820 and established a *kachcheri* there in 1833. In 1873, the creation of the North Central Province led to conflict when Anurādhapura was made its capital. Even though Governor William Gregory was motivated by respect for the city's historic heritage, Buddhist revivalists objected to the government building offices and allowing markets to spread within its precincts. The next year the British began excavating the ruins while Buddhists began raising money to restore the religious sites.

Systematic excavation was not approved until 1890, by which time the collapse of the coffee industry had slowed progress. Some Buddhists protested against the archaeological excavations there and tried to prevent an Anglican church from being built near the ruins. Walisinha Harischandra, a former law student, took up residence in the city in 1899 and began protesting against what he considered desecration of the sacred city. On June 9, 1903, there were an estimated 20,000 pilgrims in the city when a disturbance broke out; pilgrims attacked a Roman Catholic Mission and a meat stall.

The government passed an ordinance in 1889 transferring temple properties from the custody of the monks, who were alleged to be mismanaging them, to elected trustees. Prominent Buddhists suggested that management would not improve unless a government official supervised it, but the secretary of state refused to allow it. When this ordinance predictably failed, the government proposed to require GAs to supervise the management of Buddhist temple property. One civil servant reportedly resigned in protest. Finally, in 1931, the government issued the Buddhist Temporalities Ordinance, according to which all revenues and expenditure of Buddhist temples were to be supervised and examined by a public trustee. The public trustee was intended to recover the cost of the administration from temple revenues, but in practice the administration was carried at public expense.

The central figure in the Buddhist Revival was Anagārika Dharmapāla (1864–1933), born Don David Hewavitarne. His father was a wealthy entrepreneur and both parents' families supported *bhikkhus* associated with Buddhist protests and the Buddhist Theosophical Society (BTS). Although raised a Buddhist, he attended a missionary boarding school. In the 1880s he adopted Theosophy, but he eventually rejected what he called the "Theosophical occultists." After a visit to Bodh Gaya in India in early 1891, he established the Maha Bodhi Society (MBS). Much of his effort was devoted to raising funds to restore the site and litigating in British Indian courts to return control of its ruins from Hindu to Buddhist hands. Olcott and Dharmapāla disagreed over this campaign, and Olcott resigned from the MBS in July 1896. He preached that Buddhism was a rational, scientific religion.

Other Sinhalese revivalists, such as the novelist Piyadasa Sirisena, advocated a return to traditional ways. They hoped to overturn what he considered an inferiority complex of the Sinhalese, and in doing so they blamed other Lankan communities, whom they accused of expropriating the wealth of the country. Dharmapāla's anti-Indian and anti-Tamil speeches and writings appeared in his journal *Sinhala Bauddhaya*. One of their major grievances, the increasing consumption of alcohol, had political overtones, as the manufacture and distribution of the local liquors were a government monopoly, and the excise duties on them were a major source of government revenue. The temperance movement brought about the first political confrontation of Sinhalese nationalists with the British in 1915.

TAMILS AND MUSLIMS

The Tamil language is the basis of the Sri Lankan Tamil identity, but it evolved throughout the colonial era. Literary Tamil is a classical language with a substantial body of poetry and scripture. Western missionaries promoted the study of literary Tamil by translating Christian texts into Tamil, studying the classics themselves, and enthusiastically promoting its beauty and subtlety. The interest in Tamil studies cut across political and religious lines; Christian and Hindu Tamils, in Ceylon and India, advocated the increased use of more formal literary structures rather than the colloquial ones appearing in newspapers and other popular media. Some Hindus objected to the role of missionaries in Tamil studies and to the conversion of Hindus to Christianity. They believed that the Tamil identity was based on Saivite Hinduism as well as language.

English-educated Tamils increasingly studied the history and culture of Jaffna and emphasized that they had an identity distinct from that of the Tamils of India. The American Mission Press published works on Jaffna such as Claas Isaakszoon's *Country Laws* in 1841. Simon Casie Chetty (1807–1860) published a series of articles on Tamil culture in 1848 and 1849, including a history of Jaffna and a catalog of books in Tamil. He also published the *Tamil Plutarch* in 1859. These histories were based on the *Yālppānavaipavamālai,* a seventeenth-century chronicle written by Matakal Mayilvakanappulavar for the Dutch colonial administration. Henry Francis Mutukisna, the first Tamil barrister, edited an English version of the *Tesavalamai* in 1862. Christopher Brito published an English translation of the *Yālppānavaipavamālai* in 1879.

Casie Chetty, Brito, and Mutukisna were "Colombo Chetties," descendants of relatively recent Protestant immigrants from south India. The most prominent Hindus were the family of Arumuganathar Pillai Coomaraswamy (1783–1836), who was chief Tamil translator to the government and the first Tamil member of the Legislative Council. His son Muttu Coomaraswamy (1820–1879) was the first Hindu to be called to the English Bar, and his grandsons Ponnambalam Ramanathan and Ponnambalam Arunachalam dominated Lankan politics in the early twentieth century.

By the end of the nineteenth century the Tamil language became the dominant marker of Ceylon Tamil identity, but it did not unite all Tamil speakers. The emphasis on the history of Jaffna not only distanced the "Jaffna Tamils" from the Sinhalese-speaking majority, but from Tamil-speaking Muslims, Hindus, and Christians outside the northern peninsula. The government no longer recognized the Colombo Chetties as a separate community after 1871, and they in response tended to deny the identification with Tamils. Plantation Tamils were considered foreigners by the Lankan Tamils as much as by the Sinhalese. The Jaffna Tamils considered Tamils of the east coast and Colombo to be part of the same community, despite distinct caste, marriage, and kinship structures. They sometime considered themselves "Batticaloa Tamils" or "Colombo Tamils." Tamil-speaking Muslims resisted Lankan Tamil attempts to characterize them as Tamils who had converted to Islam and emphasized their religious identity over the linguistic one.

Muslims comprised about 6 or 7 percent of the population and were diverse. The majority of Muslims were of south Indian origin and spoke Tamil. The British distinguished between those families who claimed descent from early Muslim trading communities in the island or "Ceylon Moors," and the "Indian Moors," who retained ties to India. Muslims who emigrated from India included people from various parts of that country; in addition there was a Malay community of Muslims whose ancestors came to the island in the service of the Dutch. The Tamil-speaking Muslims had an uneasy relationship with the Tamil leadership, who wanted them to emphasis their common interests against the Sinhala-speaking majority.

SOCIETY AND CULTURE

As small as the Anglicized elite was, it was divided by race, class, region, and ethnicity. Traditional Tamil and Kandyan elites had few challenges to their social status, and most entrepreneurs and professionals came from established families. The Low Country Sinhalese were the primary beneficiaries of British colonial policies, however, and many new families with aspirations to elite status emerged. The social order was complex and still has not been completely resolved in contemporary Sri Lanka. A disproportionate number of successful Low Country Sinhalese entrepreneurs came from the *karāva* caste.

In the long run the future belonged to wealthy *govigama* men outside the *mudaliyār* class; caste status, their greater numbers, and intermarriage made the Senanayake, Wijewardene, Jayewardene, and other families politically dominant by the time of independence.

In the 1880s, the government reversed the policy of recruiting candidates from prominent families outside a small circle of families. Governor Arthur Gordon appointed only men from a few select families that he considered the colony's aristocracy. This resulted in the appointment of some notably incompetent *mudaliyārs* and hostility from the families excluded from office. It also had limited success in creating a body of Lankan elites loyal to the crown: Maha Mudaliyar Solomon Dias Bandaranaike, for example, remained loyal, but his son S.W.R.D. Bandaranaike became a leader of the movement for independence.

An example of a successful outsider was Thomas Edward de Sampayo, a son of the *mudaliyār* of the *navandannō* caste; he won the University Scholarship in 1877 and became an English barrister in 1881. He was frequently mentioned in the newspapers as a candidate to become the Sinhalese Member of the Legislative Council—something neither the British nor the *govigama* elite would countenance. Even when he was acting Chief Justice of the Supreme Court, *govigama* lawyers avoided pleading cases before him on grounds of caste.

John Pereira was from a wealthy *durāva* family in Colombo and became famous teacher at Colombo Academy and St. Thomas. His wife was a Dutch Burgher, and his children Walter and Charles were successful lawyers who were considered Burghers in their youth. Later they converted to Buddhism and asserted their Sinhalese identity. Walter Pereira was denied the position of Attorney General on grounds of race, and Charles Pereira became a important nationalist leader.

The era gave opportunity for people of diverse origins. One of the great success stories was that of Karuppiah Thondaman, from the regionally dominant *kallar* caste of the princely state of Pudukottai in India (reportedly connected to the royal family). He came to Ceylon as young man earning 13 cents a day in about 1870. He became a *kangāni* and built a fortune initially by earning bonuses for getting high turnout of laborers. This he invested in transportation, moneylending, and trade. In 1909 he bought the estate on which he was a *kangāni* in 1890. By the time of his death in 1940, he was a multimillionaire. His son Saumiyamoorthy became one of the richest and most powerful men in Sri Lanka.

POLITICAL REFORM

The man who was to emerge as the leader of the Low Country Sinhalese was a *karāva* lawyer, James Peiris (1856–1830). His grandfather had been the most successful arrack renter and trader of the 1840s, but his father died bankrupt—a victim of holding the arrack rents along the Colombo-Kandy road when the railroads displaced the carters who had provided much of the taverns' custom. His wealthy relations financed him to the best education the colony could offer, and in 1877, he won the University Scholarship and proceeded to a brilliant success at Cambridge. After being called to the English Bar in 1881, he returned to Ceylon in 1883. His marriage to an heiress made him financially secure. He served as a Member of the Colombo Municipal Council from 1898 to 1908 but, like his contemporaries, did not lobby for constitution reforms until 1908.

In that year, he drafted a memorial on constitution reform to the secretary of state. Its requests were moderate: to have unofficial members elected on a territorial basis and to have enough of them on the legislative and executive councils to have some influence on government business. Governor Henry McCallum treated it with contempt, claiming that the Anglicized elite would not represent the people as well as British officials did. The secretary of state agreed, and only minor changes were made. Four seats were elected on a very restricted franchise: two European, one Burgher, and one at large. The last was symbolically important because the "educated Ceylonese" seat, as it came to be known, was the first legislator elected in a crown colony by a non-European election, but it had no effect on the governor's autocracy. Governor McCallum also formed a Finance Committee, in which the unofficial members were able to take part in discussions of revenue and expenditure.

The election of 1912 for the educated Ceylonese seat pitted Ponnambalam Ramanathan against Dr. Hilarion Marcus Fernando, a very highly qualified Sinhalese *karāva*. There were fewer than 3,000 voters in a population of about 4.5 million. Ramanathan won by a vote of 1,645 to 981. Since over half of the voters were Sinhalese, even if all Tamil voters voted for Ramanathan, at least one-fourth of the Sinhalese would have had to vote for him. This could be a tribute to Ramananthan's national standing compared to the less experienced Fernando, or, as some have argued, *govigama* voters may have preferred to vote for a high-status Tamil *veḷāḷa* rather than a *karāva*.

RIOTS OF 1915

Lankan politics became much more active after the British took brutal reprisals against Sinhalese Buddhist elites following widespread rioting by Sinhalese Buddhists against the businesses of the Coast Moor community in June and July 1915. The events have been reexamined in light of Sinhalese Buddhist riots against Tamils in the 1970s and 1980s, but there are still divergent interpretations of the events.

The origins can be traced, first of all, to sentiments among Sinhala-educated Buddhists that the English-educated elite had paid little attention to before the twentieth century. These included the hostility to the dominant position of Coast Moors in retail sales in Sinhalese villages, which was stirred up by the xenophobic writings of Anagārika Dharmapāla and others. The other was the temperance movement, which had become an important issue in the revival of Buddhism.

There is no doubt that the consumption of alcohol in the form of arrack had increased steadily in the nineteenth century. Although the major markets for arrack were plantation laborers, urban workers, and carters, Buddhist leaders believed that intemperance was spreading among Sinhalese villagers. The sale of arrack was a very profitable government monopoly, and both the government and those who rented the rights to distill and sell arrack had an interest in increasing consumption. Missionaries, and even some governors, had long supported a temperance movement. Buddhist leaders also campaigned against the sale of arrack, but in this case attacked it as a Western vice supported by the foreign government. There was a very active temperance movement from 1903 to 1905, which had widespread support among ordinary Sinhalese villagers and tacit approval from the government.

In 1912 prominent Buddhist laymen began to hold temperance meetings throughout the Sinhalese districts and to join prominent local Buddhists in a network of Temperance Societies. The motives at this time were mixed. There does not seem to have been a strong philosophical commitment to temperance; they did not campaign against imported liquor, of which some of the most active supporters of the temperance movement were themselves inordinately fond. The most successful arrack renters were *karāvas,* and some *karāvas* believed that other elites were motivated by antipathy to their caste's wealth. They opposed the government's attempts to separate the sale of toddy and arrack, one of a number of high-handed government actions opposed by many Lankans, and this might have been the most convenient issue to raise. Above all, wealthy English-educated Buddhists appear to have attempted to establish themselves (rather than the *mudaliyār* class) as elites by taking a leadership role in the movement—"nobodies trying to become somebodies," as the aristocratic S. C. Obeyesekere put it. It was in fact the first step in making the temperance leaders, particularly Don Baron Jayatilaka (1868–1944), Don Stephen Senanayake (1884–1952), and his brothers, into national elites. Many of these leaders were active in the observance of the centenary in March 1915 of the Kandyan Convention—and were also active in their loyal support for Britain at the outbreak of the First World War.

The anti-Muslim riots of 1915 originated in a dispute over Buddhist *perahäras* in the vicinity of mosques built by Coast Moors. Their mosques had expanded with the prosperity of the community at the same time that loud processions were becoming an important aspect of the Sinhalese-Buddhist revival. On several occasions the courts decided that the Buddhists should not make noise within 100 yards of other religious institutions, and this sometimes led to violent confrontations. In 1915, a mosque in the Kandyan town of Gampola was enlarged until it extended to the road on which the annual *vesak perahära,* celebrating the birth of the Buddha, traditionally passed. The GA had prohibited the procession; the District Judge (a Sinhalese Christian, Paul Pieris) had ruled in favor of the Buddhists, but the Supreme Court overturned his decision in February. An appeal to the Privy Council was being prepared when Buddhist violence against Muslims erupted on May 28 in Kandy and spread rapidly. This continued through June 6, 1915. Rioters, many of them criminal elements exploiting the opportunity, damaged 86 mosques and looted more than 4,000 shops. Seventeen Christian churches were also attacked. About 35 Muslims were killed and 198 injured.

Governor Robert Chalmers at first hesitated to act and then overreacted, deciding in a fit of wartime hysteria that the riots were a conspiracy by the leaders of the temperance movement, perhaps with German instigation. Possibly hundreds of people, mostly temperance workers, were shot dead by patrols under martial. Prominent Buddhists, a virtual "who's who" of later Sinhalese politicians, were tried by court-martial and sentenced to death, deportation, or long terms in prison. After the arrests, they were forced to pay compensation for riot damages or risk criminal prosecution and punitive taxation. Ramanathan made a passionate defense of the Buddhist leaders, first in the Legislative Council and then in England. Governor Chalmers was eventually recalled.

The suppression of Sinhalese political activity had exactly the opposite effect from what was intended. The loyalty of the Anglicized Sinhalese Buddhist elite was questioned, and they began to question colonial rule. Those arrested included the future Prime Minister Don Stephen Senanayake and his brothers, the two brothers of Anagārika Dharmapāla (one of whom died in prison), labor leader A. E. Goonesinha, and the Buddhist scholar Don Baron Jayatilaka.

The events also had a lasting effect on the Muslim leadership. In the face of the violence and the continuing hostility of Anagārika Dharmapāla and others, they became more conservative and supportive of the British. This was at a time when Muslims worldwide were critical of the British rulers for their treatment of Islam in the collapse of the Ottoman Empire—young Muslims who supported the Khilafat movement, which opposed British policy in the Middle East, were removed from N.H.M. Abdul Cader's Ceylon Muslim Association. The Ceylon Moors also distanced themselves from the Coast Moors, who were the main target of the riots. Abdul Cader, for example, tried to make the managers of the Maradana Mosque a Ceylon Moor rather than a Muslim body when it was created by legislation in 1921.

Ramanathan was reelected in 1917 by an even wider margin than in 1912, this time defeating a *govigama* opponent. Ramanathan's brother Arunachalam retired from the CCS in 1913 and devoted the remainder of his life to social service and politics. He founded the Ceylon Social Services League and Ceylon Workers' League in 1915, and was a leading figure in the creation of the Ceylon National Congress (CNC) in 1919 and was elected its first president.

7

Sinhalese and Tamil Nationalism

The formation of the Ceylon National Congress (CNC) in 1919 seemed to be the belated beginnings of a Lankan nationalist movement. Lankan leaders briefly worked together for reform, but the leadership divided, and the CNC became an organization dominated by conservative Low Country Sinhalese elites. Constitutional reform continued to come from British initiatives, the most important of which was the Donoughmore Constitution of 1931, which gave real power to a State Council elected on nearly universal franchise.

The Donoughmore Constitution was an ambitious British reform that created a State Council of 50 elected members (plus 8 nominated members to represent minorities and the British, and 3 officials). The officials administered the subjects reserved to the colonial government (defense, foreign relations, law, justice, and finance), but the remaining government departments were placed under the control of committees composed of State Councillors. The State Council gave experience of democratic politics to the public and real power, with a promise of full independence, to the politicians. Elections were held in 1931 and 1936. Some candidates ran under party labels, but virtually all were local notables running as individuals. Rather than appealing to voters on a national basis, politicians built their constituencies of ethnic lines. The period ended with Sinhalese leaders in firm control of the State Council.

POLITICS IN THE 1920s

The key figure from 1917 to 1921 was Ponnambalam Arunachalam. He retired from the CCS in 1913 and devoted his efforts to social reform. When the Ceylon Reform League (CRL) was founded in the wake of the 1915 riots in May 1917, the predominantly Colombo-based Sinhalese Buddhist leaders elected him president. The CNA became politicized under the leadership of Arunachalam's brother Ponnambalam Ramanathan. The CNC emerged in December 1919 through the cooperation of these two organization with the Jaffna Association (JA). The JA was the most important of a number of provincial and local groups agitating for constitutional reform. It was founded in 1905 and represented the large number of English-educated Tamils based in northern Ceylon.

The CNC's proposals in December 1919 were an uneasy compromise between those who wanted territorial electorates and those who wanted communal electorates to protect minorities. Tamil leaders were assured by James Peiris, president of the CNA, and E. J. Samarawickreme, president of the CRL, that they would try to secure as large a Tamil representation as possible.

Governor William Manning (1918–25) enlarged the Legislative Council in 1920. It created an unofficial majority for the first time—23 of the 37 members—but only 11 of the unofficials were to be elected on a territorial basis (3 for the Western Province and 1 for each of the other eight), and 5 others (two Europeans, a Burgher, the Chamber of Commerce, and the Low-Country Products Association [LCPA, an organization composed primarily of Low Country Sinhalese planters]) were elected as representatives of special interests. There were 7 members nominated by the Governor—two Kandyans, one Muslim, one Indian and three "Unrepresented Interests." The unofficial minority was an illusion, since the governor's appointees voted with the government. Leaving nothing to chance, the governor also had the power to declare any issue to be one of paramount importance, for which only official members could vote.

When the election for territorial seats took place, Arunachalam planned to contest a Western Province seat, expecting to have the support of the CNC. Instead, Peiris contested the seat and Arunachalam withdrew his name. The CNC won nine territorial constituencies and the LCPA seat. Within the Legislative Council they agitated for further reforms, while they continued to build a political base among the Sinhalese Buddhists by creating *mahājana sabhas* or "people's councils." These declined after the organizer, F. R. Senanayake, died in 1924. By this time the nationalist movement had fragmented. Low Country Sinhalese *govigama*s dominated the CNC, and they failed to widen their appeal. Workers joined the Ceylon Labour Union founded by A. E. Goonesinha in 1922, Tamil politicians gravitated to the Tamil *mahājana sabhas* founded in August 1921, and Kandyan politicians became disillusioned with low-country leadership.

Governor Manning took advantage of nationalist disunity to pass further reforms in 1924 that exacerbated communal differences. He enlarged the Legislative Council to 49 members, only 12 of whom were officials. Of the 37 unofficials, 11 were elected by communal electorates, and 3 were nominated. The communal electorates were three Europeans, two Burghers, one Lankan Tamil for the Western Province, three Muslims, and two Indians. The franchise was still based on literacy and a property or income qualification, and the voting population increased to about 4 percent of the population.

Few leaders were pleased with the communal electorates. The 23 so-called territorial seats were consciously designed as seats for Sinhalese and Tamil notables, in a ratio of approximately two to one. The CNC promised Kandyan leaders that no Low Country Sinhalese would contest Kandyan seats, but several did, and only three Kandyans were elected in 1924. Kandyans then formed the Kandyan National Assembly which demanded autonomy for the Kandyan districts in a federal state. The Burgher electorates included anyone who considered himself a Burgher, despite the Dutch Burgher claims that only patrilineal descendants of Dutch colonials should be eligible. The Indian electorates, in contrast, were narrowly defined, excluding plantation laborers and other people of Indian origin who were domiciled in Ceylon. Peri Sundaram, who emerged as the spokesman for the Plantation Tamils in the State Council, was disqualified as a candidate for the Indian seat on the grounds that he was not an Indian.

From 1924 to 1930 Lankan politics was in turmoil. Politicians clashed with heads of departments. Because they had little influence on legislation, the CNC members of the Legislative Council began acting like an opposition. They used the finance committee as a forum for criticizing government policy by interrogating department heads, who previously had administered policy with no scrutiny.

The situation worsened with the appointment of Hugh Clifford as governor in 1926. He had opposed constitutional reforms as Colonial Secretary from May 1907 to September 1912. Most of his career had been in colonies that were governed through traditional elites, and he had no sympathy for Anglicized elites. He claimed that the 1924 constitutional reforms were a dismal failure. His frustration culminated in a bitter, secret 135-page despatch in November 1926 that attacked the character of the members of the Legislative Council. He acknowledged the abilities of the Councillors with backhanded compliments but characterized them as opportunists who used politics solely for personal advancement. He considered the people of the island to be inevitably divided by race, religion, and caste.

The Colonial Office was embarrassed by Clifford's wild accusations, which had more to do with his prejudices and failing mental health than Lankan politics, but they thought that there was justification for early reform. In fact the Legislative Council in this period attempted to deal with serious issues, such as education (particularly the language of instruction), workers' wages and benefits, and land settlement.

Ceylon's University College opened in 1921 in Colombo. It prepared students for external degrees of University of London. By 1928, the Legislative Council was debating ambitious plans to create a world-class university in Kandy.

The Legislative Council attempted to deal with the inequities of the school system. The Anglicized elite spoke English at home and were educated in Christian missionary and denominational schools. The schools levied fees, which closed them to the majority of the population, and they received greater government grants. Plantation laborers and lower castes, particularly in the Tamil districts, had little access to education. There was a consensus that education in Sinhala and Tamil should be made more readily available and that Sinhala- and Tamil-speaking students should have the opportunity to learn in English. There was no question of challenging the dominance of the elite, but English education would provide access to government employment and professional and commercial careers.

The Legislative Council debated questions that have still not been fully answered: Where would the English teachers come from? How does one determine the mother tongue? Is it the language spoken in the home or the language identified with one's race, or should parents decide? What was the place of religious instruction in the curriculum? The reformers supported moral education, but Christian educators were reluctant to admit that Buddhism, Hinduism, or Islam could provide it. Should the lower castes be educated? Some conservatives rejected the idea. The question of education became highly politicized during the State Council.

DONOUGHMORE COMMISSION

In August 1927, the Secretary of State for the Colonies appointed a special commission led by the Earl of Donoughmore to visit Ceylon and report on the working of the existing constitution and on any amendments that were needed. News of the commission was greeted by widespread criticism by politicians and the newspapers, particularly since it was not a Royal Commission and it contained no Lankan member.

The Commission worked hard at their tasks; they held 43 sittings and examined 164 witnesses and delegations from November 13, 1927, to January 18, 1928. They received hundreds of written representations (not all of which have been preserved). Members of the leading organizations were given preferential treatment, but the commissioners considered the testimony they heard and read seriously.

What they found was an enormous outpouring of grievances by spokesmen for every communal identity in the island. Their complaints were directed not so much at the Sinhalese majority but at the notables of their own communities. Lower castes among the Sinhalese protested against abuse by the *govigamas.* Tamil-speaking Lankans of various groups (Chetties, *bharatas,* Christians, Eastern Province Tamils, and lower castes) resented the domination of Tamil politics by upper-class Colombo *veḷḷāḷas*. Plantation Tamils did not want to be represented by wealthy Indian merchants. Kandyans, Malays, Portuguese Burghers, Catholics, and others all wanted separate representation. No system of communal representation could have satisfied the witnesses—and there was no assurance that the witnesses faithfully represented the people on whose behalf they spoke.

The Commission proposed a radical departure from the 1924 reforms that they had been sent to investigate. It recommended an experimental system of administration by executive committees in a State Council elected by nearly universal adult franchise. It also included a series of recommendations to protect communal interests, including a bill of rights, the power of the governor to veto legislative proposals that discriminated against any particular community, nominated members to represent minorities, and electorates small enough to give minorities a voice. They intended universal adult franchise to allow people to resolve grievances through politics. Their report repeats again and again that the wider franchise would serve the interests of the minorities better than communal representation.

This aspect of the reforms proved to be a failure on two counts. First, access to political power among all social categories tended to be limited to the same stratum of wealthy, urban, English-educated notables who monopolized representation under the Legislative Council, a feature of Lankan politics that only began to change in 1956. Second, politics became increasingly polarized, as the notables depended on appeals on ethnic lines to maintain their position; inevitably, Sinhalese representatives to the State Council soon dominated political life, as they have continued to do to the present.

When the reforms were implemented, the proposals were watered down in ways that increased the power of the Sinhalese elite. Elected seats were reduced from 65 to 50, nominated members were reduced from 12 to 8 (4 of which were used to appoint Europeans), and the votes of Lankans of Indian origin were further restricted. All these were done in a successful attempt to secure approval of the reforms from the Sinhalese members of the Legislative Council. Even then the State Council might have overcome division on ethnic lines if enough politicians would have appealed across ethnic lines to wider constituencies. This did not happen, and the minorities began to find common cause against the Sinhalese majority.

Universal franchise opened up the possibility of participation of the Plantation Tamils, nearly 15 percent of the population. More than 80 percent of them were plantation laborers, and in addition, a considerable proportion of the urban laboring population originated on the plantations, especially after

1921, when changes in labor laws made it easier for plantation laborers workers to leave. A growing proportion were second- or third-generation Lankans.

Sinhalese politicians objected to equal rights for Plantation Tamils, since this would have given them substantial political power in the planting districts and would have placed Kandyans in a minority in some of the upcountry districts. The CNC refused to approve the Donoughmore Constitution until their votes were restricted. Governor Herbert Stanley was in a difficult spot because the government had promised to recognize the rights of Indians lawfully domiciled in Ceylon, and the Government of India would not accept less. In the end, he let the Sinhalese politicians believe that the number of Plantation Tamils who were domiciled in Ceylon would be relatively small, and the Donoughmore Constitution was passed on the strength of Sinhalese votes in the Legislative Council, 19–17.

THE FIRST STATE COUNCIL

Elections were held in June 1931, except in four Tamil districts that boycotted them. Only C.W.W. Kannangara (Education) joined Don Stephen Senanayake (Agriculture and Lands) and Don Baron Jayatilaka (Home Affairs) as chairmen of committees on the Board of Ministers from the Ceylon National Congress. The other committee chairmen were chosen to represent regional and ethnic interests and proved to be ineffective. They sat on a Board of Ministers with little coordination except that provided by Senanayake as Chairman of the Board and Jayatilaka as Leader of the House.

Politically the committee system had mixed results. It gave committee members, especially the ministers, opportunity to promote pet projects, but the Committees competed with each other for finances. This discouraged both the cooperation of Ministers and the formation of political parties. The first political party, the socialist Lanka Sama Samaja Paksha (LSSP), was founded on December 18, 1935.

As more Plantation Tamils registered to vote, Sinhalese politicians demanded further restrictions. Senanayake in particular bombarded the Colonial Office with his own interpretation of the voting laws. When it became clear that almost all Plantation Tamils had a Lankan domicile, Sinhalese politicians demanded that they also prove a Lankan "domicile of origin" (the domicile at one's birth) and an "abiding interest" in the colony. These concepts were introduced into legislation by the State Council.

The State Council implemented a number of reforms that the colonial administrators might not have done. It passed an income tax, which gave them revenue to invested in public services. They oversaw a rapid transition to a predominantly Ceylonese civil service. A Public Service Commission advised the governor, who suspended the recruitment of British civil servants in March 1932. Even the key positions of GAs of the Central and Western Provinces were opened to Lankans in 1941.

The proportion of students attending school grew steadily, and more students advanced past a primary education to secondary school. The Land Commission implemented a more generous policy toward alienation of Crown Land, especially village expansion. They encouraged the growth of cooperatives, and they protested again imperial preference in tariffs, which restricted cheaper imports, especially from Japan.

Government took an increasing part in the provision of health and welfare services. The government had already provided some medical care for plantation laborers. These facilities, which were heavily used by the Kandyan population, became the model for the further expansion of public health. Nurses and midwives reduced maternal and infant mortality rates.

British business interests continued to lobby for favorable legislation on such matters as foreign exchange, planning, labor, and infrastructure through associations like the Employees Federation, various Chambers of Commerce, Ceylon Estate Employers Federation, commercial banks, and the London-based Ceylon Association, but with less success. Now newspapers, labor unions, professional organizations, Income Tax Payers Association, and the Rent Payers Association had more influence.

Sinhalese nationalist politicians took up the notion of reviving the once-fertile Dry Zone by restoring irrigation works and settling cultivators. They followed the recommendations of a Land Commission that had met from 1927 to 1929. It recommended the appointment of a Land Commissioner to control the sale of Crown Land, the reservation of land for "village expansion" rather than selling it to speculators, and the colonization of the Dry Zone to turn landless villagers into independent peasant proprietors.

Senanayake pressed for the creation of colonization schemes in the Dry Zone. This achieved a number of benefits for Sinhalese politicians: It strengthened their claim to be worthy successors to the British; it linked them to a growing Sinhalese nationalism that glorified the ancient civilization; and it was a means of appealing to the Kandyan Sinhalese, who were the people identified as suffering most from landlessness. The Land Settlement Ordinance of 1931 gave title to peasants who occupied land for one-third of a century, including *chenas*, and the Land Development Ordinance of 1935 implemented many recommendation of the Land Commission. They succeeded to some extent but at an extraordinary cost for irrigation, incentives, and infrastructure, much of it in scarce foreign exchange, and benefitted relatively few people.

ECONOMIC CONDITIONS

The State Council made little headway against the crisis created by the Great Depression. The 1920s had been a boom time for the economy as exports increased rapidly. Prices of the major export crops plummeted during the depression, however, and were made worse by rapid expansion and unrealistic expectations. Workers, particularly plantation laborers, suffered as the plantations, commercial sector, and government all cut back on employment.

Plantations had recruited far more new laborers than they needed in the 1920s for fear that India would restrict emigration. After November 1932 only workers with guaranteed jobs or relatives on plantations were allowed to return to Ceylon. In 1934, planters convinced the government that economic conditions justified additional immigration, which exacerbated island-wide unemployment. The numbers of urban workers in Colombo also increased in the 1920s, particularly in the harbor and railway yards. A majority were Sinhalese Buddhists, but others were Tamils who had left the plantations.

In the 1920s the Sinhalese labor leader A. E. Goonesinha and K. Natesa Aiyar, a Brahmin from south India, organized urban laborers. A number of strikes were held, but the depression undermined the strength of unions and the movement split on ethnic lines. Goonesinha became increasingly anti-Indian and, along with Sinhalese politicians, blamed Indians for causing unemployment among the Sinhalese. In 1931 Natesa Aiyar founded the All-Ceylon Estate Labour Federation in the planting districts, where he attracted large crowds and helped laborers prepare petitions to the Indian Agent, but was not allowed to enter the plantations.

Under pressure from India, the government implemented minimum wage rates for plantation laborers. The rates were low—laborers generally earned more under various incentive schemes—but the minimum wage provided them some protection during the depression. The government allowed plantations to reduce wages several times, and did not return to the 1929 level until 1941.

The economic crisis exacerbated ethnic relations as Sinhalese politicians exploited the feeling among the Sinhalese that minorities were, on one hand, taking their jobs while dominating banking and moneylending on the other. Legislation was passed to protect occupation to which the Sinhalese considered themselves entitled such as land ownership, rice cultivation, retail trade, and gem mining. Under colonial law, all people were British subjects, but Sinhalese nationalists considered the minorities to be foreigners.

The first State Council appointed a commission on banking. British banks did not loan money directly to Lankans. Instead, they loaned to Chettiar bankers from India, who reloaned the money to Lankans at higher interest. Even this source of credit dried up first from a banking scandal in 1925, and then from the depression. The State Council created a State Mortgage Bank in 1934 so that landowners could get loans without depending on the moneylenders. This helped urban property owners, but the State Mortgage Bank did not move into rural credit. A Central Bank was established in 1939 to regulate the colony's finances, but it was restricted by European commercial interests; it could not finance investment or loan money on immovable property, and initially was not allowed to make foreign exchange transactions except with India.

The business community included Muslims from Malabar, Nattukottai Chettiars from Tamil South India, and Afghans, Sindhis, Borahs, and Memons from West India. They dominated shopkeeping, pawnbroking, peddling, and petty moneylending. The small trading class had little connection to the big financiers and bankers, but Sinhalese politicians lumped them together as foreigners who sided with British imperialists.

A number of measures were enforced to break their monopoly on certain professions. Pawnbroking transactions were regulated by new procedures for recording, bookkeeping, interest rates, and the redemption of goods pawned. Under the Agricultural Quota Ordinance, Indian importers of rice and textiles were required to to purchase local products at a fixed price. Gem mining was a virtual monopoly of the Sinhalese, but trade in gems, including exports, was dominated by Muslims. Legislation was passed intended to prevent the Muslims from controlling gem cutting.

The State Council missed an opportunity to promote the economic development of the colony: Two engineers served on the Committee on Communications and Works (Stephen William Dassanaike and Devapura Jayasena Wimalasurendra), but chairman H. M. Macan Markar, son of a wealthy Muslim jeweler, showed little interest in their proposals. He closely adhered to the policies of Senanayake and Jayatilaka, and is remembered primarily for stating publicly in 1938 that he preferred that Ceylon be ruled by the Sinhalese.

Wimalasurendra advocated industrialization as the solution to the island's poverty. His work in the Public Works Department since 1916 had focused on developing the island's potential for hydroelectric power. In 1924 the Legislative Council approved his plan for the Laxapana ("100,000 lamps") power plant, which was abandoned in 1927. He became a member of the Executive Committee of the CNC and was elected to the State Council, but resigned in July 1931.

As a State Councillor, Wimalasurendra pressed unsuccessfully for resumption of the Laxapana Project and criticized the expenditure on peasant colonization, arguing for more efficient investment in agriculture. He proposed the creation of an Electricity Board, which was passed in 1935 but dissolved in 1937, not to be reestablished until 1969. He suggested many potential industries that could be developed in Ceylon, from the use of the island's graphite in locally produced pencils to the manufacture of plywood chests for the tea plantations. He was defeated for reelection in 1936.

THE PAN-SINHALESE MINISTRIES

The general elections of 1936 produced the first members elected to the State Council as representatives of a political party as Philip Gunawardena and

Dr N. M. Perera won seats as members of the LSSP. The Donoughmore Constitution did not encourage the formation of parties, because candidates were restricted to the small group of English-educated elites and because the committee system required members of the State Council to form alliances within their committees.

The Sinhalese State Councillors distributed themselves on the committees in order to dominate all the committees and proceeded to appoint only Sinhalese ministers. They justified this action as a means to improve their bargaining position with the British for change in the constitution. In this they succeeded. For the remainder of British rule, the Board of Ministers negotiated privately with the British Government. They also needed to make room on the Board for key members of the CNC leadership, particularly S.W.R.D. Bandaranaike as Minister of Local Administration and G.C.S. Corea as Minister of Labour, Industry and Commerce. It is not likely that the leadership was thinking of the long-term consequences of their actions; it suggests that the Ceylon National Congress leadership expected little change in the ruling order. This fueled the suspicions of the Tamils and led to G. G. Ponnambalam's demand for a system of balanced representation that would prevent the Sinhalese from dominating the minorities.

Jayatilaka, the Leader of the House, Don Baron Jayatilaka, made his way to London for the Coronation in 1937 and lobbied with the secretary of state on constitutional reform While he was in England, a constitutional crisis broke out. A radical young Australian tea planter named Mark Bracegirdle was arrested by the police, who intended to deport him. The police were the responsibility of Jayatilaka's Department of Home Affairs, but it was effectively controlled by European officers. The Board of Ministers protested that the governor was taking police action without reference to the Home Minister but were embarrassed to learn that the Inspector General of Police (IGP) had done so. Jayatilaka's failure to act effectively damaged his reputation, and he was gradually eased out of the Congress leadership. The use of special powers by the governor became a lively political issue.

Meanwhile, Governor Andrew Caldecott arrived with instructions from the secretary of state to examine the working of the constitution and to report on it. Governor Caldecott had a reputation of being sympathetic to the people of the country and soon proposed reforms that opposed communal representation and recommended that a "normal" Cabinet replace the Executive Committees and the Board of Ministers.

In 1939 there was a wave of strikes on tea plantations in the Central Province and Uva. One of these, Mooloya Estate, was led by the All Ceylon Estate Workers Union organized by the LSSP. The police opened fire on a band of workers, killing one of them. Governor Caldecott agreed to a Commission of Inquiry. The strike was settled in January 1940, and Jayatilaka requested the IGP to allow the postponement of three Mooloya cases pending before the

Magistrate's Court at Kandy. The IGP refused, and the governor supported him. The Board of Ministers resigned to call attention to the anomaly of a police department refusing to consider the wishes of the elected government and the governor siding with the head of a department responsible rather than the State Council.

The British patronized Senanayake because they thought he was the alternative to a left-wing government that would threaten British investments. He was able to convince the British that he was above communal conflict.

TOWARD INDEPENDENCE

Negotiations toward increased self-government and eventual independence took place between Governor Caldecott and the Board of Ministers, but the future of the colony became a matter of public debate, and parties inside and outside the State Council took actions that influenced later policy in the areas of religion, language, education, citizenship, and ideology.

Sinhalese-Buddhist nationalists increasingly advocated the creation of a state modeled after their vision of an idyllic past in a growing body of fiction and journalism. Piyadasa Sirisena in particular advocated a return to what he thought was an ideal Buddhist society. Later novelists such as W. A. Silva and Martin Wickramasinghe painted a more realistic view of a society. Sinhala-educated Lankans were subjected to a view of the future in which Buddhism would be not only the official religion but the inspiration for governing; Sinhala would be the official language; missionary and denominational schools would be abolished; and the state would promote the cultural heritage of the Sinhalese. The Anglicized elite, eager to win support from the Sinhalese voters, did little to discourage these ideas. They needed their electoral support and seem to have believed that communal feelings would give way eventually.

Some politicians of all ethnic communities favored English as the official language indefinitely, as the link language between communities and as the essential language of law, government, finance, business, higher scholarship, and international relations. Sinhalese nationalists and some Muslims wanted Sinhala to become the official language, and most Tamil and Muslim politicians favored both Sinhala and Tamil as official languages. The advocates of Sinhala or Sinhala and Tamil were concerned both about the unfair advantages the colonial society gave to the English-educated and the difficulty for the *swabasha*-educated of functioning in English.

In light of future developments, it is significant that Sinhalese nationalists differed as to *which* Sinhala should be the national language. Spoken Sinhala differs greatly from literary Sinhala, and the various forms of the written language differ from each other. *Bhikkhu*s and scholars wrote in a style that incorporated many loan words from Sanskrit and Pāli. Journalists and novelists had been developing over a century literary forms closer to the spoken language. Writers under the leadership of Munidasa Kumaranatunga demanded that the schools teach *Hela,* a version of Sinhala that reduced words to a form that obliterated all traces of their Indian origins.

In the State Council, the Executive Committee for Education under C.W.W. Kannangara (1884–1969) pushed for free education. Born and educated a Christian, Kannangara converted to Buddhism and was Minister of Education in both State Councils. His education ordinance in 1939 removed control of education from the Christian-dominated Board of Education to the Executive Committee. It created English-medium central schools in all parts of the island, which provided the opportunity for a rigorous education to all children. Religious instruction was allowed in government schools, but not as part of the regular curriculum. Kannangara encouraged the study of Sinhala and Tamil in anticipation of a transition from English to *swabasha* in government departments. It was proposed that Sinhala rather than Tamil should be the medium of instruction in estate schools, but this led to no action.

Senanayake had campaigned tirelessly for restrictions on the votes of Lankans of Indian origin, not distinguishing between Indians temporarily resident in the island and those who had lived there for generations. As a planter himself, Senanayake opposed limits on immigration that would threaten the supply of cheap labor. In 1940 he finally won over the government, and one-fourth of the registered voters of Indian origin were stricken from the rolls, declining from 225,000 in 1939 to 168,000 in 1943.

The State Council had passed a series of laws that discriminated against people of Indian origins by restricting many activities to Ceylonese, defined on a racial basis. Ceylonese were given preference in enterprises such as retail shopkeeping, import trade, fishing, and bus services. Non-Ceylonese businesses were required to hire Ceylonese employees. Indian businesses were not given relief for double taxation in the Income Tax Ordinance of 1942.

In 1938 people of Indian origin constituted more than one-fourth of all workers in government employment. The following year a state council resolution led to the "compulsory retirement" of about 25,000 Indians. By 1941, Indians were reduced to 12 percent of government employment. In retaliation, India prohibited immigration to Ceylon beginning in August 1939. Under the ban, unskilled laborers of Indian origin could not travel to Ceylon, and those who traveled to India could not return. Although a few exceptions were made, the ban was effective: From August 1, 1939, to November 30, 1940, there was a net emigration about 65,000 people of Indian origin to India. The ban was lifted in 1942 because Indian laborers, who were needed for war work in Ceylon, continued to emigrate to India.

8

The Coming of Independence

Sri Lanka's independence from Britain on February 4, 1948, was a peaceful transition from the colonial rulers to the Anglicized upper-class elite, who already had already been substantially self-governing since 1931. This elite adapted smoothly the British-style parliamentary democracy created by the Soulbury Constitution. There never was any doubt that the political leadership would be drawn from a handful of prominent Sinhalese elites, but D. S. Senanayake, who succeeded D. B. Jayatilaka as leader of the State Council, consciously attempted to include minority supporters in the United National Party (UNP) after independence. In 1956, which coincided with the presumed two thousand five hundredth anniversary of the birth of the Buddha, S.W.R.D. Bandaranaike contested the election on a direct appeal to Sinhalese Buddhist emotions that gave his Sri Lanka Freedom Party (SLFP) a landslide victory. The process of creation of a Sinhalese government that began with the "pan-Sinhalese" Board of Ministers in 1936 culminated in this victory.

The Board of Ministers became stronger in the 1940s. More Lankans held high office in government departments and cooperated with the State Council better than British civil servants had. The governor rarely exercised his veto power. The elections that were scheduled for 1941 were postponed, the first of several times a Lankan legislature would extend its term of office. During World War II, the British relied increasingly on the State Council for wartime cooperation. During the final negotiations for independence, the British accepted the Ministers' draft of a constitution without dissent.

WARTIME GOVERNMENT

The colony was under a military government during World War II; Admiral Geoffrey Layton governed through a War Council consisting of military officers, the governor, the Board of Ministers and the Civil Defense Commissioner. For the last he appointed the Auditor General, O. E. Goonetilleke. He was the most able Lankan official of his time and a close ally of D. S. Senanayake. Ceylon was an important base of operations in the Allied offensive against the Japanese and a major source of rubber, foodstuffs, and other materials vital to the war effort. The island was virtually untouched by the war. On Easter Sunday 1942, a small-scale air-raid struck Colombo. It did little damage, but many civilians deserted the city in panic. Four days later carrier-based planes attacked the harbor of Trincomalee.

Before the war, Marxists were the most organized and articulate politicians; the war made a profound difference to them. Those leftists who continued to follow the lead of the Soviet Union were expelled from the LSSP, and it became an openly Trotskyite party. The government arrested LSSP leaders who did not go into hiding. S. A. Wickramasinghe and others founded the United Socialist Party, which in 1943 became the Communist Party of Ceylon. The group supported the war effort once the Soviet Union was attacked; it affiliated with the CNC, which went into decline after Senanayake withdrew from it in protest. In 1945 the LSSP split over personal differences and the question of cooperation with non-Marxist parties. The new LSSP, headed by Philip Gunawardena and N. M. Perera, favored cooperation, whereas the Bolshevik Leninist Party (BLP) led by Colvin R. de Silva and Leslie Goonewardene opposed it. Although the left collectively remained influential in Lankan political life, fragmentation meant that the possibility that they could form a government declined rapidly.

Other politically active groups included S.W.R.D. Bandaranaike's Sinhala Maha Sabha, which had provincial associations linked with it throughout the Sinhalese-majority districts; G. G. Ponnambalam led the All Ceylon Tamil Congress (TC), which argued for a 50-50 scheme of "balanced representation"; and A. E. Goonesinha's Ceylon Labour Party.

In November 1940 the governor included D. S. Senanayake, S.W.R.D. Bandaranaike, and G.C.S. Corea in a government delegation to New Delhi to discuss the status of Indian immigrants to Ceylon. It was a significant event because the British gave the Board of Ministers the right to speak for the country on a topic of external affairs. Ominously, however, the question was one of the first in which Sinhalese politicians competed for Sinhalese support by taking extreme positions on an ethnic issue. The Ceylon Indian Congress (CIC) also sent a delegation to New Delhi headed by Peri Sundaram, but it had no official standing. Bandaranaike and Senanayake both appealed to their Sinhalese constituencies by anti-Indian speeches in the State Council.

The British declared in 1941 that the constitution would be examined by a Commission after the war. The State Council demanded Dominion Status, and the British responded that Ceylon would get "full responsible government" for internal civil administration when the war ended.

The war had been profitable for people who were not on fixed incomes. The armed forces spent money freely throughout the island. Anyone with anything to sell to the military prospered; intermediaries who procured the goods and services they demanded did even better. Ceylon became the largest rubber-producing area for the allies, and trees were "slaughter-tapped"—extracting the maximum amount of latex even though the trees' ability to recover was destroyed. The prosperity continued into the postwar period as blocked payments were disbursed.

The losers were the state and any employees whose pay was tied to an unrealistic official cost of living index. By 1946, clerical workers were desperate, and the abrupt termination of money spent by the armed forces added hardship throughout the country. Housing shortages multiplied the discontent.

Competing unions sprang up. The Communist Party founded the Ceylon Trade Union Federation. N. M. Perera led the Ceylon Federation of Labour after his release from detention. Under the threat of a general strike, the Board of Ministers hesitated, then passed repressive legislation, which included the use of the military against the strikers. Perera was arrested and then was released, and the strikes were settled. The government blamed politicians for inciting the workers. There were large-scale strikes in 1947 just before the General Election under the new Soulbury Constitution. Government clerical workers were told that state employees did not have the right to strike, and when they did, their strike was suppressed.

LANGUAGE AND EDUCATION

As independence neared, the State Council debated the official language of the new nation and the education of its citizens. Universal free education was a popular issue during the State Council. Senanayake opposed the idea and obstructed its passage, but the State Council passed it while he was out of the country. Most of the politicians had been educated in English in the elite schools; those who opposed it on the grounds of cost, or of caste and class considerations, were reluctant to speak out.

In June 1943, J. R. Jayewardene moved a resolution to make Sinhala the official language. He supported amendments that would allow schools to teach children in their mother tongue and would include Tamil as an official language in the Tamil-speaking areas. Both he and Dudley Senanayake, the son of D. S. Senanayake, voiced the fears of those who objected to giving Tamil official status: The Tamil language had advantages from the proximity of the large, Tamil-speaking population of India, which produced publications, films, and radio broadcasts in a quantity that Sinhala could not match. If Tamil had parity with Sinhala in Ceylon, Senanayake argued, Sinhala might become a dead language.

The State Council passed the Free Education Act in 1945. This removed fees from English-medium schools and created scholarships to the expanding Central Schools. Fee-levying schools had to choose between eliminating fees and accepting grants, or continuing as fee-levying schools without public support. Ordinance No. 20 of 1947 abolished fees for all schools except "denominational," most of which were Catholic schools. At about the same time, school examinations were administered and graded in Ceylon rather than in England as they had been until the war. The Act was amended in 1947 to include instruction in the religion of the parent in the curriculum.

The reforms were costly; they provided for free books, uniforms, and midday meals. In 1925–1926, education made up 7.1 percent of total government expenditure; in 1947–1948 it had risen to 18.9 percent.

These reforms did not diminish the demand for English. In the years immediately following independence, some Sinhalese and Tamils learned each other's language, but both were much more likely to learn English as a second language—the number of English-speakers increased dramatically from 6.5 percent of the population at the 1946 census to 9.6 percent at the 1953 census.

In 1950 education was made free through the university, and higher education was expanded to meet the anticipated demand. The University of Ceylon at Peradeniya began offering liberal arts classes in October 1952. There was a great increase in secondary education, particularly the Central Schools (Madhya Maha Vidyalayas), which gave rural Lankan youth access to high-quality education—sometimes more rigorous than that offered in the complacent and less disciplined elite schools. They were joined by many Senior Schools (Maha Vidyalayas), which taught only the lower levels.

SOULBURY CONSTITUTION

The ministers prepared a draft of the Constitution with the aid of Sir Ivor Jennings, Vice-Chancellor of the University of Ceylon. The Soulbury Commission arrived in December 1944, but the Board of Ministers refused to give evidence, because they wanted the Commission to consider only their proposals and not meet with representatives of minorities. They met privately with the Commission, which accepted their draft almost entirely. It was put into effect in 1946 and became the constitution two years later with appropriate changes. The lack of consultation on the constitution undermined its legitimacy, and opposition governments kept alive the issue of rewriting it until it was finally replaced in 1972.

S.W.R.D. Bandaranaike and J. R. Jayewardene, who had been considered radical young politicians, followed Senanayake's leadership and pushed the CNC into acceptance of the terms of the transfer of power. They joined the United National Party (UNP), which Senanayake created in September 1946.

Ceylon's path to independence was deceptively easy. The colony appeared to the British to be a safe bet to succeed compared with other British colonies. It was undamaged by the war and had both monetary reserves released after the end of hostilities and a profitable plantation economy. The leadership was conservative and experienced in democratic politics and in a British-style administrative structure. The people were relatively well educated and healthy. The Colonial Office shared the fear of the conservative upper classes that the only alternative to the CNC would be a leftist coup d'etat.

The reality differed. The economy was fragile because the plantation economy proved to be less profitable when the protection of the British Empire was removed. The terms of trade turned against the colony as export prices declined and the cost of essential food imports rose. The political leadership was drawn primarily from a few wealthy low-country *govigama* families who had learned to use democratic institutions to perpetuate their power. The provision of health, welfare, and education was a major feature of their strategy to maintain their control. It absorbed government revenues that were needed for investment in the new nation's future.

Senanayake had convinced the Colonial Office that the minorities would be protected in a Sinhalese government under his leadership, but the transfer of power did not resolve the basic political issues that divided the society. The parliamentary system guaranteed that the Sinhalese Buddhist vote would determine who ruled the island. Many of these voters were led to believe that independence gave them the power to recreate an idyllic society that would redress the real and imagined grievances of Buddhists under colonial domination. Sinhalese leaders were unable or unwilling to establish the need to recognize the rights of minority groups. The leaders of other communities also tended to rely on their ethnic community rather than to create a pluralistic Sri Lanka. (Although the nation was not officially named "Sri Lanka" until 1972, it seems appropriate to discontinue the use of the colonial name "Ceylon" after independence).

POLITICS 1947–1951

The UNP easily won the first parliamentary election in 1947 with about 40 percent of the votes and formed a government with the aid of independent members. The leftist parties and their allies won about 20 percent of the vote (a count they never reached again) and about one-fourth of the seats in the first election, despite a delimitation of seats that underrepresented the urban areas, where they had their greatest strength. After the election, politicians jockeyed for parties and constituencies to secure influence in Parliament.

The three Marxist parties (LSSP, CP, and BLP) benefited from discontent over the current economic crisis and opposition to the way the British handed power to Senanayake and his conservative allies. Fears of a leftist takeover of the government proved unjustified when most of the leftist politicians turned out to be happy to use the electoral system to maintain their personal positions. In 1950 the BLP reunited with the LSSP under the leadership of N. M. Perera. Perera became the leader of the opposition, but Philip Gunawardena opposed the merger and formed his own Viplavakari Lanka Sama Samaja Party (VLSSP). The left remained fragmented and abandoned its revolutionary goals, but they were able to influence policy within parliament.

In 1951 Saumiyamoorthy Thondaman, the son of Karuppiah Thondaman, renamed the CIC the Ceylon Workers' Congress (CWC). Despite the loss of Plantation Tamil citizenship, Thondaman remained a force in Lankan politics until his death in 1999.

Senanayake held the new nation together by uniting a broad segment of the Anglicized elite against leftist opposition and avoided the breakdown of the constitutional regime that had taken place in other post-colonial states. He did not have any positive solutions, however, for overcoming its dysfunctional colonial legacy—an English-speaking government in a Sinhala and Tamil nation, an overly centralized administration, and economic dependence on the export of plantation crops. The constitution itself exacerbated the problems by placing political power in the hands of the majority community.

Senanayake's UNP included members of all ethnic groups, as did the left parties. They were all, however, representatives of the Anglicized elite that had prospered under colonial rule, and party leaders represented the Sinhalese-Buddhist majority. The *swabasha*-educated intelligentsia remained suspicious of these English-speaking members of the upper class. Senanayake resisted the Sinhalese extremists, and Tamil politicians generally supported his administration.

The rural Sinhalese electorate became even more decisive with the acts that disenfranchised many plantation laborers: the Citizenship Acts of 1948, the Indian and Pakistani Residents (Citizenship) Act of 1949, and the Parliamentary Elections (Amendment) Act of 1949. These were the culmination of the anti-Indian policies of the State Council period and made stateless many people whose families had lived on the island for generations. Their disfranchisement gave greater representation to the Kandyan Sinhalese because the delimitation of constituencies continued to be based on total population: 26 percent of the population elected 44 percent of the members of parliament.

A section of the TC headed by S.J.V. Chelvanayakam broke away and created the Ilangai Tamil Arasu Katchi (Lanka Tamil Government Party, called

"Federal Party" in English, but now known by its initials ITAK) in September 1951. The ITAK cited the continuing support of the TC for the government even after the disenfranchisement of the Indian Tamils as a reason for the split, but the TC claimed that it was a matter of personal differences.

None of the political developments threatened D. S. Senanayake, who ruled with little effective dissent until 1951. The left parties were split into too many quarreling factions to create a cohesive opposition. It seemed as if Sri Lanka might have a one-party system like Jawaharlal Nehru's Congress party in India. This was shattered, first, when S.W.R.D. Bandaranaike defected to the opposition and, second, when Senanayake died suddenly in March 1952. Dudley Senanayake led the UNP to a sweeping victory in July 1952, but conditions then rapidly deteriorated.

Bandaranaike was pushed to a relatively minor role in the government for a number of reasons. He had long-standing differences with Senanayake, who was grooming his son Dudley to succeed him. He also faced the rivalries of Sir John Kotelawala and J. R. Jayewardene. Bandaranaike's proposals, such as those for the creation of elected district councils, were disregarded. He was considered a leftist as well as a Sinhalese nationalist. He finally joined the opposition with five followers on July 12, 1951.

ECONOMY 1947–1951

Sri Lanka had no clear economic policy. This has been called a "liberal trade regime" or "open economy" in hindsight because it did not implement the socialist policies that the CNC had advocated before independence. In fact, the UNP allowed the economy to drift and squandered the relative prosperity the new nation enjoyed—its real per capita income was higher than that of Thailand and South Korea until the 1960s. Except in the area of rice production, the economy weakened.

Sinhalese politicians had convinced their constituents that the economic hardships of the immediate postwar period were caused by British and Indian control of the economy. They had continued to dominate much of the import and export trade, retail trade, and banking despite the legislation of the State Council. The UNP found scapegoats rather than dealing with economic problems.

During World War II, there had been a movement toward a modern economy. The government had started 15 factories to manufacture goods that could not be imported, including plywood, paper, ceramics, acetic acid, and rerolled steel. Without competition, and with an Industrial Products Act that required consumers to purchase their products, they had no incentives to become efficient. After the war, they had no protection from imports and were closed down, except for plywood, leather, ceramic, and glass factories. The cement and paper factories were located in Tamil areas owing to a lack of interest by Sinhalese politicians.

The Plywood Corporation, one of the few industries to survive the war, is an example of the problems that beset manufacturing. The idea of producing tea chests in Sri Lanka had been discussed often in the 1930s but resisted by the planters, some of whom were directly involved in their import from the London Plywood Chest Association. The Corporation had high overhead costs from mismanagement. It sold the chests through government distribution offices, and it lost money on a huge amount of perishable glue it purchased in 1947 that spoiled before it could be used. When it was finally offered to private investors, there was no interest.

Some private entrepreneurs emerged during World War II. Lankans rebuilt tires, manufactured cookies and soap, and supplied the military with every kind of commodity. Many of these were Sinhalese nationalists who then suffered when the UNP discouraged domestic enterprise and allowed the import of competing products. The Ministry of Industries opposed private exploitation of the island's rich mineral sand deposits and a proposed tire factory. It competed with private producers of coconut oil. In contrast, foreign businesses, particularly the large companies that controlled the tea industry, were encouraged.

The rubber industry faced a crisis when the British stopped purchasing rubber after the war. Productivity declined from trees that had been slaughter tapped as part of the war effort. Synthetic rubber factories began to be built in the industrial nations. The Korean War produced a brief revival of rubber prices.

The UNP inherited food subsidies and health facilities that were expanded during the war. They were continued in part to undermine support for leftist parties. As economic conditions deteriorated, it became an increasing burden on the budget. Furthermore, a lax trade policy allowed the country's foreign exchange reserves to dwindle as wealthy Lankans imported luxury consumer goods. The government was forced to reduce welfare expenditures, although the subsidized rice ration was maintained.

The Korean War produced a commodity price boom. In 1950 and early 1951 Sri Lanka's export prices rose almost 40 percent, and external reserves and the domestic money supply increased. The boom was short-lived, but the UNP responded by increasing food subsidies. Subsidies accounted for about one-fifth of all government expenditures.

When export prices declined and import prices rose in 1951, the budget and foreign exchange deficits grew astronomically. This economic decline took place against the background of an extraordinarily high population growth rate of more than 3 percent a year: After independence the birth rate increased, and government welfare policies lowered mortality.

ECONOMIC PLANNING

There were attempts to implement economic planning in this period, but they were overcome by political expediency. The development plans were a Six-Year Development plan in 1948, a report of the World Bank Mission in 1951, and the Government's Six Year Programme of Investment for the period 1954–1955 to 1959–1960. The Central Bank also issued annual reports. The Six-Year Development Plan consisted merely of the 1947–1948 and 1948–1949 budget speeches. It was prepared primarily to be used as the basis for aid negotiations under the Colombo Plan.

In 1951, at about the time export prices were plummeting, the first of many World Bank missions visited the island. Its 829-page report contained many of the recommendations and suggestions that have become familiar: Increase revenue by raising taxes, especially income taxes; reduce expenditures by gradually phasing out food subsidies and subsidized services; increase productivity by tax incentives to producers; develop the infrastructure in the harbor, railroads, and roads; and encourage family planning. The Six-Year Program of Investment was a synthesis of the proposals made by the World Bank mission.

John Exter, an economist with the U.S. Federal Reserve system, recommended the establishment of a Central Bank in 1949. It was established the following year, with Exter as its first governor. It was given power to control the banking system and regulate the money supply in order to stabilize the value of the rupee and to preserve its use for international transactions. It was also asked to promote high levels of production, employment, and income and to encourage the development of productive resources. It quickly proved capable in the former but not the latter.

From the early 1950s on, budget deficits have been normal in Sri Lanka. Tariffs provided more than half of government revenue in the 1950s. Export duties increased after 1953. In 1950 and 1951 most restrictions on imports were removed, but the higher revenue from import duties was offset by increased government expenditures on imports.

COLONIZATION SCHEMES

The one area in which the new nation succeeded was in the increased production of rice. Much of this was in new settlements in the Dry Zone, called "colonization schemes." This was an inefficient use of scarce revenue. In the short term, the colonization schemes had political benefits for the UNP among the Sinhalese voters of the southwest, but in the long run, the settlement of Sinhalese in the previously heterogeneous Dry Zone became a major grievance of the Tamils.

Buddhist politicians hoped to repopulate the Dry Zone with Buddhist peasant cultivators. This notion began with nationalist criticisms of British colonial policy toward the peasants, which they claim destroyed peasant society. Some Buddhists claimed that the colonization schemes had a historical importance, as the "reconquest" of land that once was the fertile center of the ancient civilization. The culturally biased Department of Archaeology was enlisted to buttress these claims.

In a colonization scheme, the government created an irrigation system, selected the settlers, granted them land, and provided them with means of survival until their crops enable them to become independent self-sufficient paddy farmers. Alternative strategies, such as commercial land development of cash crops, might have returned more for the investment and certainly would have been preferred by the people of the old, or *purana,* Dry Zone villages.

POLITICS 1951–1956

In addition to the budget crisis caused by falling export prices, unemployment increased. The UNP's pledge to maintain welfare expenditures help reelect them in July 1952, but Senanayake attempted to reduce subsidies on rice, free lunches for schoolchildren, and public services such as transportation, postal service, and electricity. The LSSP led an island-wide *hartal* (general strike) in August 1953. Although he controlled two-thirds of the seats in Parliament, Dudley Senanayake resigned.

Bandaranaike, despite the weakness of his SLFP, led the opposition to Senanayake's cousin Sir John Kotelawala, who succeeded him. Kotelawala's blunders paved the way for Bandaranaike's emergence. Kotelawala's intolerance of Tamils, Indians, and non-*govigama* castes offended many. He removed an effective Tamil leader, G. G. Ponnambalam, from the cabinet for personal reasons and replaced him with a less capable Tamil, Kandiah Vaithyanathan. Tamils resented that he allowed no vote of thanks in Tamil to Queen Elizabeth II when she visited Parliament in 1954. He put greater restrictions on resident Indian permit holders. Indians and Lankans of Indian ancestry were arrested and detained on the pretext that they were illegal immigrants.

Most of all, he outraged Sinhalese Buddhists by his flamboyant Westernized lifestyle and lack of interest in their concerns. On a visit to Jaffna in September 1954, he stated that he would change the constitution to give Tamil parity with Sinhala and repeated it three weeks later, despite protests from Sinhalese areas. Although Kotelawala reneged on his promise when a motion to that effect was introduced in Parliament, his promise marks a turning point in the question of language policy.

Bandaranaike had also supported parity of Sinhala and Tamil in 1952, but he opportunistically declared that the SLFP favored only Sinhala as the official language, with a "reasonable use of Tamil." The Ceylon Muslim League and the All Ceylon Moors Association, whose members were mostly Tamil-speakers, also supported Sinhala as the official language if Tamil and English were also recognized. In 1956 the UNP belatedly adopted "Sinhala-only."

Foolishly thinking that he could win an early election, Kotelawala dissolved Parliament 15 months early in February 1956. Bandaranaike campaigned on the language issue. He proposed to make Sinhala the language of administration in the country rather than English. He seems to have thought of himself as representing the ordinary Sinhalese, who could not communicate with the government in English. When the UNP entered the debate, the issue tended to become not over whether there should be an alternative to English but whether there should be an alternative to parity for Tamil and Sinhala.

Buddhism was the second issue in the 1956 campaign. The All-Ceylon Buddhist Congress (ACBC) created an unofficial Buddhist Commission of Inquiry in 1952. Its report, published as *The Betrayal of Buddhism,* accused the UNP of neglecting Buddhist interests. Catholics saw it as an attack on them because it called for the nationalization of aided schools, many of them Catholic, and recommended such things as the prohibition of nuns working in government hospitals. Buddhist leaders wanted political control in the hands of Buddhists in order to foster Buddhism and promote the Sinhalese-Buddhist heritage.

The 1956 election saw the emergence of *bhikkhus* as influential actors in Sinhalese politics. In the 1930s *bhikkhus,* inspired by Anagārika Dharmapāla, became active in society rather than concentrating on their traditional ritual obligations of chanting protective verses, accepting alms, and performing funerals. As described by anthropologist H. L. Seneviratne, they tended to become active in two directions, each following part of Dharmapāla's prescription. The first group, centered at Vidyodaya, devoted their efforts to *gramasamvardhana* (village development). They promoted such virtues as temperance, crime prevention, teaching, and self-help programs. This effort has faded.

Other *bhikkhus,* from Vidyalankara, have taken active participation in the political process. Ven. Walpola Rahula published the intellectual arguments for the *sangha* to be the spokesmen for the Sinhalese people in his 1946 book, *Heritage of the Bhikkhu.* This was a response to statements by Senanayake that *bhikkhus* should stay out of politics. Rahula argues that it is the responsibility of the *bhikkhu* to prevent the decline of Buddhism in Lankan life. The activist *bhikkhus* argued that they could serve Sinhalese culture in a variety of occupations and activities. They tended to be hostile to Christian missionaries and schools and to Tamils, and they advocated socialism.

FOREIGN POLICY

D. S. Senanayake signed defense agreements with the United Kingdom, which were criticized by many politicians. He feared a threat from India, which Sri Lanka could not resist alone. Although personally Senanayake was pro-Western and anti-communist, he was also anti-colonial. He opposed the Dutch war on Indonesia, recognized the People's Republic of China (PRC), and refused to take sides in the Cold War.

The foreign ministers of the Commonwealth of Nations met in Colombo in January 1950 and drafted a tentative plan for the economic development. The Colombo Plan allocated nearly $340 million of Commonwealth funds for Sri Lanka, primarily irrigation works and hydroelectric plants.

In 1952 Sri Lanka negotiated a barter agreement with the PRC under which China provided desperately needed rice for Sri Lanka's rubber. The United States opposed the agreement, and Sri Lanka resisted American pressure to end it.

Kotelawala was openly pro-Western and anti-communist. He allowed American airplanes carrying French troops to Indo-China to land in Sri Lanka. He made belligerently anti-Communist speeches at a conference on Indo-China in Colombo in 1954, and again at the Bandung conference in 1956. He declined to join the Southeast Asia Treaty Organization, knowing that it would create strong opposition. The Soviet Union nevertheless considered it to be pro-Western and vetoed its admission to the United Nations until December 14, 1955.

THE 1956 ELECTION

The 1956 election is a landmark not only in Lankan history, but in the history of post-colonial states. A free democratic election removed a government that had been handed power by the colonial ruler and that had maintained its authority in two elections. The transfer of power was smoothly handled. Bandanaike's Mahajana Eksath Peramuna (MEP), a coalition of the SLFP, VLSSP, and others won 40 percent of the vote and 51 of the 95 seats. The UNP was reduced to 27 percent of the vote and only 8 seats, fewer than the LSSP (14) and the ITAK (10).

The sweeping victory of the MEP created a de facto two-party system in which the SLFP and UNP competed for Sinhalese voters, who controlled 80 percent of the seats in Parliament. Between them the two parties divided most of the Sinhalese vote, but their leaders needed support from the left (SLFP) or Tamil parties (UNP) while holding on to their Sinhalese-Buddhist base. In opposition, both parties resisted solutions to ethnic problems and advocated additional privileges for Sinhalese Buddhists. In the context of economic deterioration, this had the dual effect of discrimination against non-Sinhalese Buddhist Lankans and of making the victims of discrimination scapegoats when governments failed to meet the peoples' raised expectations.

The MEP coalition of leftist parties and anti-UNP candidates in 1956 appealed to the frustrations of rural Sinhalese, who were disillusioned because independence had not redressed the inequities of the colonial era. The MEP promised to restore Buddhism, Sinhalese culture, and Sinhala to a predominant position in the nation. In response the UNP, J. R. Jayewardene, in par-

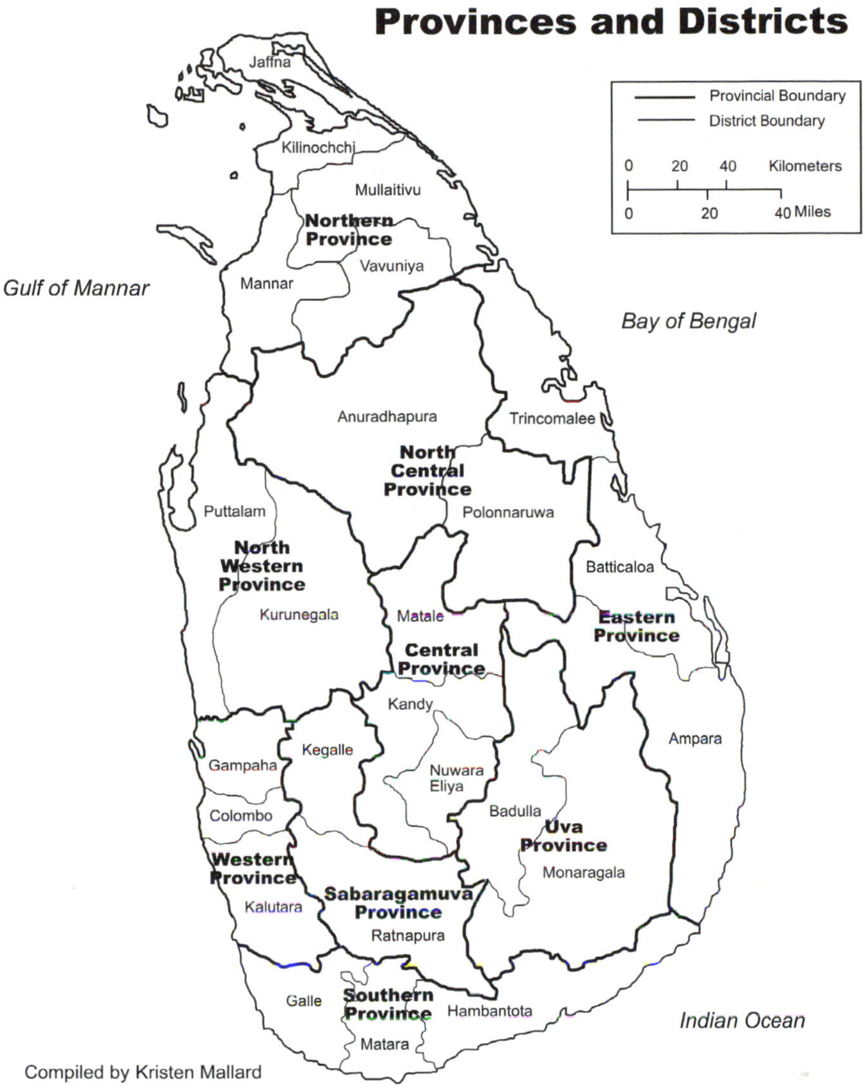

ticular, began competing for Buddhist support. Since then, the party in opposition has been able to undermine all solutions to ethnic issues by opposing them in the name of the Sinhalese Buddhist majority. Voters' response to these appeals is indicated by the high voter turnout. In 1956, for example, 69.0 percent of registered voters cast their ballots. Turnout increased in March 1960 to 77.6 percent, 75.9 percent in July 1960, 82.1 percent in 1965, and 85.2 percent in 1970. In each election, the voters defeated the incumbents.

The election demonstrated that a party could win on the strength of Sinhalese votes only. Bandaranaike was careful to include Muslims, Burghers, and Christians in his government, but no Tamils, for the first time since independence. He also included two *karāvas* and two *salāgamas*. One of the latter, C. P. de Silva, was the leader of the house, a brilliant administrator, and Bandaranaike's second in command. In August 1959 he was poisoned at a cabinet meeting but survived, one month before Bandaranaike was assassinated. Had he recovered in time, he would have been in line to be the interim prime minister.

9

Triumph of Sinhalese Nationalism

S.W.R.D. Bandaranaike's brief term (1956–1959) was torn by controversy on economic policy and the language issue. Sirimavo Ratwatte Bandaranaike (1960–1965) implemented policies to improve the lives of her Sinhalese constituents, particularly growing numbers of youth who faced fewer opportunities in a rapidly growing population at the same time that Sinhalese nationalist rhetoric was promising them a brighter future as a result of her language policies and a state-controlled economy. In fact, unemployment soared, particularly of educated youth, and state corporations drained revenue from an already weakened economy. Little attention was paid to the similar distress of Tamil youth. Dudley Senanayake (1965–1970) made some attempt to amend the language policy but was unable to overcome Sinhalese opposition. Agriculture improved during his administration, but he left office with the country on the verge of a crisis. Sirimavo Bandaranaike was returned to office in 1970 with radical plans to transform the nation.

MEP GOVERNMENT

When he took office in 1956, as he had promised, S.W.R.D. Bandaranaike made the "Sinhala Only" bill his first priority. The draft bill included provisions for the use of Tamil and English that he had to remove under pressure from Sinhalese extremists. The ITAK reacted with protests and demonstrations. On

June 5, when it was introduced, 200 demonstrators marched on the Galle Face Green near Parliament and a complete *hartal* was held in Tamil-majority areas. Sinhalese mobs then attacked Tamils in Colombo; violence broke out in Trincomalee and Jaffna. The worst violence took place in the Gal Oya colonization scheme, where Sinhalese thugs massacred an estimated 100 to 150 Tamils.

Bandaranaike delayed enforcement of the "Sinhala Only" act and tried to win over moderate Tamil support with promises of fair treatment. The ITAK met at a conference at Trincomalee and announced four demands on August 19, 1956: (1) a Federal constitution; (2) parity of Tamil and Sinhala; (3) citizenship for Tamils of Indian origin; and (4) the end of colonization by Sinhalese in Tamil-majority regions. They gave the government a year to comply, but Bandaranaike faced more persuasive opposition from Sinhalese extremists complaining of the delay in enforcing the act and demanding enactment of more of their agenda.

Bandaranaike and S.J.V. Chelvanayakam met for over a month in 1957 and produced a compromise, the Bandaranaike-Chelvanayakam Pact (BC Pact). Chelvanayakam accepted far less than federalism and the parity of Tamil, and Bandaranaike agreed to give regional councils substantial powers. It was attacked by opportunist politicians on both sides, especially G. G. Ponnambalam and Junius Richard Jayewardene. The BC pact was the best—and possibly the last—opportunity to begin to resolve ethnic issues. The terms were a reasonable compromise, and both men appeared to have enough credibility with their own communities to gain acceptance.

The BC pact would have been only a beginning, however. The two English-educated men did not seem to consider the difficulty of communicating between Sinhala-educated and Tamil-educated populations when everyone would be educated to a high degree in only one of them. They seem to have presumed that English would be the link language indefinitely.

The 22 administrative districts had replaced the nine provinces as the largest administrative units in 1955. In May 1957 the MEP prepared a draft of a Regional Councils bill that would combine districts into regions. It was a vague and weak proposal; the councilors would not be elected but chosen by urban and municipal councilors.

Jayawardene was the main UNP strategist. He was a descendant of Tambi Mudaliyar, whose descendants were never considered the social equal of the first-class *govigamas* despite their wealth and accomplishments, particularly as lawyers. He built up the party strength, and when Dudley Senanayake came out of retirement to contest the 1965 election, Jayewardene served as his deputy until Senanayake died in 1973. In October 1957 he organized a UNP protest march from Colombo to Kandy that was banned after it threatened to become violent. In 1955 Bandaranaike had mobilized Sinhalese-Buddhist nationalists to defeat the UNP when they were dealing with the language issue; now the UNP made vicious attacks on his attempts to do the same. In fact

Bandaranaike seemed to have widespread support for the BC pact among the Sinhalese.

In 1958, racial vandalism by both Tamils and Sinhalese was getting out of the control of the leaders. For example, Tamils defaced the Sinhala character *Sri* on automobile license plates, and Sinhalese painted over Tamil lettering on signboards. Bandaranaike and Chelvanayakam met in April to discuss the BC pact. Faced with protests by militant *bhikkhus* who camped in the street near his house, however, Bandaranaike capitulated and abrogated the pact.

The ITAK responded with a threat of mass civil disobedience. Before this could be organized, violence broke out throughout the country beginning May 22. The violence initially was the rape, beating, arson, and murder directed at Tamils, but Tamils soon retaliated against Sinhalese. By May 26 attacks had become a general race war. Bandaranaike vacillated when reports began to reach him. He made a radio address to calm the people but left the impression that Tamils had started the violence. Finally on May 27, Governor-General Oliver Goonetilleke declared a state of emergency and restored law and order.

Many of the violent acts were the actions of criminal gangs on both sides, which seized the opportunity for destruction and looting. Many of the anti-Tamil attacks were by disadvantaged Sinhalese in the vicinity of the colonization schemes, landless wage-laborers, and illegal squatters. The destruction of the Buddhist pilgrimage site at Nainativu and other attacks near Velvettiturai were apparently the work of gangs working on behalf of the area's smugglers.

After the violence subsided, Bandaranaike pushed the Tamil Language (Special Provisions) Bill through Parliament over the private objections of members of his own party. The Sinhalese-Buddhist nationalists who had worked for his election became increasingly dissatisfied with his government. Some pro-Sinhala and pro-Buddhist policies his cabinet had promised were never implemented, owing to the incompetence of those ministers.

In 1958 disputes between right-wing and left-wing members of the MEP crippled the government, which almost collapsed when Philip Gunawardena, the Minister of Agriculture, left the government with three other leftists. With only 47 votes in a house of 101 members, Bandaranaike prorogued Parliament in May 1959. It met again in June, but the coalition fell apart after Bandaranaike was assassinated in September 1959. In dissatisfaction with Bandaranaike's inability to implement a pro-Buddhist policy and with the leftist tendencies of his party, a *bhikkhu* shot him. W. Dahanayake served as prime minister for two months and Parliament was dissolved in December.

The Bandaranaike government continued to discriminate against Tamils in numerous ways. For example, in 1961, the Government Scholarship in Science at British Universities was given to the Sinhalese student V. K. Samaranayake instead of the Tamil Ganesar Chanmugam. Samaranayake declined the award because he felt Chanmugam deserved it and only took it when Chanmugam insisted. (Both men went on to distinguished careers: Chanmugam as an astrophysicist at Louisiana State University and Samaranayake as Director of the Institute of Computer Technology at the University of Colombo and Chairman of Sri Lanka's Council for Information Technology.) Likewise, Nagalingam Ethirveerasingham of Jaffna won a gold medal in the high jump at the Asian Games in 1958 but was not made captain of the national team until public pressure was put on the government.

SLFP 1960–1965

Dudley Senanayake became prime minister again briefly after the general elections of March 19, 1960, aided by the decision of the LSSP to compete against the SLFP. Despite increasing rice subsidies in order to win popular support, Senanayake faced strong opposition from the left and from Tamils after he did not act on the Tamil language issue. By the end of April 1960, parliamentary democracy seemed to have failed, and many feared a coup d'etat by either the right or the left. It did not happen, and the UNP government called new elections in July.

The SLFP won the July election because it reunited behind Bandaranaike's widow, Sirimavo, and because the left parties agreed not to contest seats where the SLFP could defeat UNP candidates. Mrs. Bandaranaike was a member of the Kandyan aristocracy and had no previous political experience. The regime survived an attempted right-wing coup d'etat by elements within the military in 1962, but the three main leftist parties withdrew their support and formed a United Left Front (ULF) in 1963. In early 1964 the government was forced to back down in a confrontation with a militant left-wing trade union.

The ITAK attempted unsuccessfully to play the two Sinhalese parties against each other. They supported the UNP in March 1960 and the SLFP in July. Both parties looked toward the Tamil political parties for support but were unable to make any concessions to their demands because the party out of power appealed to Sinhalese-Buddhist opposition. Before the March 1965 elections, the ITAK entered into a secret pact with Dudley Senanayake to support him in Parliament in return for Tamil language and other rights. Senanayake was unable to implement the agreement because 15 members of his own government threatened to revolt, and the ITAK withdrew from the coalition.

In March 1964 Mrs. Bandaranaike prorogued Parliament for nearly four months; in June she added the LSSP to the government to head off a trade union challenge. This marked the point at which the traditional left renounced its revolutionary aspirations and was incorporated into the mainstream. The coalition government formed in 1964 was short-lived, however, losing a vote of confidence in Parliament in November 1964 when 14 members of the SLFP defected and voted with the opposition.

On December 31, 1960, a bill was passed making Sinhalese the only official language of the country and took effect the following day. Representatives of the Tamil-speaking minority led mass demonstrations against the measure in early 1961. To cope with the situation, a state of emergency was declared, ITAK was forbidden to operate, and strikes were declared illegal. Sinhalese–Tamil relations continued to be strained until January 1966, when Tamil was made the administrative language in the northern and eastern parts of the island. Sinhala as the only official language meant that government servants were required to know Sinhala or learn it within a stipulated time. The policy was a severe blow to Tamils, for whom the civil service was a main source of employment. In 1956, Tamils held 30 percent of the jobs in the administrative services. By 1975, that number had fallen to 5 percent.

The change in official language policy coincided with radical changes in the educational system that magnified its effect. Free education had resulted in a rapid expansion of the student population in Sinhala and Tamil. Bandaranaike nationalized more than 2500 private schools in 1960 and 1961 without compensation. The nationalization of schools was a particularly serious problem for Jaffna because nearly all the schools were under Hindu or Christian private management, with financial assistance from the government. Instruction in government schools, including the newly nationalized ones, was required to be in the "mother tongue," defined as the language of one's ethnic identity, not the language one spoke at home. Non-Sinhalese students were thus prevented from studying Sinhala, which was the only means to government employment. Even students educated in Sinhala saw little improvement in their prospects for a generation.

Universities admitted the first Sinhala- and Tamil-medium students in 1959. Schools (called *faculties* in Sri Lanka) of medicine, science, and engineering were added in the 1960s. Enrollments grew rapidly, and the number of campuses increased, but competition for admission to the scarce positions was intense. Vidyalankara and Vidyodaya *pirivenas* were reconstituted as universities, and the Higher Education Act No. 20 of 1966 placed them under a common administrative structure. A National Education Commission in 1961 recommended religious quotas to university admissions and public service to compensate for presumed Buddhist disadvantages.

Sinhala-educated Buddhists were led to believe that these changes in language policy and education would create a new elite that would displace the Anglicized, predominantly Christian elite. Employers tended to prefer English-speaking employees and many senior government officials continued to administer their departments in English. In some cases the discrimination against those educated in Sinhala increased. People who learned English later in life spoke with a telltale accent, and this reduced their chances for employment. The language issue exacerbated the unemployment problem caused by a growing population and lagging economy; growing numbers of youth, well-educated in Sinhala or Tamil, had no visible future prospects.

Ethnic tensions increased when it became clear that a decade of "Sinhala only" did not provide the results expected by Sinhala-educated youth. Tamil-educated youth faced even greater problems, although Tamils were much more willing to learn Sinhala than vice versa. With no hope of displacing the English-educated elite, Sinhalese nationalists increasingly blamed Tamils for their distress. Both Tamil and Sinhalese youth began to look to radical solutions to their plight.

Both the military and the police, which had attracted minorities during the colonial eras, became predominantly Buddhist through implementation of the Sinhala language act. Army officers who were Sinhalese Christians took retirement under the language act, even though they were fluent in Sinhala, because they thought their careers had no future. The police had been about three-fourths Christian. In 1962 police and military officers staged a coup attempt against Mrs. Bandaranaike; they were apparently motivated by opposition to communal policies, led not by Tamils but by Sinhalese Christian officers.

UNP 1965–1970

The UNP won the March 1965 election with a wide range of support from Sinhalese-Buddhist nationalists to Tamil parties, most of them united only in opposition to the SLFP's turn to the left. The UNP called this a "national government" but seldom was able to rise above the Sinhalese-Buddhist agenda. In February 1966 the army staged another abortive attempt at a coup, led this time by Buddhist appointees of the SLFP who appear to have feared a return to secular armed forces. The UNP attempted unsuccessfully to deal with ethnic problems and made little headway against the nation's economic problems.

In the Senanayake-Chelvanayakam Pact of March 24, 1965, Senanayake agreed to implement the Tamil Language Special Provisions Act No 28 of 1958. This was the act adopted by Bandaranaike to enable Tamil to be the language of administration and records in the North and Eastern Provinces, to allow for legal proceedings there to be conducted in Tamil, and to establish effective district councils. Senanayake also promised to amend the Land Development Ordinance to give preference in new colonization schemes to landless villagers in the Northern and Eastern Provinces. The Tamil Language Regulations passed by a vote of 72 to 40. It faced public opposition both from Sinhalese-Buddhist militants, who opposed any modification of Sinhala-only, and from Tamils, because it made no provision for the use of the language outside the north and east.

Senanayake found it necessary to placate his Sinhalese Buddhist supporters. He denied the remaining privately managed Catholic schools the right to charge tuition fees, and he introduced a calendar substituting Buddhist Poya Days (the phases of the moon) for Sundays. The latter interfered with the country's external relations and was discontinued by the United Front (UF) government after 1970. He also allowed the government to publish a selection of Anagārika Dharmapāla's inflammatory speeches and writings under the title *Return to Righteousness*.

The Buddhist *sangha* became an indispensable political force for the Sinhalese parties. They were able to resist attempts to use the power of the state to reform the *sangha*. As did the MEP before them, the UNP faced opposition from militant Buddhists, who demonstrated against Tamil language provisions. On one occasion, the police shot and killed a demonstrating *bhikkhu*.

Both the UNP and SLFP increasingly used Buddhist symbolism at public functions and promoted Buddhist activities. Ancient sites, especially Anurādhapura, were restored as Buddhist shrines rather than archeological sites. At Sīgiriya, for example, the Department of Archaeology restored (with UNESCO assistance) a later Buddhist monastery at the rock fortress, one of the island's greatest historical sites, rather than restoring the ancient palace complex or even excavating the rest of the site. In the 1960s and 1970s statues of the Buddha were erected at many intersections in Colombo—requiring passengers to leap to their feet and bow their heads while the cars careened around turns.

TAMIL RESISTANCE

The ITAK was the dominant Tamil party after 1956, but its ineffectiveness divided the Tamil leadership. A 1961 civil disobedience campaign had widespread support among Tamils, but the ITAK led no mass movements after then. Attempts to stage a direct action campaign in late 1964 came to nothing. Chelvanayakam and M. Tiruchelvam continued to believe that the only option for the Tamils was to work within the Sinhalese-dominated government to redress their grievances.

More militant voices among Tamils began to be heard. Former CCS officer Chellappah Suntharalingam, who had been a minister in the first UNP government, began talking about a separate state and later published a map in the 1970s of what he called "Eylom." Member of Parliament V. Navaratnam also resigned from the ITAK. Some Tamil activists contemplated the possibility of taking control of a "Tamil Homeland" by force when they met secretly to create the *pulippadai*, or "Tiger Army" in 1961. Some of the participants later joined militant organizations, but their meeting led to nothing at this time. The ITAK undermined militant resistance to discrimination against Tamils when it joined the UNP government in 1965 and Tiruchelvam was appointed Minister of Local Government.

A draft District Councils Bill was prepared in 1968. Tamils objected to the lack of elected councilors and to the inability of the councils to select settlers for colonization schemes. The Bill was opposed by the SLFP, LSSP, and CP.

THE ECONOMY

The economic policies of the MEP were based more on the need to keep the support of Sinhala-educated local elites than on ideology. Government made concessions to local entrepreneurs by restricting imports, providing loans from banks, and granting tax holidays. The policies led to the production of some light consumer goods—candy, cookies, matches, and so on, usually of low quality—but no industrial breakthrough. In this area the UNP and SLFP policies differed little.

S.W.R.D. Bandaranaike had promised to nationalize all essential industries. The port of Colombo and bus services were nationalized in 1958. Mrs. Bandaranaike went much further, nationalizing the largest commercial bank (the Bank of Ceylon), insurance companies, and the import and sale of petroleum products. The import and distribution of essential commodities was placed under the Co-Operative Wholesale Establishment(CWE). State Corporations were a massive drain on the revenue; poor planning and mismanagement made them inefficient. The Sugar Corporation produced sugar of such low quality that much of it was used only to produce low-quality alcoholic beverages. Most observers believe that S.W.R.D. Bandaranaike would have shown more restraint had he lived.

As the trade deficit grew ever larger, the Central Bank imposed controls to reduce imports, beginning with nonessential goods such as automobiles, alcoholic beverages, and luxury goods in August 1960. Soon higher import duties were extended to other imports as well.

The UNP invested in agriculture, both in irrigation and colonization, which ran at a loss, and in capital inputs, such as high-yielding varieties of rice, fertilizer, and pesticides, which contributed to a substantial increase in rice production. Tamil cultivators complained that there was no corresponding investment in the vegetable crops that were the mainstay of the Jaffna economy. The UNP also introduced plans for the diversion of the Mahaweli Ganga to provide both irrigation water and hydroelectric power.

Nationalization also contributed to ethnic tensions, as a disproportionate share of the industries nationalized were those in which Tamils predominated, such as the import of consumer goods. When the port of Trincomalee was nationalized in 1967, for example, it displaced many shipping companies owned by Tamils with Tamil employees and placed the harbor under mainly Sinhalese management.

Mrs. Bandaranaike implemented policies that appeared to shut Tamils out of careers in public service and the professions at a time of massive unemployment. These policies resulted in discriminatory university admissions policies and favoritism, nepotism, and corruption in government appointments. They were enforced on the rationale that the Tamils were overrepresented in higher education and government employment due to a British colonial policy of "divide and rule." The combination of extraordinary patronage powers for the government in power and the expansion of the role of the government in the economy made this a very potent policy.

COLONIZATION OF THE DRY ZONE

The settlement of landless Sinhalese villagers in the Dry Zone has been a focus of ethnic conflict because the Sinhalese and Tamil politicians perceive the policy in directly opposite ways. To Buddhist leaders it is a means both of revitalizing the lands of the ancient Buddhist kingdom (destroyed, many believe, by Tamil invaders) and of alleviating land hunger in the Wet Zone of the island (created, Sinhalese politicians claim, by British colonial divide and rule policies that favored the Tamils). To the Tamils it is confiscation of their traditional homeland provided at an enormous cost to public revenues. The room for negotiation between these two points of view is minuscule. It is restricted further by encroachments of Sinhalese villagers, facilitated by Buddhist monks and military forces, and by encroachments of plantation Tamils facilitated by Tamil separatists, but in this case resisted by military forces.

By the late 1960s the government had alienated 304,355 acres of land to 67,122 allottees in colonization projects. It contributed to a substantial increase in paddy production, but at a high economic and social cost: The financial return was low, so that it was done at the expense of public investments that would have had benefited more people; the living conditions of the colonists remained low because the allotments were too small for growing families; it did not significantly alleviate population pressure in the Wet Zone; and it added to ethnic conflict because the colonists were predominantly Sinhalese even when the existing population was Tamil-speaking or mixed.

Colonization schemes did not integrate the Tamil-majority and Sinhalese-majority areas but further divided them. The population of Tamankaduwa (now renamed Polonnaruwa), is a prime example. Up to 1911 it consisted primarily of traditional *(purana)* villages, of which 22 Sinhalese-speaking and 36 Tamil-speaking. It had a population of only 20,900 in 1946, of whom 55.9 percent were Sinhalese, most of them colonists. By 1981 the district had a population of 263,000, of whom 90 percent were Sinhalese and almost entirely Buddhist.

The Tamil population of Trincomalee District was 81.8 percent of the total in 1827, but by the census of 1963, the percentage of Tamils had dropped to 39.1 percent, whereas the earlier Sinhalese population had risen from 1.3 percent to 29.6 percent. In Trincomalee District, the Sinhalese population increased from 20.7 percent in 1946 to 33.6 percent in 1981.

Tamil politicians had protested even before independence that these colonies confiscated their "traditional homeland" at an enormous cost in public revenues and transferred them to Sinhalese cultivators. They objected to discrimination in settlements in Gal Oya, Allai, and Kantalai projects in the Eastern Province and repeatedly pointed out how such preference to settlers from other provinces violated the Land Settlement Ordinance of 1935. The Federal Party made colonization a political issue for Tamils from the time of its founding in 1949. This grew into a myth of a "Tamil Homeland" (*pārampariyamāna tāyakam;* literally, hereditary motherland) in the Northern and Eastern Provinces. This process of state-aided colonization was seen as a threat not only to the political status of Tamils in the affected areas, but also to existence of the Tamils as a community with its own linguistic and cultural identity.

FOREIGN POLICY

Sri Lanka adopted a policy of nonalignment (following India) in the Cold War, with the tendency to lean against former colonial powers (e.g., in 1956 it opposed Britain and France when Egypt nationalized the Suez Canal, but it looked the other way when the Soviet Union crushed the Hungarian Revolution). This outraged U.S. Secretary of State John Foster Dulles, whose family had sent missionaries to Jaffna, but the United States nevertheless agreed in early 1958 to provide the country with technical assistance and a grant of about $780,000 for economic projects. Sri Lanka played an important role in the Non-Aligned Movement (NAM), particularly during Mrs. Bandaranaike's administration.

Britain withdrew from its bases in Sri Lanka in 1957 as the government took over the Trincomalee naval base and the Katunayake airport. In 1958 the Soviet Union and Sri Lanka signed trade and economic agreements, increasing the USSR's presence in the country. Shortly afterward the country accepted a loan of about $10.5 million from China.

During the SLFP administration in 1962, the government nationalized the assets of American oil companies, but it failed to take adequate steps to pay compensation. Subsequently, U.S. president John F. Kennedy applied the Hickenlooper Amendment to suspend aid to Sri Lanka. American technicians who had been working to improve the Katunayake airport, for example, were recalled. But when Dudley Senanayake's government was installed, a settlement was worked out with the U.S. companies, handled by J. R. Jayewardene. Eventually, the government paid them Rs 55 million, which was then worth about US $5.5 million.

THE STATELESS

About 171,000 Indian expatriates from Sri Lanka were given Indian citizenship before 1964. India considered the bulk of the people of Indian origin in Sri Lanka to be Lankans, as most of them were born there and had no homes in India. Indian Prime Minister Jawaharlal Nehru refused to agree to a negotiated settlement to the problem of nearly a million people who had become 'stateless.' After Nehru's death, Sirimavo Bandaranaike negotiated an agreement with his successor Lal Bahadur Sastri. Under this agreement, Sri Lanka agreed to give citizenship to 300,000 of the estimated 975,000 people of recent Indian origin in Sri Lanka, and 525,000 would become Indian citizens, over a period of 15 years. The two nations later agreed to give citizenship to an equal share of the remaining 150,000.

In early 1968, the UNP passed the Indo-Ceylon Implementation Bill. It made concessions to the CWC and the ITAK, which supported the government by, promising that there would be no compulsory repatriation (and if it did occur, any such person would have a legal right to appeal) and that registered citizens would be placed in a separate register. The government also agreed to grant Lankan citizenship without waiting until those to whom Indian citizenship had been granted left for India. (Originally, the grant of Lankan citizenship was contingent on this.)

The government finally called for applications until May 1, 1968. By early 1970, more than 450,000 people had been repatriated to India under the agreement, in addition to about 50,000 Indians who left to avoid a residence tax. There remained more than 630,000 in Sri Lanka. Of these, the government had agreed to give citizenship to 375,000 but was only slowly doing so.

1970 ELECTION

The election of May 1970 resulted in a sweeping victory for the SLFP. In an uneasy UF coalition with the LSSP and CP, it won 120 of 157 seats, and Sirimavo Bandaranaike became prime minister again. The UNP had actually received more votes than the SLFP (37.9 percent to 36.6 percent). The SLFP regarded the victory as a positive endorsement of its ideology rather than a backlash against the incumbents. The new government began to move the country toward socialism, although the Marxist parties had little influence on policy. The sweeping victory of the UF in 1970 surprised the elite, who misjudged the distress among young people. The UNP was left with only 7 seats, with Jayewardene as the party leader.

1971 INSURGENCY

The future was bleak in the 1970s for most young Lankans: Poverty was growing in rural society and the opportunities for advancement were few. Rapid population growth had produced a huge cohort of Lankans for whom the economy did not provide a place, particularly for those who were well educated in Sinhala or Tamil. Political and economic power remained in the hands of the Anglicized elite and their children, who continued to learn

English at home. Higher education was an escape for some, but unemployed university graduates became a growing problem. Even when Sinhala- or Tamil-educated youths learned English, their accents gave them away and they could be dismissed as a country bumpkin *(goḍayā)*.

Lower middle-class Sinhalese youth, particularly the educated segments of large, disadvantaged castes such as the *vahumpura* and *batgam,* turned to a radical organization, the Janata Vimukti Peramuna (JVP, People's Liberation Front), which promised a radical socialist revolution and a Sinhalese-dominated society and provided a highly disciplined organization to achieve both. It was founded in May 1965 in response to the rejection of revolution by the leftist parties. Rohana Wijeweera led the JVP. He had attended Lumumba University in Moscow before being expelled. He became disillusioned successively with both Russian and Chinese communism and lived for some time in North Korea. The JVP program was summarized in their "Five Lectures," which were anti-imperialist and anti-capitalist, and promised the transition to socialism in a state highly regulated on behalf of the ordinary Sinhalese people. They opposed both the Anglicized elite and Tamils, who they said were the wealthy landowners and businesspeople who exploited the people.

The JVP was prepared to rise up against the UNP, which it thought was planning to remain in power in 1970 with U.S. intervention. They initially supported the UF government, but it disappointed the radical youth with its slow progress toward their socialist agenda. Instead, the government increased the police force by 55 percent in the summer of 1970 and on March 16, 1971 arrested Wijeweera and declared a State of Emergency. Nevertheless, the JVP decided to overthrow the government on April 2, 1971 and three days later attached 93 police stations and reportedly planned to kidnap or assassinate Prime Minister Bandaranaike. They only captured five police stations, and they failed to free Wijeweera or to seize military bases. They anticipated that the young Sinhalese Buddhists in the security forces would rise up with them, but this did not happen. It was brutally suppressed; more than 16,000 suspects were incarcerated, and estimates of the death toll range from 1,200 (official) to more than 10,000 (JVP). Many of the leaders and followers were sentenced to jail; Wijeweera was sentenced to 20 years in prison but released by the UNP in 1977. A study of the people incarcerated suggests that the strongest support for the insurgency came from unemployed or underemployed Sinhalese Buddhist men in their teens or early twenties who had attended a Maha Vidyalaya.

The insurgency of 1971 failed, but it had lasting consequences. The government passed a series of reforms that made the government more centralized and more authoritarian. The State of Emergency remained in effect for six years. The government expanded the role of the military as defender of the government against internal threats. The armed forces increased from about 10,000 in 1971 to 18,000 in 1973. Military aid from India, the Soviet Union,

United States, Pakistan, and others equipped them better. The government remained suspicious of the potential of the military to overthrow the elected government, however, and troops received little training except in internal security and counterrevolutionary tactics.

Ideologically driven changes were made in the curriculum and examination system at the elementary and secondary level to deal with the problem of educated unemployment. The emphasis was to be on practical education instead the liberal arts. English language was made compulsory from grade six onward, and subjects such as cultural studies and socialism were introduced. The purpose was to reduce the gap between the privileged and the poor and between urban and rural. Subjects in which rural students were at a disadvantage, such as science education, were deemphasized in the national examinations.

Universities were brought under central control. Sri Lanka had a high rate of literacy but one of the lowest percentages of university students in Asia. After the 1971 insurrection, the percentage of youths with higher education was lowered further by the Higher Education Act of January 1972, which reduced the teaching of the humanities in universities. The gap between the number of qualified applicants and admissions continued to increase; by the mid-1970s only about 20 percent of qualified students were admitted. A disproportionate number of Tamil students had been admitted to the university previously, and to increase the proportion of Sinhalese students, communal quotas for university entrance were created by "standardizing" test scores.

Standardizing scores of university entrance exams was a disaster for many Tamil youth. Tamils for generations had taken advantage of education as a means to a livelihood. Standardization meant that very few qualified Tamils could attend the university. On top of the frustrations faced by all Lankan youth, this drove young Tamils to the conclusion that their aspirations for the future could only be fulfilled within a separate Tamil state.

10

Authoritarianism and Ethnic Conflict

In 1970 Sri Lanka had not settled its ethnic problems, and time was running out for a solution. Economic crises and social unrest continued to plague the nation, and a new generation of youth was impatient with the failure of the ruling elite to create a prosperous society. Sinhalese youth first expressed their hostility in an insurgency in March and April 1971. Tamil youth began to see the creation of Eelam, a Tamil state on the island, as their best hope for success. Although ideologically poles apart, Sirimavo Bandaranaike and J. R. Jayewardene both fell back on appeals to the Sinhalese-Buddhist nationalists to cover their economic and political failures, and both became increasingly authoritarian despite maintaining democratic forms. Both created new constitutions, in 1972 and 1978, respectively, to reflect changes in the society. Nevertheless, the Sinhalese-Buddhist majority as a whole became increasingly frustrated with the inability of their increased political power to change the society. The elections of May 1970 and July 1977 resulted in sweeping victories for the SLFP and UNP, respectively. In both elections, the victors regarded their victory as an ideological triumph rather than a backlash against the incumbents.

1972 CONSTITUTION

The 1972 Constitution fulfilled a longstanding desire to replace the colonially imposed Soulbury Constitution with an autochthonous constitution. The

UF had promised in its election campaign a new constitution that would protect Buddhism and transform Sri Lanka into a socialist state. Bandaranaike convened the lower house of Parliament as a Constituent Assembly to draft it in July 1970. The new constitution went into effect on May 22, 1972. It renamed the nation "Republic of Sri Lanka (Ceylon)" and retained the structure of a parliamentary democracy, although a unicameral National State Assembly (NSA) replaced Parliament. (The Senate had been abolished in 1971.) The major changes were an increase in the authority of the government to act without constitutional restraints, the introduction of socialist principles, and a constitutional foundation to the pre-eminent position of Sinhala and Buddhism.

The constitution abolished the Public Service Commission and the Judicial Service Commission, which had limited politicians' patronage powers. It strengthened the legislature by making all laws passed by the NSA valid until repealed by the Assembly and not subject to judicial review. Both the civil service and the judiciary came under political control. The constitution had a chapter on fundamental rights and freedoms, but it nullified this by removing the protection of civil and human rights that existed under the Soulbury Constitution. It has been suggested that the JVP insurrection, which broke out as it was being drafted, influenced the authoritarian nature of the constitution.

Marxist members of the coalition insisted that their socialist agenda be included in the "Principles of State Policy." The preamble committed the state to guaranteeing full employment, redistributing wealth to all citizens, and developing state and collective forms of property. The absence of any protection of private property raised fears among property owners. The constitution clearly was aimed at moving the nation further in a socialist direction, although the specifics were not. The Marxist parties themselves differed over policies, and Bandaranaike's rhetoric showed an infatuation with Post–Cultural Revolution China.

Chapter II of the constitution states, "The Republic of Sri Lanka shall give to Buddhism the foremost place and accordingly it shall be the duty of the state to protect and foster Buddhism." It also made Sinhala the official language without allowing the use of Tamil as a constitutional right. These implemented promises to Sinhalese-Buddhist nationalists that the SLFP had made since 1956 but raised opposition from the Tamils and secular Lankans. ITAK members of Parliament had withdrawn from the Constituent Assembly in protest in June 1971, and many Tamils began to turn to more radical political solutions.

UF GOVERNMENT

The UF government began by promising to create a socialist society and ended by implementing reforms to encourage foreign private investment. The economy (described further in Chapter 11) deteriorated steadily. The government blamed this on the deteriorating terms of trade, but the rising prices of imports only changed a impending disaster into an immediate one. To deal with dissent, the government turned increasingly authoritarian.

An International Monetary Fund mission in 1972 pointed out that it would be impossible to sustain the continued growth of social services without a substantial increase in export earnings, but political pressure prevented a satisfactory response. A five-year plan for 1972–1976 was designed to develop the economy, which proposed increased investment from restrictions on consumption and higher saving, but no reduction in welfare expenditures. It also projected unrealistic returns from the state corporations.

New state corporations were established to handle several economic activities, particularly the import-export trade. The CWE was assigned a greater role in handling internal trade. The Ceylon Shipping Corporation was established as the national shipping line in retaliation against private companies for raising their rates without consulting the government. The Business Acquisition Act, passed in 1971, enabled the government to take over any private sector business by notification. Restrictions were imposed on Agency houses, through which foreign companies managed the plantation sector.

The most radical economic change was the nationalization of the land through two land reforms under which the government acquired more than a million acres of privately held land. These reforms, described in the chapter 11, led to the demise of the UF coalition. The LSSP wanted to take a larger part in the legislation and implementation of the nationalization of plantations. They expected that it would be placed under the Minister for Plantation Industries, a LSSP party member, but Mrs. Bandaranaike instead delegated it to the SLFP Minister of Agriculture and Lands. The Marxist parties wanted further nationalization, which many SLFP leaders opposed.

When the press criticized the government, it put restrictions on the press. It took over the Lake House newspapers, which had been outspoken critics of the government in 1973. The newspaper group became a public company in which the previous owners were allowed to own no more than 25 percent of the shares. It created a Press Council with the powers of a court to prosecute newspapers. The media were prohibited from publishing whatever the government considered "official secrets." In 1975 it closed five newspapers in the Dawasa group on the grounds that they were closely associated with the UNP's protests against the government.

Food shortages in 1973 led to drastic measures to promote cultivation. Government ministers exhorted the rural population to grow more food crops, especially paddy and substitutes for it such as manioc and sweet potatoes. The Emergency (Cultivation of Food Crops) Regulation No. 2 of 1973 empowered officials to appropriate cultivable land.

Mrs. Bandaranaike took an active part in foreign affairs, particularly in connection with the NAM. The UF government shifted its foreign policy to the left in May 1970, recognizing East Germany, South Vietnam's Revolutionary Government, North Vietnam, North Korea, and the Sihanouk Government-in-exile. This was called "radical neutralism." A related topic was the idea of making the Indian Ocean a "zone of peace." Sirimavo Bandaranaike presented this idea at summit meetings of the NAM and at the United Nations in 1971. The proposal was in part a criticism of the United States, which had established a naval base on the island of Diego Garcia. Mrs. Bandaranaike visited China in June 1972 and received an enthusiastic reception. China granted project and financial aid, including interest-free loans that helped alleviate the country's foreign exchange problems. Better relations with India resulted in the settlement of a disputed claim to the uninhabited island Kachchaitivu in Sri Lanka's favor. At the end of her term, when Colombo hosted the fifth NAM Summit in August 1976, Mrs. Bandaranaike had retreated from her party's radical stance and worked to move the organization toward the center again.

At the end of 1976 there was a serious confrontation with government departments that went on strike in support of striking railway workers. The government refused to negotiate while the strikes were on and used the armed forces to prevent demonstrations under emergency regulations. The government ended the strike, but not until making concessions to the railway workers. The SLFP, no less than the UNP, considered the peasantry rather than the urban working class as their primary constituency and believed that the workers were politically motivated and unsympathetic to the difficulties of the peasants.

Economic and social policy also shifted to the right. Marxism in Sri Lanka suffered a blow when Dr. S. A. Wickremasinghe was expelled from the UF Coalition in September 1973. He was the loser in a factional dispute in the CP with Pieter Keuneman, the Minister of Housing and Construction. The Marxists in the government continued to press for the further nationalization of the economy. The final split with the LSSP came about when Mrs. Bandaranaike took offense at what she believed to be unfair criticism of her late husband and herself in a speech by Minister of Finance N. M. Perera in 1975. Their confrontation exposed other differences between the two, and the prime minister removed Perera and other LSSP ministers, who then crossed over to the opposition. The expulsion of the LSSP increased the authority of her son Anura Bandaranaike and the new Minister of Finance, Felix R. Dias Bandaranaike.

TAMIL SEPARATISM

Unlike 1960 and 1965, the ITAK had no role in the government after 1970. Its manifesto for the 1970 election opposed separatism. The ITAK had asked for parity for Sinhala and Tamil, citizenship rights for stateless Plantation Tamils, a secular state, a guarantee of fundamental rights for all citizens, the abolition of caste and untouchability, and decentralization of the government. These were rejected, and the ITAK withdrew from the Constituent Assembly. Under pressure from extremist youth, however, mainstream Tamil politicians became radicalized in the 1970s. Politicians like S.J.V. Chelvanayakam and A. Amirthalingam began using separatist rhetoric in their speeches and met with Indian leaders to lobby for support. After the promulgation of the 1972 constitution, the Tamil parties came together in a coalition to form the Tamil United Front (TUF).

The Constituent Assembly paid little attention to the wishes of the Tamil United Front MPs, which boycotted the Assembly temporarily in protest. The name *Sri Lanka* itself exacerbated ethnic conflict: *Lanka* would have been acceptable in either language, but *Sri* is uniquely Sinhala and had already contributed to Tamil protests for its use on automobile license plates.

Government policies in the 1970s created recruits to the many—estimated up to 40—revolutionary Tamil groups founded in the late 1960s and early 1970s. Bandaranaike, for her part, in 1970 and 1971 began taking increasingly repressive measures against Tamils such as refusing to allow them to using foreign exchange to study in India and banning the import of south Indian Tamil films, books, and magazines from Tamil Nadu. The first terrorist act by Tamil militant youths was a bomb placed in the car of Somaweera Chandrasiri, a Junior Minister who was visiting Jaffna in August 1971. He was not in the car when it exploded. On June 4, 1972, militants shot and wounded a strong supporter of the SLFP and killed his driver.

Vellupillai Prabakaran (b. 1954) emerged as the leader of the militant youth. He quit school at age 16 to become a full-time revolutionary in the Tamil Students' Federation, which he founded with seven others. Prabakaran attacked a carnival on September 17, 1972, with bombs, intending to kill Alfred Duraiappah, an SLFP politician and the mayor of Jaffna; he later killed Duraiappah in July 1975. On March 5, 1976 he led a bank robbery, using crude homemade guns and bombs. He eventually claimed responsibility for 11 high profile murders. The LTTE was not a leading group because its members were considered to be politically inept. Other, more powerful groups included the Tamil Liberation Organization (TLO) started in 1969 by Nadaraja Thangavelu (Thangadurai) and Selvaraja Yogachandran (Kuttimani). Kuttimani, like Prabakaran, was from Velvettiturai, a haven for smugglers from the *karaiyar* caste. On May 5, 1976, Prabakaran's Tamil New Tigers (TNT) changed its name to the Liberation Tigers of Tamil Eelam (LTTE).

The death of nine Tamils in Jaffna on January 10, 1974, was a turning point for many Tamils. The Fourth International World Tamil Conference was held from January 3 to January 9, despite opposition from the Bandaranaike government. The following day a meeting was held to present awards to participants. It was held outdoors to accommodate the overflow crowd of about 10,000 people. The police informed the organizers that the meeting exceeded the terms of their permit, but the organizers believed they had permission. Suddenly, about 40 police attacked the crowd of about 50,000. Seven people were electrocuted by downed power lines, and 50 people were injured. Bandaranaike neither condemned the brutality nor expressed any regret at the violence; the police were not punished but rewarded with promotions.

The revolutionary youth were tolerated by the Anglicized Tamil elite (who called them "the boys") in defiance of the security force abuses against Tamils. As the number of terrorist incidents increased, it created a dilemma for Tamil politicians. The TUF was unwilling to condemn the militants as long as discrimination against Tamils was increasing, but they wanted to work within constitutional means. In 1975 the TUF began to demand autonomy for the Tamil-majority provinces, and on May 14, 1976, Tamil leaders met at Vaddukoddai *(Vaṭṭukottai)*, resolved that the creation of a "free, sovereign secular socialist State of Tamil Eelam . . . has become inevitable in order to safeguard the very existence of the Tamil nation in this country," and renamed their party the Tamil United Liberation Front (TULF). Some Tamil politicians opposed the resolution and remained in the Sinhalese parties or left to restore the Tamil Congress after the 1977 elections and the CWC did not endorse the resolution.

The Vaddukoddai Resolution put the TULF in a dangerous position. It fell short of endorsing revolutionary violence, but it called upon the youth to "throw themselves fully into the sacred fight for freedom." It contains the same sort of dubious historical claims, exaggerations, and logical inconsistencies that were used to argue that the Sinhalese-Buddhist nation encompassed the entire island. Eelam, for example, was both a territorial unit (the arbitrary borders of the Northern and Eastern Provinces) and a cultural one—all people identified as Lankan Tamils in the island and beyond. The Tamils received the resolution with great enthusiasm, but it made solution to the crisis more remote.

1977 ELECTION

The UNP struggled to regroup after the 1970 debacle. Ranasinghe Premadasa, the MP for Colombo Central, created a Colombo Citizens Front to challenge Dudley Senanayake. Premadasa was a member of the *hinnāva* caste, considered extremely low by the *govigama,* but he was indispensable to the party because of his charismatic appeal to Sinhalese voters and his ruthless but effective party leadership. In March 1973 the Citizens Front proposed reorganization of the party in order to strengthen branch organizations. Senanayake died suddenly in April 1973; huge crowds attended his funeral, which was interpreted as a protest against the government. J. R. Jayawardene then organized a series of campaigns. He protested the takeover of the Lake House newspapers, the handling of food shortages, and the two-year extension of the government's term. He accused a group within the SLFP called the Janavegaya ("People's Force") of planning a left-wing coup. The group allegedly included the prime minister's daughters, Chandrika and Sunethra, and Sunethra's husband, Kumar Rupasinghe. These campaigns helped Jayewardene to inherit the party leadership rather than Premadasa.

The 1977 election had been postponed two years to allow Mrs. Bandaranaike to rule for a full term under the new constitution. As leader of the opposition, J. R. Jayewardene protested by resigning (he had won the bye-election), but the delay helped him in several ways. He had time to consolidate his position within the UNP after the death of Dudley Senanayake, the economy continued to deteriorate, and during that time, the SLFP split apart on factional lines. Bandaranaike prorogued Parliament on February 10, 1977, and dissolved it on May 18, 1977.

The UNP increased its share of the vote from 37.9 to 50.9 percent and won 140 of 168 seats. J. R. Jayewardene took over the government, which remained in his control until 1989. Riots followed the election. They were triggered by fighting between police and civilians in Jaffna; Sinhalese in the south then looted and burned Tamil homes for two weeks. The official death toll was 112, with 25,000 Tamils left homeless, although unofficial estimates are much higher. Observers generally assume the 1977 riots were instigated by members of the SLFP to embarrass the UNP and to force Jayewardene to declare a state of emergency, since he had made the frequent emergencies under Mrs. Bandaranaike a campaign issue. President Jayewardene ordered troops to shoot curfew violators on sight, toured victims' homes, and publicly offered them his full protection.

By 1977, Sri Lanka had disappointed many people, who had seen it as the most hopeful of the new nations. Its economy had fallen behind many Asian nations, it had been unable to integrate its diverse population, and the state had turned more autocratic as conditions worsened. The 1977 election seemed to show that democracy had prevailed. The doctrinaire left was rejected decisively; Tamil voters overwhelmingly chose the parliamentary Tamil leadership over the militant separatists; and the conservative UNP was back in power. A sweeping victory by the UNP at local government elections in May 1979 confirmed its mandate. Tragically, President Jayewardene, in his inability to deal with the crises, turned more authoritarian and set the nation on course to a civil war.

Jayewardene was 70 years old when he was elected, and many younger politicians competed to be his successor, not knowing that he would outlive most of them. There is an undercurrent in Sinhalese Buddhist nationalism of resistance to the domination of the wealthy *govigama* elite. Jayewardene used this by appealing to non-*govigama* support to a greater extent than the SLFP. He made Premadasa Leader of the House and Minister of Local Government, Housing and Construction When Jayewardene became president by Constitutional amendment on February 4, 1978, Premadasa became prime minister. Likewise, Cyril Mathew, Minister of Industries, had a strong base in the large *vahumpura* caste. Mathew and other *vahumpura* caste leaders claimed higher status than the *govigama* accorded them because no member of the caste had converted to Christianity. Jayewardene had to tolerate Mathew's violent anti-Tamil actions in 1981 and 1983, until he was finally dismissed in 1986 to maintain support from the *vahumpura* caste.

UNP leaders did not consider Premadasa and Mathew eligible to succeed Jayewardene. The leading contenders were Upali Wijewardene, Lalith Athulathmudali, and Gamini Dissanayake. Wijewardene was a first cousin of Jayewardene and a wealthy entrepreneur. He wanted a seat in Parliament, but Jayewardene refused to allow this because he did not compete in the 1977 elections. Instead, Wijewardene began in 1980 to publish newspapers that were critical of the government, particularly Premadasa. He became Director-General of the Free Trade Zone (FTZ) and was in 1982 considered a likely successor to Jayewardene. That year his private jet mysteriously disappeared after taking off from Kuala Lumpur in Malaysia. Rumors circulated, linking Premadasa with his death, but no evidence has been made public.

Athulathmudali was the son of a member of the first State Council and a brilliant lawyer, who had been the first Lankan president of the Oxford Union and earned a master's degree from Harvard Law School. He had been a lecturer in the faculty of law of the University of Singapore and began practicing law in Sri Lanka in 1964. He was elected to Parliament in 1977 and held several portfolios, most importantly Minister of National Security. Dissanayake was the only new UNP Member of Parliament in 1970, from Nuwara Eliya, where he had broad support from Tamil as well as Sinhalese voters. In 1978 he was appointed Minister of Lands, Land Development and Mahaweli Development and directed the Accelerated Mahaweli Program (AMP). Both men used their important ministries to further their political ambitions.

Jayewardene manipulated the personal ambitions of these men to maintain his control within the party. He was 20 years older than Premadasa, who was 16 years older than Dissanayake and 10 years older than Athulathmudali. Some *govigama* politicians opposed the appointment of Premadasa as deputy leader of the government rather than Athulathmudali or Dissanayake because it made him Jayewardene's presumptive successor.

The foreign policy of the UNP was driven by its economic policies. Jayewardene was openly pro-West, courting private investment as well as development aid. Jayewardene ridiculed Bandaranaike for her anti-West, anti-imperialist rhetoric. Ironically, he inherited the chairmanship of the NAM and was responsible for planning the Havana Summit in the fall of 1979. Sri Lanka took an active part in the debate on Cambodia. Sri Lanka supported the decision to allow the deposed Pol Pot delegation to participate in the conference and supported it in the debate at the United Nations headquarters in September 1979. Most overseas visits by Jayawardene and Prime Minister Premadasa were directed toward obtaining economic aid and private investment.

1978 CONSTITUTION

The UNP opposed the 1972 Constitution as a threat to democratic institutions and produced another version after its own landslide victory in 1977. It created a directly elected president as head of state and established proportional representation, which was intended to balance the representation of the two major parties in Parliament. It also created a list of "fundamental rights" similar to the U.S. Bill of Rights, although these rights were qualified and restricted by legislation. Using the power of its huge majority in parliament, the UNP amended the constitution six times by 1983, mainly to extend its own life to 1989 without a parliamentary election and to counter Tamil separatism.

Jayewardene had made it clear from 1966 on that he believed that the solution for Sri Lanka was a Gaullist-type executive president in combination with a parliament; the 1972 constitution, he thought, gave parliament too much power. The executive president was far more powerful than the prime ministers had been. For example, Parliament could not question his or her conduct; the prime minister and all ministers would be appointed by the president and could be dismissed or reassigned, or the number of ministers changed without consultation and the president could even govern without a cabinet. Jayewardene used his power to implement new economic policies, described in Chapter 11. His aim was to dismantle the welfare provisions that had expanded steadily since independence and to replace them with economic reforms that would stimulate growth.

Proportional representation has prevented a recurrence of the sweeping majorities that happened as in 1970 and 1977 by giving more representation to the party that came in second, but it introduced the further problem of marginalizing smaller parties other than regional parties like the TULF. Initially, the threshold limit for election was set very high for parties (12.5 percent), later reduced to 5 percent. Minority candidates and minor parties have little hope of election except in alliance with one of the two parties .

There was dissent to the constitution from SLFP, which opposed the method of selection of the executive president, the loss of "supremacy" by the NSA and the system of proportional representation. S. Thondaman raised questions on demands of Plantation Tamils.

The system of proportional representation changed the nature of elected office. The Fourteenth Amendment to the constitution in 1988 increased the number of Members of Parliment from 196 to 225, the additional 29 members selected in proportion to the total votes received by each party from lists provided by the parties. This meant that candidates compete with members of their own parties for their rank on the lists. It also changed the role of the Member of Parliament. Up to this time, MPs had been preoccupied with constituency service and development work, but now the former was undermined because they represented a district rather than electorates, and the latter was lost to the Provincial Councils, which have sweeping roles in development.

The constitution of 1978 was an attempt to present compromise formulations of religious and language policy. For example, the constitution gives "the foremost place" to Buddhism, while guaranteeing "freedom of thought, conscience and religion." Likewise, there is an entire chapter on language, which attempts to strike a compromise. Sinhala is the "official" language, but Tamil is a "national" language used in Tamil-speaking areas. The 1972 constitution had required the state to foster "Buddhism," but the 1978 version says to "protect and foster the Buddha Sasana." (*Sasana* refers to the teaching of the Buddha, and can be given a narrower interpretation than the English term.) The 1978 constitution asserts, as in 1972, that "The Republic of Sri Lanka is a Unitary State."

UNP-TULF NEGOTIATIONS

Jayewardene seems to have believed in 1977 that his political mandate, economic growth, and repression of militant separatists would enable him to find a negotiated settlement of Tamil grievances. In fact, opportunities for peace declined steadily from 1977 to 1983. Economic growth was uneven and disruptive. The number and severity of incidents attributed to Tamil separatists increased, and government fostered resistance by becoming increasingly violent in its attempts to defeat the terrorists. Negotiations broke down as the UNP could not make concessions that were opposed by Sinhalese-Buddhist nationalists.

The TULF victory in Jaffna District in 1977 was the most sweeping of any party in any election in Sri Lankan history (72.1 percent of the vote in Jaffna District and 68.9 percent of the entire Northern Province). It won the second largest number of seats in the 1977 election, which put the head of a separatist party in the anomalous position of being the leader of the loyal opposition. The Tamil voters had chosen a democratic, constitutional means of achieving autonomy. The TULF was apparently in a good position to negotiate redress of Tamil grievances.

Jayewardene made some concessions to redress minority grievances. Tamil was made an official language in the 1978 Constitution. The system of proportional representation had a potential to make minority MPs more influential by preventing the sweeping majorities that had occurred in 1970 and 1977. Economic liberalization was expected to help Tamil businesses by replacing state control of the economy in Sinhalese hands with free competition. The constitution removed the distinction between "citizens by descent" and "citizens by registration" by which Plantation Tamils were stigmatized; the government belatedly removed the prohibition on Plantation Tamils participating in local elections. Most importantly, he promised that elected Development Councils would be created in every district in the country.

The District Development Councils were a major disappointment because Parliament did not give them the autonomy needed to satisfy Tamil minimum demands. The District Development Councils Act was approved in August 1980, and the first elections were held on June 4, 1981. The Councils found, however, that they did not have the financial resources to promote local development, nor did they have the authority to initiate development projects. The government delayed in delegating powers to the district ministers, during which time centrally appointed bureaucrats resisted their efforts. The UNP claimed that over time the financial problems, if not the degree of autonomy, would be resolved.

Jayewardene negotiated with the TULF, but relations became increasingly strained. The 1978 constitution provided that a MP who changed parties would vacate his or her seat. When a TULF member, C. Rajadurai, and one other MP wanted to join the government, it rushed through the Second Amendment to the Constitution to allow it over the objection of the opposition led by the TULF. The TULF itself weakened their negotiating position by failing to oppose the terrorist activities of the militant separatists, which increased the hostility of Sinhalese extremists. In particular, A. Amirthalingam, the leader of the TULF, made comments on a visit to India in March 1979 that seemed to support the militants.

Negotiations took place against the background of increasing violence. The militant Tamil groups murdered 20 police officers, 3 politicians, and 13 civilians (mostly police informers) from 1975 to 1981 in the Northern Province. The government declared an emergency under the Public Security Act on July 11, 1979. The TULF charged that the emergency was used to suppress legitimate political activity in the North. At the same time it passed the Prevention of Terrorism (Temporary Provisions) Act, No. 48 of 1979 (PTA), which became a permanent law by Act No. 10 of 1982. It gave security forces wide powers such as preventive detention throughout the country. Incitement of communal violence became punishable by imprisonment for 5–10 years. The security forces, however, had already displayed their lack of discipline and training in their brutal suppression of the JVP insurrection in 1971 and in their strike-breaking actions. Now they were asked to suppress Tamil terrorists, at a time when they were almost entirely Sinhalese Buddhists who spoke no Tamil and were exposed to a constant barrage of propaganda from Sinhalese-Buddhist extremists. This resulted in many abuses by the security forces such as extrajudicial killings, disappearances, abuse of detainees, and arbitrary arrest and detention.

Communal violence preceded the Development Council elections in Jaffna. The UNP candidate for the Jaffna development council was fatally shot and a policeman was also killed. The frustrated police rioted; they burned down the central market and some politicians' homes and vandalized monuments. Most importantly, they burned down the exceptional Jaffna Municipal Library, a symbol of Tamil education and scholarship.

Six weeks later, gangs of Sinhalese hoodlums assaulted Tamil laborers, particularly those who had moved off the plantations to work in Sinhalese towns and villages. More than 5,000 Tamil refugees moved from the planting districts to Tamil-majority districts. These were timed to intimidate the "stateless" Tamils shortly before the period in which they could apply for Indian citizenship was to expire. When Jayewardene learned that members of his government were involved in the 1981 violence, he offered to resign.

PRESIDENTIAL AND PARLIAMENTARY ELECTIONS

Parliament's term was due to end in August 1983, and President Jayewardene's own term was due to end only in February 1984. In 1982, however, Jayewardene decided to hold an early presidential election, as permitted by the Third Amendment to the Constitution. He won this election on October 20 with 52.9 percent of the vote and proceeded to hold a referendum that extended the life of Parliament until 1989 with 54.7 percent of the vote.

There were several reasons for holding the elections early. The one given publicly by the UNP itself was that 1983 and 1984 were expected to be transitional years in his policy of economic liberalization. The possibility existed of a new Parliament undermining the changes, and the UNP did not want to allow that. There is no evidence that this was likely, however, and other factors seem more important. The referendum allowed the UNP to maintain its five-sixths majority in Parliament. This enabled the government to continue to change the Constitution at will and gave the party immense patronage power to build support.

In 1982 the opposition was fragmented and might not have been in 1983. In October 1980 Mrs. Bandaranaike had her civil rights removed after the Supreme Court found that she abused her power during her years as prime minister; she was expelled from Parliament and barred from voting or standing for election for seven years. In 1982 factions were still fighting for control of the SLFP. The Marxist parties disintegrated after the death of N. M. Perera in August 1979. The SLFP candidate was Mrs. Bandaranaike's kinsman Hector Kobbekaduwa, after the party had rejected a common candidate who could be supported by the left parties. Colvin R. de Silva of the LSSP also ran but attracted few voters. The TULF did not participate in the presidential election of October 1982 because its leaders believed the alternatives to Jayewardene would have been worse. Rohana Wijeweera, the JVP leader released from prison, won more than 4 percent of the vote.

The two elections had the effect of discrediting Jayewardene and weakening democracy in Sri Lanka. In both cases the president appeared to have once again manipulated the Constitution cynically for partisan advantage. The presidential election does not seem to have been unusually corrupt; the majority seems, in fact, to have been relatively low considering the propaganda campaign of the state-controlled media, the ineptitude of the opposition, and what appears to have been a genuine support for economic liberalization.

Accusations have been leveled at the government for the conduct of the referendum, however. The state of emergency remained in effect, which enabled Sri Lankan government to detain opposition leaders, seal their presses, and intimidate their supporters. Claims of widespread voter impersonation were levied. The referendum was a severe blow to parliamentary democracy in Sri Lanka. It changed the conduct of elections by institutionalizing the use of force and legitimizing the incumbents' use of the powers of government to sway the electorate.

OUTBREAK OF CIVIL WAR

The outset of civil war can be dated from the widespread mob violence against Tamils that began on Sunday evening July 23, 1983. The previous night the LTTE ambushed an army patrol in Jaffna and killed 13 soldiers. The government immediately flew the bodies to Colombo and gathered the victims' families at Colombo's main cemetery for a hastily organized mass funeral. The gathering erupted into an anti-Tamil rampage before the funeral could be held. There is no doubt that people within the government planned an attack on Tamils and were using the funeral to instigate it.

On Monday Tamil homes and businesses were systematically targeted by mobs led by persons believed to be associated with the UNP's trade-union organization, the Jathika Sevaka Sangamaya (JSS). Eyewitnesses reported instances in which shops owned by Sinhalese were not damaged, but the property of their Tamil renters was destroyed. It is certain that the violence extended far beyond the planners' intent.

The week-long rampage in Colombo can be divided into six phases: mob violence on Sunday night; systematic intimidation of Tamils and destruction of Tamil property on Monday; looting, arson, and murder on Monday afternoon and Tuesday, tapering off on Wednesday; a lull on Thursday; and rumor-driven panic on Friday. Violence spread during the week to all Sinhalese-majority areas, especially the towns of Kandy, Nuwara Eliya and Badulla. It continued in Trincomalee, where the armed forces harassed and assaulted Tamils and burned their homes and shops for more than a month.

Mobs went beyond arson and looting to murder. The official death toll was 367, but unofficial estimates are as high as 3,000. Police and troops stood by, and in some cases assisted the mobs. The mobs murdered 53 Tamil political prisoners in the Welikada Prison. It resulted in enormous damage to Tamil-owned property; it created 135,000 refugees, 30,000 of them going to Tamilnadu; the adverse international publicity undermined the economy by discouraging tourism and foreign investment. Damage was estimated at $100 million.

The victims were loyal, conservative Tamils who lived among the Sinhalese, many of them supporters of the UNP government. Many were in fact Colombo constituents of the president (in Wellawatte) and the prime minister (in the Pettah).

President Jayewardene failed to control the security forces and hesitated several days before making a public appearance; when he did speak publicly, he blamed the Tamil separatists for inciting violence and referred to the Sinhalese as victims. His actions suggest that he feared opposition from extremists within the UNP more than from the separatists. He rushed into effect the Sixth Amendment to the 1978 constitution, which prohibits the advocacy of a separate state in Sri Lanka by individuals or parties. This forced the TULF out of Parliament by making the platform on which it was elected illegal, removed Eelam from formal political debate, and left the militants in control of the separatist movement.

11

Economic Liberalization and the Quality of Life

Sri Lanka is lifting itself out of poverty at a slower pace than most East and Southeast Asian nations. This has been a major disappointment, since Lankans and foreign observers alike expected it to be one of the success stories among postcolonial states. In 1948 prospects for economic growth appeared to be outstanding. The country had suffered little damage from war or anti-colonial protest; its population was relatively healthy and literate; plantation crops provided substantial foreign exchange (including substantial reserves that had been blocked during World War II); the infrastructure created for the plantation economy was available to the new nation; and the people had been virtually self-governing since 1931. Instead, governments have made many bad economic decisions and have not been able to control the waste, mismanagement, and corruption that have undermined even the most promising policies.

There have been dramatic shifts in government strategy over the years; these are labeled by their ideological orientations, but in most cases they have been determined more by economic necessity and political expediency than by ideological commitment. In the first generation after independence, the government was unable politically to reduce the extensive public services and subsidies that had grown during the State Council period. These were justified as a means of improving the "quality of life." The unfavorable balance of trade in the 1960s forced strict controls on imports and foreign exchange. This has been described as an import-substitution strategy. When attempts to industrialize faltered in the late 1960s, the government claimed to be giving priority to agriculture. The economic chaos of the 1970s under the UF government was called socialism. The reversal of policy after 1975, particularly the mixed bag of reforms implemented by the UNP in 1977 and continued by subsequent governments, has been held up as a model of economic liberalization. This chapter puts those reforms in their historical context and examines the relationship of the economic changes to the political history of Sri Lanka.

ECONOMY TO 1970

From 1948 to 1960 high export prices created an artificial prosperity. In terms of purchasing power, Sri Lanka's per capita income was by far the highest in South Asia and was higher than that of Thailand or South Korea. The UNP was able to devote government revenue to welfare, education, and consumption rather than investment. Few restrictions were placed on imports. Prosperity depended on the export of a limited range of agricultural industries—mainly tea, rubber and coconut. These had been developed by foreign investors and were cultivated in large part by a labor force that was denied citizenship. Little was done to restructure the colonial economy, even after it was clear that foreign exchange reserves were dwindling and a rapidly growing population was creating economic problems for the future. The extension of rice cultivation remained a priority for the UNP. Its rudimentary July 1948 economic plan advocated import substitution as an economic strategy, but investment was less than 10 percent of gross national product (GNP). Manufacturing grew at only 1.3 percent a year, and its share of the GNP was about 5 percent.

The MEP government of 1956 was not ideologically committed to socialism, but the aristocratic S.W.R.D. Bandaranaike adopted leftist rhetoric and promised to nationalize all foreign-owned plantations and to take over key industries. It projected a growth rate of 5.9 percent a year from import-substitution and increased government participation in manufacturing. A State Industrial Corporation Act provided the mechanism by which the government started new industrial undertakings. Corporations were started for iron and steel, oil, rubber, sugar, hydroelectric power, mineral sands, and other products. State Trading Corporations refused to allow import licenses to potential competitors and became monopolies. Budget deficits grew because exports lagged while the terms of trade worsened. Government expenditure increased as the government found it impossible to reduce welfare programs or to resist striking workers. Bandaranaike, beset by political crises, had not advanced industrialization very far when he was assassinated in 1959.

Import substitution decreased the country's dependence on imported consumer goods, but it required increased imported capital goods and raw materials, especially when the corporation was based on foreign aid with strings attached. Inefficiency and corruption raised prices. The rubber corporation, for example, was built with Russian aid. In addition to the cost of Russian technicians, parts and equipment, the corporation decided to use only local rubber. In the end, it cost more foreign exchange to produce automobile tires than it would have cost to import them from Singapore or Thailand, where they were produced with Japanese equipment. Import substitution never achieved its potential in Sri Lanka.

By 1960 foreign exchange reserves were exhausted and the Central Bank attempted to deal with the foreign exchange crisis. It imposed selective controls to reduce imports of nonessential goods (e.g., automobiles, alcohol, cosmetics), followed by steeper duties on other imports, including petroleum, tobacco, watches, and textiles. In January 1961, foreign exchange was tightly controlled, 49 luxury goods were banned, and most other imports had licensing requirements that amounted to quotas.

In 1963 the government created a Foreign Exchange Budget Committee at the Ministry of Finance to allocate foreign exchange on the basis of "national priorities"; further foreign exchange controls were imposed in 1964, along with a moratorium on repatriation of profits and dividends, and restrictions on overseas education and foreign travel. In addition to its trade balance deficit, the country also had a large deficit in its domestic budget. The government attempted to reduce the rice subsidy program but had to give in to opposition from the left and the trade unions.

By 1965 extensive exchange and import controls had transformed Sri Lanka's economy into a protectionist regime despite its continuing dependence on foreign trade. The Bank of Ceylon and insurance companies were nationalized. The operations of foreign bank branches were restricted.

The UNP government from 1965 to 1970 limited its economic initiatives to increasing agricultural productivity. Thirty years of colonization had brought 600,000 acres of new land into cultivation, and the control of malaria in the colonization schemes made their improvement feasible. Although this was achieved at a high cost for irrigation, land clearing, and construction, it now was beginning to repay some of the cost. The government distributed high-yielding varieties of seed, subsidized fertilizers, provided extension services, and offered price incentives. The government's guaranteed price scheme provided a market when prices fell. Agricultural credit and crop insurance were also available. As a result, annual rice production increased from about 50 million bushels to 77 million bushels. Production of "subsidiary crops" such as potatoes, chillies, onions, and maize also increased.

These policies were justified as means to promote import-substitution industrialization; in fact, it appears to have been the only way to deal with the shortage of foreign exchange when the country still depended on food imports to feed its people.

A SOCIALIST EXPERIMENT

The economic situation worsened in the 1970s. The balance of payments deficit increased, particularly after the global increase in oil prices. The price of imported food also increased, and by 1973 the country was unable to feed itself. The world prices of Sri Lanka's exports fell while import prices rose, turning the perennial shortage of foreign exchange into a crisis. Nevertheless, the government continued to pursue structural changes in the economy, particularly after the JVP insurrection.

The government introduced a series of desperate measures. The prices of necessities were increased, the sugar ration was halved, and the government increased the price of the second measure of rationed rice by 40 percent. As the price of rice increased, people switched to flour, which also was in short supply. In September 1973, Bandaranaike reduced the weekly rice ration to half a measure (one pound). Breadlines formed at State Cooperative retail stores.

In February 1974, the government imposed a ban on the transport of paddy and rice by private individuals without a permit and placed a ceiling on the amount of rice that could be held by individuals to prevent farmers and traders from hoarding rice and to facilitate the Paddy Marketing Board's monopoly.

State control of the economy exacerbated the situation by discouraging markets and by increasing overhead costs in every industry. The Paddy Marketing Board had discouraged the growth of rice production. The Ceylon Fisheries Corporation was created in 1964 to develop deep-sea trawler fishing, process fish, and market it. It constructed harbors and imported fishing gear. Nevertheless, per capita fish consumption fell in half, from 48.6 pounds in 1966 to 24.1 pounds in 1974.

Bandaranaike's five-year plan presented in November 1971 seems to reflect both the influence of post–Cultural Revolution China, and also the threat of revolutionary violence displayed by the JVP insurrection. China apparently had transformed its people into a new socialist society in which people willingly reduced consumption in order to provide savings. Zhou Enlai, premier and foreign minister of the PRC, reportedly told Bandaranaike that "giving free rice, free health services and education is not socialism." The five-year plan proposed radical land reform, limits on agriculture and urban property ownership, ceilings on disposable income, compulsory savings, and the reduction of subsidies. These were intended both to provide revenue for development and to transform society.

The Land Reform Law No. 1 of 1972 placed a ceiling of 50 acres total or 25 acres of paddy land on private land ownership. Landowners could place this amount in the names of each of their family members, which led to abuses.

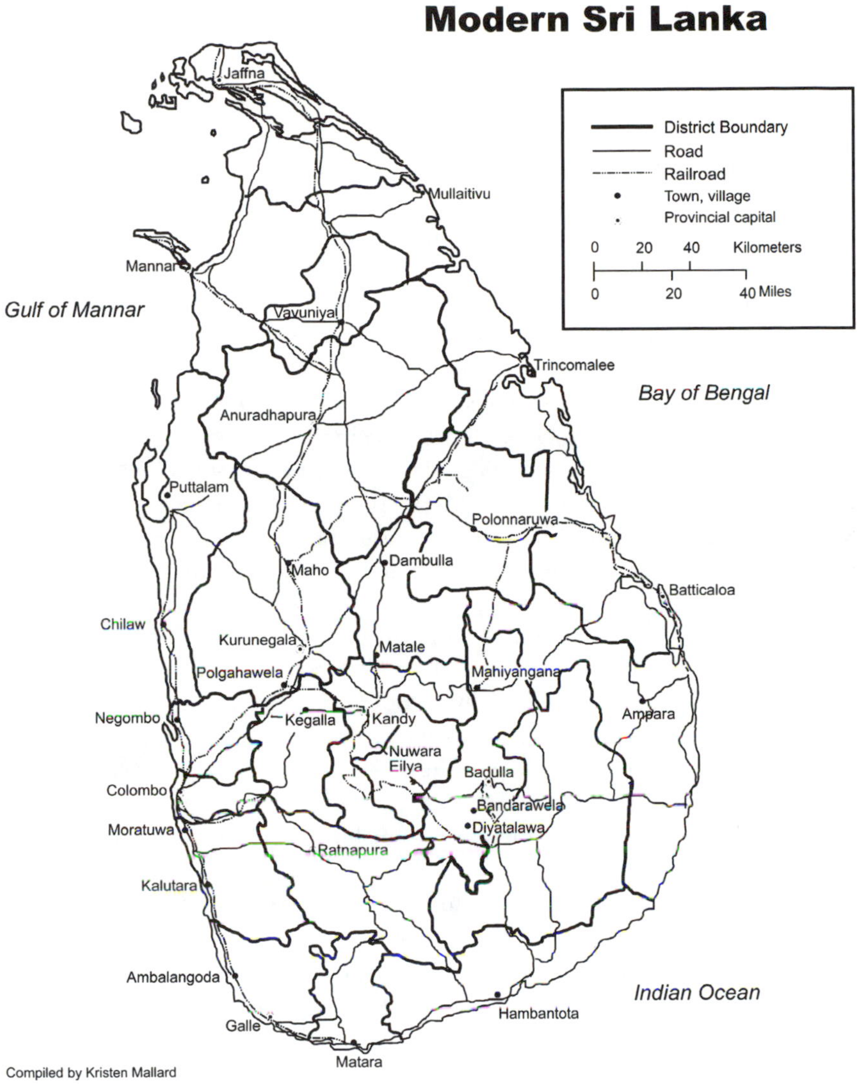

Compiled by Kristen Mallard

The excess was taken over by a Land Reform Commission, which had the power to redistribute it. Only a fraction was actually distributed to landless peasants, most of it in small lots for homesteads. The Land Reform (Amendment) Law No. 39 of 1975 nationalized land owned by private companies, which had been exempted from the 1972 law. The Agency Houses that managed most of the plantations were also taken over.

The Land Reform Commission took control of more than 415,000 acres of plantation lands (292,000 acres of tea, 110,00 acres of rubber, and 13,000 acres of coconut and other tree crops), more than one-third of the land under these crops. Although many foreign plantation owners had sold their property to local investors by this time, it marked the end of foreign ownership of plantations, which had played such an important part in the island's modern history. Nationalization placed a heavy economic burden on the nation, first for compensation for the nationalized lands and then from the loss of production owing to politicization of the State Plantations Corporation and its mismanagement of the plantations. It also resulted in the displacement of many Plantation Tamils.

Social pressure and constant government propaganda tried to convince individuals to contribute their private wealth to Bandaranaike's development programs. This was a disaster; there was little support for many of the programs, and people who were coerced into giving up their money and property resented both the government's failure to control corruption in the bureaucratic elite and the evasion of the new laws by SLFP party leaders.

The years 1974 and 1975 were a low point in the economy. Sri Lanka couldn't provide enough food to feed its population; the economy was riddled with inefficiency, waste, and corruption; and investors were discouraged by excessive regulation.

Many Lankans left the country to find better opportunity overseas. The Compulsory Public Service Act (No. 70 of 1961) forced professionals to serve in Sri Lanka for five years before they could leave the country. People who traveled abroad at public expense were required to sign a contract to serve for 1–10 years on their return. Laws required citizens working abroad to remit a portion of their earnings to Sri Lanka. Many doctors and engineers found their way to the West, and skilled and semiskilled laborers emigrated to the Middle East.

There was a great increase in the number of beggars from fewer than 8,000 in the early 1960s (many of them of the *roḍiya* caste, who were professional beggars) to about 25,000 in 1977, even though the number of *roḍiya* beggars appears to have declined. Many of the increase were plantation laborers who were dispossessed after the nationalization of the plantations. The incidence of infanticide by parents who could not feed their children increased, particularly among plantation laborers.

The shift to economic liberalization can be dated from 1975, when Felix Dias Bandaranaike became Minister of Finance and began the reversal of the socialist policies of the early UF with a budget aimed to provide incentives for production in the private sector. He removed many controls and taxes on private enterprise, and tried to encourage foreign investment. In 1976 he announced 429 new projects in the private sector. To encourage investment he proposed tax concessions and legal protection for export-oriented foreign investment, which had to be withdrawn in the face of political opposition. The projects made little headway prior to the 1977 election.

From 1951 to 1977 the GNP per capita grew only 2 percent per year. The island's economy lost ground not only to the industrial nations but to many Third-World nations that had been less prosperous at independence.

QUALITY OF LIFE

S.W.R.D. Bandaranaike had expanded social welfare programs that contributed to these high measures of social well-being. These included pension programs, free medical care, nutrition programs, and a series of subsidies of important food and fuel items. As a result, education, medicine and health services, food, transportation, clothing, and housing were all available at free or subsidized prices. It was a welfare state, and there is no doubt that many, perhaps even a majority, of the population lived better as a result of it. However, the cost of these programs was so great that they diverted revenue not from the rich to the poor but from investment to consumption. The country continually depended on foreign aid and deficit financing to cover their cost.

Despite the low income of Sri Lanka, the country measured well on indices that measure the quality of life. In the 1980s Sri Lanka scored very high on the Physical Quality of Life Index (PQLI), which was composed of a composite of three indicators: life expectancy, infant mortality, and literacy. Sri Lanka has not fared as well on the United Nations' Human Development Index (HDI), which in addition measures school enrollment and GDP per capita (in purchasing power parity). In 2003 Sri Lanka was ninety-first among nations on the 2003 HDI—lower than China or the Philippines, and well below Thailand and Malaysia. Until 1977, Sri Lanka also had a more equitable distribution of income and wealth than was found in other Third-World countries. Although there is a wide gap between the rich and the poor, it was not as large as that in other developing nations.

After independence, the birth rate remained high while malaria eradication contributed to a rapid decline in death rates. Population grew at about 1.8 percent a year from 1931 to 1946 but increased to 2.8 percent in the 1950s. In the short run, population growth put pressure on the cost of welfare and education; in the long run, employment was to become a much greater problem.

ECONOMIC LIBERALIZATION

When J. R. Jayewardene became president, he quickly introduced a series of economic reforms that were summarized at the time as the "open economy." The reforms were a mixture of development strategies and political expediencies that sometime overlapped and sometimes contradicted each other. The first of these were the so-called market-friendly policies advocated by the International Monetary Fund (IMF), World Bank, and aid donors. Some times called the "Washington consensus," they consist of liberalization of trade and foreign investment; correcting prices by devaluating the currency and increasing interest rates; privatization of state-owned enterprises; deregulation of the domestic market; and balancing the budget. Many of these policies were long overdue and were received well by Lankans who saw the failure of the opposite approach in the previous administration.

The second strategy was that of government intervention to protect selected industries and to achieve social goals, as implemented by Japan and adapted by South Korea, Taiwan, Singapore, and others. This involved not balancing the budget but massive increases in spending, particularly in the AMP, housing, and urban development.

In practice, actual implementation of the proposals was politically determined. Although the UNP had a massive majority in Parliament, Jayewardene needed to keep the loyal support of his MPs. For government backbenchers, this meant access to patronage power, particularly of government jobs to distribute to followers and kinsmen. There were more government MPs than ever before, and most of them were newly elected ones who expected that this was the time for them to display their power to constituents.

Jayewardene had a further problem: He needed to allow each of the leaders of the party to use the power of the state to build their national following, often through identification with one or more economic policies. Thus Prime Minister Ranasinghe promoted *gam udawa* (village reawakening) housing schemes throughout the Sinhalese districts. Gamini Dissanayake made the AMP his personal campaign. Lalith Athulathmudali, as Minister of Trade and Shipping, reformed the Colombo port administration and had the CWE create a highly publicized scheme of buffer stocks of food to keep prices low. Cyril Mathew protected the state corporations as Minister for Industries and Scientific Affairs and used the militant union he controlled, the JSS to break strikes. In a manner comparable to the Board of Ministers in the State Council, Jayewardene had to placate each of these potential successors to the presidency.

The first wave of economic liberalization replaced quantitative restrictions on imports with tariffs, with the intention of lowering them. Average import duties increased from the late 1970s to the mid-1980s before declining thereafter. The rupee was devalued by 40 percent and then allowed to fall from about 9 rupees to the U.S. dollar in 1978 to 102 rupees in 2006. Interest rates were adjusted above the rate of inflation; foreign banks were allowed to open branches in Sri Lanka for the first time since 1961.

The immediate effect of liberalization was to open the coffers of aid donors. Sri Lanka asked for, and usually received, massive grants of foreign aid, to the point that it became the highest aid recipient per capita in the world.

The greatest success of liberalization came in export processing zones created by the Greater Colombo Economic Commission (GCEC) to attract export-oriented foreign investment. The first Free Trade Zone (FTZ) at Katunayake near the International Airport opened in June 1978. A second FTZ was located in Biyagama in 1982, and a third in Koggala in June 1991. Investors were allowed complete foreign ownership of investment projects; a tax holiday for up to 10 years; duty exemption for the import of inputs; industrial services at subsidized rates; and unlimited access to foreign currency credit. A guarantee against nationalization of assets without compensation was written into the 1978 Constitution.

The FTZs became very attractive to garment manufacturers that had used up their quotas under the Multi-Fibre Arrangement (MFA) and wished to use Sri Lanka's quota. Garment and textile exports grew from less than US$10 million in 1977 to $280 million in the mid-1980s to $1.2 billion in 1992 and $2.3 billion in 2004. Besides bringing foreign exchange into the country, the FTZs provided employment for young unskilled women at low wages. Most of the raw materials—up to 90 percent for some products—had to be imported, however, so the net foreign exchange earnings are lower than the gross receipts. The overall impact of the FTZs is hard to gauge. Attempts to attract higher value-added industries have not been successful, and no entrepreneurs have come forward with locally produced inputs of a quality high enough to vertically integrate the FTZ.

Sri Lanka made little progress in other aspects of the market-friendly agenda. Privatization of state industries was a UNP campaign promise, but it could not overcome resistance from within the party, especially from Cyril Mathew. Instead, the government attempted, with mixed success, to make them more efficient. No attempt was made to balance the budget; expenditures doubled from 1977 to 1978. The "socialist" UF government spent on the average about 31 percent of GNP; the "capitalist" UNP spent more than 40 percent of GNP by1980. Budget deficits also increased.

PUBLIC INVESTMENT

The UNP government spent vast amounts of money on construction projects with the aim of jump-starting the economy. The single largest expenditure during the Jayewardene era was the AMP. This was an adaptation of a 30-year master plan of development of hydroelectric power and irrigation on Sri Lanka's one large river that had begun in the previous administration. In 1977 and 1978 the UNP promised that it would implement the entire 30-development plan proposed in 1968 in 6 years. The original plans proposed to irrigate 654,000 acres of land and settle 1.5 million people. The project was scaled down several times and when it was completed in 1988, it included four major dams, and a fifth dam for hydroelectric power, with an installed capacity of 400 megawatts. It was intended to irrigate an estimated 390,000 acres of new lands, most of them in the Eastern Province in the Mahaweli and adjacent Madurai Oya basins, on which 140,000 Sinhalese families would settle.

The AMP exacerbated ethnic conflict because it created colonies of Sinhalese cultivators in areas that many Tamils believed to be part of the Tamil Homeland, Moreover, the scaled-down version of the Master Plan excluded areas that were near Tamil urban centers. Jayewardene and Gamini Dissanayake, as Minister of Mahaweli Development, emphasized that these settlements were to be idyllic Sinhalese Buddhist communities that would recall the mythical past of the ancient civilization. Despite the overblown rhetoric, most settlers found very little development of the social infrastructure when they arrived.

The civil war has disrupted the colonies because some of them are vulnerable to terrorist attacks from the LTTE and require military protection. This adds to farmer discontent from their small holdings, lack of *chēna* land, inequality resulting from differential access to resources, poor infrastructure, and legal restrictions on the sale and inheritance of allotments.

The second largest area of public investment is housing. Prime Minister Premadasa's housing and urban development programs cost about one-fourth of AMP expenditures during Jayewardene's first term. The most successful project was Aided Self-Help Rural Housing, which Premadasa combined with his program of village reawakening *(gam udawa)*. Villagers did most of the construction with government funding. Money for wells, public buildings, and even clock towers (to encourage punctuality) was provided. Despite a budget cut demanded by the IMF, more than 50,000 new houses had been completed by December 1982. The program was presented with an appeal to Sinhalese-Buddhist nationalism, but the favoritism for UNP supporters tended to exacerbate political factionalism.

Urban development was another priority, particularly the creation of a new capital, Sri Jayewardenapura-Kottē, bordering Colombo on the west and twice its size. This was centered on a magnificent parliament built by noted architect Geoffrey Bawa entirely from Sri Lankan funds. Colombo remains the financial capital. President Jayarwadene opened it on April 29, 1982. Expenditures also included money for road and rail networks, additional public buildings at Sri Jayewardenapura, and the beautification of Colombo.

The massive expenditure on these three projects over such a brief time span created problems. There was little accountability on spending, and the opportunities for corruption were enormous. The rapid increase of money in circulation sent inflation spiraling out of control. As always government expenditures were used to reward political supporters, but the vast advantages given to UNP loyalists in this period dwarfed previous cases.

TOURISM AND REMITTANCES

Two other sources of income provided desperately needed foreign exchange: tourism and the remittances of overseas Lankans. Tourism has been a priority for Lankan governments since the 1960s, but it was hindered in the 1970s by lack of capital for investment in hotels and other facilities. After 1977 it became both a favorite of local and foreign investors and a new destination for global tourists. By 1979 arrivals during the height of the season stretched the hotel capacity. The number of rooms grew and by 1984 tourist arrivals peaked at about 325,000 and tourist receipts exceeded $100 million. The civil war reduced arrivals dramatically, but they increased again after 1989, peaking at about 450,000 in 1994, before Eelam War III discouraged tourists again. The cease-fire in 2002 brought tourism to much higher levels—the tsunami of December 2004 struck at the height of the highest tourist season ever.

Tourism has had many critics. Many thought Sri Lanka should cater only to "first-class" tourists and were disappointed when many tourists turned out to be working-class Europeans on all-expense paid charter tours, Asians, or youth attracted to the budget beach hotels. Others dislike the cultural influence of foreign tourists. Concerns have been raised about the existence of sex tourism.

The other source of foreign exchange is the remittances of overseas emigrant laborers, primarily unskilled female labor. About 800,000 Lankans work abroad, 90 percent of them in the Middle East. They send home more than $1 billion a year, which equals more than one-fifth of total export earnings and accounts for more than a one-fourth of national savings. The other, undocumented form of remittances is the money collected by the LTTE from overseas Tamils.

The initial response to the new economy was euphoric. By 1979 the English-educated elite were asking not whether Sri Lanka *would* become the new Singapore, but whether they *should* become like Singapore. Within three years, however, the economy faltered. (This influenced the decision of President Jayewardene to seek early reelection and to extend the life of Parliament by a referendum without facing a disillusioned electorate.) Government debt, inflation, and trade deficits grew out of control. Inequality became highly visible as a very wealthy group of winners at the top acquired luxuries and larger numbers of Lankans suffered dire poverty at the bottom. It reversed the situation of the 1970s, in which it was the wealthy who considered themselves deprived. People now asked if the new economy could provide sustained growth, and if it could do so, whether the political and social cost worth it.

Wages in the private sector, especially in tourism, could be much higher than public sector wages, which fell behind inflation. A university professor could raise his or her income by becoming a tour guide. Unemployed and underemployed workers—landless agricultural laborers, small landholders, self employed craftsmen, fishermen, and casual laborers—became impoverished. Ironically, plantation laborers, who had always been the poorest Lankans, were able to survive because their strong labor unions could demand higher wages and benefits. Other labor unions suffered brutal repression as strikebreakers in UNP control crushed strikes, and striking workers were dismissed. After 1983 the spiraling costs, and the political chaos, of the civil war limited the government's ability to continue economic reforms.

SECOND WAVE OF LIBERALIZATION

Sri Lanka negotiated an Enhanced Structural Adjustment Facility loan with the IMF in 1989, under which large loans were granted on concessionary terms to improve balance of payments in return for meeting targets for the liberalization of the economy. President Premadasa thus inaugurated a second wave of liberalization, although the loans were withheld at times because Sri Lanka failed to meet the targets to which it agreed. Premadasa began the privatization of state corporations but was less successful at cutting the budget deficit and reducing spending.

Premadasa began to privatize 46 state-owned enterprises in 1990. He overcame trade union resistance to privatization by giving employees a tenth of the shares free, a process he called "peoplisation." Only seven were actually sold. The largest privatization attempt was that of the 450 plantations that had been nationalized in the 1970s. Privatization in this case was motivated in part by the growing losses of the state plantation corporations. Waste, mismanagement, theft, and corruption made the cost of producing tea higher than the sale price, and the two government-owned corporations that ran the plantations were deeply in debt and were losing 400 million rupees ($90 million) a month. In May 1992 the government turned over control of 449 state-owned tea, rubber, and coconut plantations to 22 state-owned companies, which were awarded five-year profit-sharing management contracts. They in turn hired private managers. The plantation companies soon went even more deeply into debt. They lacked the capital to improve the plantations because the government had cut off funds and refused to guarantee bank loans since the end of 1994.

In October 1989, Premadasa introduced a massive poverty alleviation program called *Janasaviya,* which made direct cash payments to more than half the country's population. Theoretically, the program would stimulate growth at the local level, but some of it went into high overhead costs and the rest directly into consumption. Government transfers to households under the two programs were about 22 percent of government revenue, money that might have served the recipients better if it were invested. The *Janasaviya* program brought Premadasa into conflict with Dr. A. T. Ariyaratne, the highly respected and internationally renowned founder of the social service organization Sarvodaya, which could have helped divert some of the money into development. Ariyaratne claimed that the World Bank expected that Sarvodaya would participate, but Premadasa excluded Ariyaratne, perhaps fearing that Ariyaratne would be a political rival.

THE PRESENT SITUATION

To the surprise of some who had believed UNP campaign rhetoric, Chandrika Bandaranaike Kumaratunga made few changes in economic policies after her election in 1994. The People's Alliance (PA) had indicated during the campaign that it was committed to a market economy and to cooperation with the private sector. Her priorities were the elimination of corruption, privatization of government corporations, and control of inflation.

In 1994 both parties campaigned against the corruption of the previous era. Once elected, the PA established a Permanent Commission on Bribery and Corruption and even appealed to the United Nations for assistance. Kumaratunga set about exposing corruption in the previous administration. Critics argued that the measures it took to prevent current corruption slowed the economy without accomplishing the goal. She was also unable to prevent the exploitation of power by her own party after 17 years of exile. Kumaratunga was forced by political pressure to approve cabinet ministers that she had accused of misusing funds in their ministries.

Kumaratunga moved quickly to create a Public Enterprise Reform Commission to examine the sale, lease, or management of government firms. Privatization faced opposition within her own party, particularly from her mother, Prime Minister Sirimavo Bandaranaike (who had nationalized many industries in the first place). Many state corporations were sold or leased to private investors, including the heavily subsidized national airline Air Lanka and tea plantation companies.

The labor movement opposed privatization, particularly the state-owned telephone company Sri Lanka Telecom She ended the government monopoly on power generation and succeeded in attracting foreign investment in much-needed power plants. In 1997 the government reacquired companies that had been sold to investors financed by state-owned banks who were unable to repay their loans.

Inflation slowed initially but increased again when Eelam War III began. It peaked at 15.9 percent in 1996. The rupee halved in value relative to the U.S. dollar in this period, from about Rs. 50 to the dollar in 1995 to Rs. 102 at the beginning of 2006.

The PA criticized the *Janasaviya* program but found it was too popular to abandon. The party revived the program under the name *Samurdhi* in August 1995. The amount of direct payments to the poor increased, but the program continued to have very high overhead costs and many opportunities to abuse the program.

Tourism continues to grow irregularly and may benefit in the long run from the tsunami. Tourist arrivals passed 500,000 visitors in 2003 and might have reached 600,000 in 2005 if not for the tsunami and political unrest at the end of the year. These are still low numbers by global standards and should increase. The pattern of tourism changed as India became the largest source of tourists rather than the United Kingdom.

President Mahinda Rajapakse presented a new "populist" budget shortly after his election in November 2005, replacing the budget presented a few weeks earlier. It raised taxes on high incomes, companies, and luxuries such as cigarettes, liquor, gambling, and imported goods. It increased subsidies to farmers (especially fertilizer) and low-wage employees and promised to create 10,000 jobs and to build houses for 80,000 families displaced by the civil war. He removed a 15 percent tax on income from some agricultural exports and cut tax on small and medium firms to 15 percent from 20 percent. High-earning companies, meanwhile, will be taxed at 35 percent.

The future of the nation's economy is very much in doubt. A resumption of civil war would slow growth indefinitely. Even without war, political leaders are divided. Some seem to be listening to "neo-liberal" economists who would push liberalization further, but most appear to favor selective government intervention on the model of the East and Southeast Asian economies. One of the most hopeful signs is the beginning of off-shore drilling for oil.

12

Civil War

After July 23, 1983, ethnic conflict became civil war. The Government of Sri Lanka attempted to crush the Tamils and then dictate a settlement, but the militant separatists were able to increase their strength every time the government did. Their success won respect for the militants from many Tamils, even those who opposed their ruthless methods. Their insurrection was funded by financial support from overseas Tamils and by drug smuggling. The war up to the end of 1994 can be divided into four distinct phases: escalation, 1983–1987 (Eelam War I); Indian intervention, 1987–1989; the reign of Ranasinghe Premadasa, 1989–1993 (Eelam War II); and the attempt to find a negotiated solution, 1993–1994, culminating in the election of Chandrika Bandaranaike Kumaratunga on a peace platform.

Violence spiraled upward after the pogrom of 1983, interrupted by periods of raised hopes for a settlement between the Sinhalese Buddhist majority and the Tamil minority. Both sides believed that the escalation of violence favored it, and extremists on both sides were unwilling to accept conditions that would bring about a negotiated settlement. In early 1983 it was believed that the extremists among the separatists were a small minority, a few hundred young men, although more were being trained in India. Soon they established bases in South India, gained international support, and developed the capacity to attack Sinhalese areas. The armed forces of Sri Lanka had been small and primarily ceremonial, but quickly grew into a larger and better equipped, but poorly trained, military.

Observers in late 1983 hoped that the unprecedented violence would shock Lankan leaders into negotiating a solution to ethnic conflict. India, which took in more than 135,000 Tamil refugees, offered to mediate. Indira Gandhi's efforts were undermined by the suspicion, later confirmed, that she had allowed her military intelligence agency, the Research and Analysis Wing (RAW), to create training camps in south India for Tamil militants and to arm them. The Government of Sri Lanka rejected a proposal, known as "Annexure C," in part because it was written by her envoy Gopalaswamy Parthasarathy in consultation with Lankan politicians. It proposed a "union of regions" within a unitary constitutional framework, the devolution of substantial legislative and executive power to these regions, and measures that would ensure adequate Tamil representation in the central government.

As the extremists began to use their bases in India more effectively, relations between the two countries worsened, particularly after the appointment of Lalith Athulathmudali as Minister of National Security. Athulathmudali equated all separatists with terrorists and used extreme measures for their suppression, resulting in high civilian casualties, which he blamed on the Tamil people for allowing the extremists to thrive. He created a 5000-strong commando force (later increased to 6,000) known as the Special Task Force (STF). Athulathmudali's interdiction of supplies and guerillas from Tamilnadu resulted in the seizure of Indian fishing vessels and tense relations between the countries.

EMERGENCE OF THE LTTE

The Tamil extremists took advantage of the confusion in late 1983 to build up their strength. The undermanned police were unable to prevent politically motivated crime, and dispossessed Tamils joined the movement. Political prisoners freed from the Batticaloa prison joined the rebels in Tamilnadu. By March 1984, there were an estimated 2,000 armed extremists in camps in Tamilnadu, with more awaiting weapons.

Eventually, the LTTE under the leadership of Vellupillai Prabhakaran prevailed over five other major militant groups: the People's Liberation Organization of Tamileelam (PLOTE), led by Uma Maheswaran; the Eelam People's Revolutionary Liberation Front (EPRLF), led by Padmanabha; the Tamileelam Liberation Organization (TELO), led by Kuttimani and Thevan; the Eelam Revolutionary Organizers (EROS); and the Eelam People's Democratic Party (EPDP). They differed in tactics, areas of influence, ideological orientation, and goals. EROS and EPRLF were openly Marxist and favored an island-wide Marxist revolution over a separate Tamil state. Personal rivalries divided their leaders, who were unable to overcome their differences at a meeting in Madras on November 10, 1983. Instead, the most ruthless and best organized group seized power through a series of bloody confrontations in Sri Lanka, Madras, and London.

The success of the LTTE can be credited to its single-minded devotion to the creation of an authoritarian government for the state of Eelam. In Jaffna they killed nonmilitant authorities such as human-rights activists, academics, and social workers, and they took control of most civilian organizations. Internationally they opened offices around the world, engaged in business and financial operations, and systematically levied funds from overseas Tamils. They indoctrinated their recruits to kill and die for the cause, including suicide bombers, and operated efficient propaganda and intelligence networks. They kept pace with the technological developments of the 1980s and 1990s and have been called a textbook case of the globalization of terrorism.

As it became stronger, the LTTE systematically destroyed its opposition. In April–May 1986, it killed 200 members of TELO, and later that year it attacked the EPRLF organization in the Jaffna Peninsula. On July 13, 1989 LTTE members assassinated Amirthalingam, and in June 1990, they murdered many senior EPRLF leaders while holding a meeting in Madras. The other groups had depended on India to supply them with weapons, and they had no alternative sources when India shut off the supply. They were unable to resist, and some of them turned to kidnapping, extortion, and burglary to raise money, which undermined their legitimacy in the eyes of the Tamil people.

ESCALATION OF VIOLENCE

Throughout 1984 the militant separatists attacked security forces, who retaliated with reprisals against Tamil civilians. On both sides atrocities appear to have been committed by undisciplined forces in the field without the approval of their senior officials. Emergency Regulation 15A enabled security forces to dispose of bodies without inquest proceedings, which facilitated extrajudicial killings.

The level of violence rose and fell. August 1984, for example, was one of the peak periods. Tamil guerrillas killed 95 people in attacks that marked the first anniversary of the 1983 riots. A suitcase bomb scheduled to be put on an Air Lanka flight from Madras to Colombo exploded in the airport on August 2 and killed 32 people, most of them Sri Lankans. On August 4 and 5, the LTTE ambushed security forces in two incidents; clashes and reprisals left another estimated 100 people dead. Hundreds of Tamil youths were rounded up in Velvettiturai. They were beaten and held incommunicado indefinitely, and about 100 shops and homes destroyed. A week later, six soldiers died when their jeep ran over a land mine. The armed forces retaliated with reprisals in the town of Mannar, killing two people and destroying 123 buildings. The same day, the Chunnakam police station near Jaffna was destroyed, and 19 Tamil prisoners lost their lives—which both sides blamed on the other. On August 13, soldiers opened fire when military vehicles spotted a van carrying militants; eight bystanders were killed at a cooperative society across the road. At sea, the navy fired at Indian fishing boats and confiscated the catch from some of them. The violence then subsided, only to revive again in December.

By the end of 1984 both the militants and the government introduced more gruesome tactics. The LTTE turned to terrorism against unarmed Sinhalese civilians, beginning with attacks on experimental settlements of convicts in or near what the organization considered Tamil territory. The worst was the massacre of 146 civilians at Anurādhapura on May 14, 1985. At the same time, a pattern of "disappearances" in government custody emerged. Large numbers of people were taken from their homes by the STF and never seen again. The government denied knowledge of these cases, but Amnesty International documented the "disappearance" of 272 people arrested by members of the security forces between June 14, 1983, and April 20, 1986.

In 1985 violence increased in the Eastern Province. The STF allegedly manipulated Hindu–Muslim riots in March and April 1985. Even during the eight-month truce from June 1985 to January 1986, most of the violations were in the Eastern Province. Violence also erupted between Plantation Tamils and Kandyan Sinhalese in the central hills of the island in early 1986. Gamini Dissanayake claimed that the extremists from EROS and PLOTE were training estate workers for terrorist activity.

In May 1986, the LTTE had emerged as the dominant group among five extremist factions after a gun battle in Jaffna during which they killed 100–200 members of TELO, including their leader Sri Sabaratnam. Apparently hoping to deal a decisive blow to a weakened LTTE, the government launched attacks from Jaffna, the west coast, and Elephant Pass but called it off after four days. In the Eastern Province fighting continued to be severe, and the government relied on "cordon and search operations" in which hundreds of Tamil youths were taken in for questioning.

ATTEMPTS TO NEGOTIATE

Negotiations had little hope of success against this background. There were three periods of negotiations before the Indo-Sri Lanka accord of 1987: a yearlong All-Parties Conference in 1984; eight months of a badly maintained ceasefire from June 1985 to January 1986; and those that resulted in an agreement brokered by Rajiv Gandhi in December 1986.

The All-Parties Conference convened on January 10, 1984, and brought together a wide range of nonpolitical organizations with divergent opinions, many representing religious organizations, in addition to the political parities. They chose to discuss broad, general subjects: the causes of ethnic violence and terrorism, the decentralization of administrative and political power, redress of the grievances of all communities, and the machinery to carry out any decisions. *Bhikkhus* and other Sinhalese Buddhist nationalists objected to any proposal that gave Tamils more powers of administration. They met off and on until December 21. In the end, the All-Parties Conference (without several parties that had withdrawn), merely revived the idea of District Development Councils.

After Indira Gandhi was assassinated on October 31, 1984, Rajiv Gandhi attempted to mediate and disavowed support for a separate Tamil state. India put pressure on the separatist groups to negotiate or face the possibility of losing their Indian sanctuary. After six months of trying, Gandhi Rajiv and Jayewardene met for eight hours in Delhi in early June 1985 and worked out the terms of a cease-fire. Two weeks later, New Delhi had used its pressure to bring the extremists to the bargaining table, and the cease-fire went into effect on June 16.

Talks were held in Thimpu, Bhutan, in early July. It was a triumph for Rajiv Gandhi: The government recognized the legitimacy of the Tamil groups, and the Tamil militants attended without insisting on a separate state. The government team consisted of lawyers and military intelligence personnel headed by the president's brother, Hector Jayewardene; the Tamil groups were divided into three factions—the TULF; a coalition of the LTTE, EPRLF, EROS, and TELO; and PLOTE. The government offered only the same proposals it had put before the All-Parties Conference in 1984, and the meetings soon collapsed. The Tamils met together and produced the four "Thimpu Principles" on July 13, 1985. The first three were the recognition of Tamils as a distinct national entity, an identified Tamil homeland whose integrity was guaranteed, and their inalienable right to self-determination. These were unacceptable to the government negotiators, but since then Tamil parties have demanded a solution consistent with them.

A fourth principle, citizenship for all Tamils in Sri Lanka, was conceded by the government under pressure from the CWC and its leader, S. Thondaman, who was Minister of Rural Industrial Development. Parliament passed a new Citizenship Act in February 1986 that promised to grant citizenship to the remaining "stateless" Plantation Tamils within 18 months.

India continued to make efforts to mediate. India seems to have hoped gestures of support for Jayewardene's government would help him to concede some autonomy to the Tamil regions without losing his own power. Instead, Sri Lanka demanded that Rajiv close all the separatist bases in Tamilnadu, a political impossibility.

PROVINCIAL COUNCILS

President Jayewardene presented new proposals to a Political Parties Conference (PPC) on June 25, 1986. They included the creation of elected Provincial Councils (PC) with responsibility for maintenance of internal law and order and land settlement. Provinces would have powers in agricultural and industrial development, elementary education, and the promotion and conduct of cultural activities. Sri Lanka would remain a unitary state; appointed governors would head the PC. Jayewardene promised that the responsibilities of the provincial councils could be enlarged though negotiations but not reduced. These proposals eventually became law after a year and a half of debate.

They were discussed in three rounds of discussions that ended on December 19, 1986. Despite extensive diplomatic efforts by India, the talks foundered over the question of the merger of the Northern and Eastern Provinces, which the militants demanded as necessary for the integrity of the Tamil homeland. The government resisted this on the grounds that the Eastern Province had a substantial Muslim (32 percent) and Sinhalese (25 percent) population. Their final proposal was to detach the Muslim- and Sinhalese-majority regions from the Eastern Province to leave the remainder a Tamil-majority province.

A compromise was negotiated on September 28, 1987. The government pushed through the Thirteenth Amendment to the Constitution and the Provincial Council Bill in November 1987 over violent Sinhalese-Buddhist protests and objections from all sides. The Supreme Court ruled favorably on the constitutionality of the measure by a 5–4 vote. The Government of India thought that the PC did not have enough power and that the government should lift emergency regulations before the PC elections.

Elections were held in 1988, resulting in UNP control of seven provinces and the EPRLF in control of the newly created Northeastern Province. The TULF said it did not contest because it could not field candidates as an "unarmed, nonviolent" party. There were 36 seats in the Northern Province and 35 in the Eastern Province. The EPRLF won all 36 seats in Jaffna uncontested, and 17 of the 35 seats in the Eastern Province; the SLMC won 17 also and the UNP a single seat in the colonist area of Amparai District. After much delay, Jayewardene proclaimed the merger of the North and East at midnight Friday night, September 9, 1988. Premadasa ordered the powers be devolved to Provincial councils in January 1989, but the process was slow. A referendum was scheduled on the unification of the North and East on July 5, 1989, but Premadasa (and his successors) postponed it.

At this time, the predominantly Tamil-speaking Muslim community became politicized after years of isolation. They had tended to support the UNP, but some Muslims turned away from the UNP after the merger of the Northern and Eastern Provinces. In 1988 Muslims increasingly supported the Sri Lanka Muslim Congress (SLMC) led by Mohamed Hussain Mohamed Ashraff. It was based in the Eastern Province. The party did well in the PC elections and won one seat in each of three districts in the general election. It gathered the third highest vote total in the latter, even though it contested only 13 of 22 electoral districts. It won seven seats in the 1994 parliamentary election.

INDIA INTERVENES 1987–1990

The negotiations over provincial councils did not prevent the resumption of hostilities between the government and LTTE, which controlled the northern peninsula, having exterminated rival separatist groups and restricted the government forces to their camps. Facing increased hostility in India, it moved most of its operations from Tamilnadu and became the de facto government of the district. The government cut off the supply of essential materials to the north and clashed with the LTTE in the Eastern Province.

On February 7, 1997, the expanded government military began an offensive to crush the LTTE in Jaffna while still negotiating with India to find new proposals. Fighting continued inconclusively for three months. The civilian population of the north suffered greatly as the LTTE used civilian hostages as firescreens and government attacks, including aerial bombardment, hit civilians. The government faced pressure from Sinhalese extremists to defeat the LTTE military and from the Indian government to stop military operations in order to bring them back to the negotiating table.

Violence against civilians reached new heights in 1987. Reprisals by security forces against civilians in the Eastern Province received international attention, including a UN Commission on Human Rights resolution calling on the country to renounce violence, seek a negotiated solution, and cooperate with the ICRC. On April 17, the militants attacked two busses and massacred 127 passengers in Trincomalee district. Four days later an explosion at Colombo's main bus station killed more than 100 people. The government blamed the bombing on EROS, but they denied it and in turn suggested that it was the act of a revived JVP.

The government in turn resumed aerial bombing of what it said were guerrilla bases in the north for three days. Sinhalese protesters, including *bhikkhus*, demanded even more aggressive measures, and the government, taking advantage of internecine battles among the militants, established a foothold in the northeast of the Jaffna peninsula and prepared to recapture the remainder of the peninsula. India, which had warned against a military solution, airdropped food and medicine on June 3, after Sri Lanka refused to allow relief shipments to come by sea. Relations between the two nations were extremely strained until the announcement of a peace accord on July 29, 1987, which Sri Lanka was too weak to refuse. Both Premadasa and Athulathmudali were hostile to Indian pressure for settling the civil war and had opposed the accord. Other government ministers supported a political settlement based on a federal solution. Dissanayake helped draft the peace agreement.

India sent 6,000 troops of the Indian Peace Keeping Force (IPKF) into Jaffna to disarm the LTTE and enforce the accord. The three parties announced a settlement on September 28, 1987. Five days later Indian troops captured 17 heavily armed LTTE members and turned them over to the Lankan Army.

They attempted a mass suicide, killing 12, and the LTTE embarked on a rampage, including massacres of Sinhalese villagers. Within days Indian troops launched a major offensive against them in Jaffna.

Violence escalated between the IPKF and the LTTE. The Indian troops were ordered to use restraint to avoid civilian casualties, to limit their own casualties, and to leave opportunity for negotiations to resume. This affected both their fighting capacity against their ruthless enemies (some of whom had been trained by India military working for the RAW) and their morale. There were estimated to be 72,000 troops at their height in February 1988, but they were unable to defeat the LTTE. Before they finally left, the IPKF had spent about about $1.25 billion on the campaign.

President Premadasa attempted to seize the anti-IPKF issue from the JVP with outrageous demands for an immediate withdrawal—something that would have damaged Sri Lanka greatly, even if it were possible. An agreement was reached on September 18, 1988. India had already made a few symbolic withdrawals, and numbers were already declining. In March 1989 there were four divisions with approximately 45,000 troops, and the final troops left in March 1990.

The final break between India and Tamil separatists came with the May 19, 1991, assassination of Rajiv Gandhi. India dismantled their aid network, and support for the Tigers among Tamil politicians evaporated. After a thorough investigation, India found Velupillai Prabakaran guilty of planning the assassination. In 2006, the LTTE attempted to improve relations with india by apologizing for it.

Annamalai Varadaraja Perumal had become the Chief Minister of the Northeast Provincial Council (NEPC) in December 1988. Perumal was a Marxist and former militant who had been a lecturer in Economics at Jaffna University. The NEPC was doomed from the start because of its close association with the IPKF, without the protection of which it could not have survived. Their heavy-handed use of IPKF favoritism created the resentment among Tamils. President Premadasa thought they were a stepping stool for Indian occupation. He placed an army officer, Lt. Gen. Nalin Seneviratne, as governor and withheld funding. The NEPC struggled despite Indian support and dissolved after a bizarre sequence of events in March 1990.

The NEPC, which had little influence outside of Trincomalee, began calling itself a national assembly and on March 3 unilaterally declared the independence of Eelam. Perumal began organizing a "Tamil National Army." Premadasa ordered the IPKF to withdraw protection from the EPRLF and Tamil separatist groups other than the LTTE to disarm. The EPRLF leaders escaped to India on March 10, and the NEPC ended. Perumal has remained under the protection of the Government of India, but the senior EPRLF leader, K. Padmanabha, was assassinated in Madras June 19.

JVP

The ban on the JVP was lifted in May 1988, and they immediately set out to mobilize support. The resumption of war produced widespread violence in Colombo, which escalated into a JVP's campaign of sabotage and assassination, intended to prevent the presidential and general elections from taking place. It repeated the pattern of its 1971 insurgency by staging raids on military facilities for arms and robberies for cash, and it recruited support within the security forces. It used Sinhalese hostility to the IPKF to attract support but terrorized any Sinhalese people who did not follow its radical reconstruction of rural society unquestioningly. Amnesty International estimates that the JVP killed more than 800 people in 1988—security forces, UNP members, and members of parties contesting elections.

With the LTTE engaged with the IPKF, Premadasa turned his security forces against the JVP. He allowed UNP politicians to recruit "home guards"—private militias of 300 supporters under personal control with no legal or judicial restraint. In November 1988 new regulations made death threats, or even carrying documents that might be considered a threat, punishable by death. In December 1988 security forces were given immunity from prosecution for actions taken in the course of their duties after August 1, 1977. Estimates of the numbers killed by government death squads, known as Black Cats, range from 12,000 to 60,000 young people during the period December 1987–1991. Supporters of the opposition, civil rights workers, lawyers, and journalists were targeted as well as JVP members.

The JVP was crushed in November 1989, when Rohana Wijeweera was killed in custody by security forces. Suspected JVP members continued to "disappear" for the remainder of Premadasa's life, and thousands continued to be held in custody. In 1992, President Premadasa warned against a renewed JVP threat, and he accused the opposition of trying to revive it. The cases against police officers accused of murder during the suppression made little progress in the courts; witnesses were killed or intimidated.

SINHALESE POLITICS

Presidential (December 15, 1988) and Parliamentary (February 15, 1989) elections were held under abnormal conditions, including violence by the LTTE and the JVP and accusations of fraud by the SLFP. In addition to the battles for supremacy within the two major parties, leftist parties began to revive in the Sri Lanka Mahajana Pakshaya (SLMP) created in 1984 by a charismatic movie actor, Vijaya Kumaratunga. His wife, Chandrika Bandaranaike Kumaratunga, the daughter of S.W.R.D. and Sirimavo Bandaranaike, left the

SLFP and became one of its vice presidents. They formed the United Left Front (ULF) with other left parties.

Kumaratunga was assassinated on February 16, 1988. His widow, Chandrika, assumed the leadership of the SLMP but left for England with their two children, staying there for about two years. When she returned she formed a new party called Bahujana Nidahas Pakshaya but soon returned to the SLFP. She defeated her brother Anura Bandaranaike for the party leadership in 1992 with the backing of her mother and the left-of-center faction of the party. In 1993 she led the People's Alliance (PA) to victory in the Western and Southern Provincial Council elections.

The UNP thought that neither Athulathmudali nor Dissanayake could defeat Mrs. Bandaranaike and thus made Premadasa their candidate. He won the direct public vote by a narrow margin of 50.4 percent, exceeding the margin required by law to win by less than 24,000 votes. Bandaranaike received 44.9 percent of the votes—much better than Hector Kobbekaduwa in 1982. Ossie Abeygunasekara was the candidate of the SLMP after the assassination of Kumaratunga but won only 4.6 percent of the votes. The turnout of 54.3 percent was by far the lowest for any national election, and appears to have worked to the disadvantage of Bandaranaike. Observers thought that she might have won if the SLFP had offered a coherent alternative to the UNP peace proposals. Premadasa received 880,000 fewer votes than Jayewardene did in 1982, but he appears to have won proportionately more Sri Lanka Tamil votes and to have continued to get strong support from plantation Tamils. Premadasa became the first head of state outside the ranks of the traditional high-caste, highly educated, and intermarried Sinhalese elite.

Premadasa faced opposition within the UNP and used his power to appoint and remove Cabinet ministers to consolidate his position. Half of Jayewardene's ministers were removed, and many of the newcomers were personally loyal to Premadasa. Premadasa kept the crucial Ministries of Defense and Policy Planning and Implementation for himself, along with the potentially sensitive ministry of Buddha *sasana,* which oversees the constitutional mandate to promote Buddhism. He named an undistinguished senior politician, Dingiri Banda Wijetunge, as prime minister and minister of finance over Gamini Dissanayake and Lalith Athulathmudali, who were given lesser portfolios. Sirisena Cooray, his close associate, was named speaker of the legislature.

President Premadasa's growing autocracy—including both an increase in violence by the state against Sinhalese politicians and a centralization of all decision making in his own hands—led to an impeachment motion in Parliament in August 1991. Premadasa had created, for example, the Security Consultancy Unit in the Ministry of Policy Planning, which secretly monitored the actions of politicians, senior military officers, journalists, and others. Its existence became public only when President Wijetunga closed it after Premadasa's death. The movement was led by Athulathmudali and Dissanayake, but had support from both government and the opposition. After intense political maneuvering, some MPs were induced to withdraw their support and the Speaker of the House M. H. Mohamed on October 8, 1991 refused to entertain the notice of the impeachment motion. Dissanayake was dismissed from the cabinet; Athulathmudali joined in a vote of confidence for Premadasa in the cabinet, but he also was expelled from the party.

RESUMPTION OF CIVIL WAR

One of the new strategies of the LTTE after the IPKF left was the "ethnic cleansing" of Muslim districts under its control. On August 3, 1990, LTTE cadres stormed two mosques in at Kattanakudy on the east coast and massacred 120 Muslims at prayer and injured more than 100, many of whom later died. On October 23, 1990, Prabakaran ordered that Muslims living in Jaffna, Kilinochchi, Mullaithivu, and Vavuniya districts should leave by October 28. Nearly 17,000 families were driven from their homes, and many are still displaced in refugee camps or with relatives. There have been accusations and counteraccusations concerning this policy; some LTTE supporters say it was done to placate east coast Tamils, but the breakaway leader Vinayagamurthy Muralitharan, known as Colonel Karuna, from the east coast denies this.

President Premadasa in December 1992 said he wanted to a find a political solution to the crisis accepted at national level and end the north-east war which he said was costing 20 billion rupees ($455 million) a year. Instead, the Lankan military attempted to defeat the LTTE in the east while containing them in the north. More than 40,000 troops pursued 1,200 LTTE cadres, most of them in the Batticaloa and Ampara districts. When the government secured the towns, LTTE retreated into the villages and the jungles, and the army gradually attempted to carry out operations there.

From 1992 to 1994 both the Lankan military and the LTTE showed that they had the ability to inflict damage on the enemy and great suffering on the people. Neither showed any likelihood that they could win the war. The Lankan military appeared to be gaining the upper hand in the east; the government held the towns, and the LTTE retreated into bases in the villages and the jungles. The government troops attacked LTTE's larger bases. But they had difficulty with operations into the jungles as the poorly trained, thinly spread, and tired troops found themselves vulnerable to ambush. The LTTE could mass large attacks on military bases in the north, but only by withdrawing cadres from the east, including their commander Karuna. Security forces captured Pooneryn from the LTTE in 1992, and the LTTE captured it back the next year.

The army had some successes against the LTTE in 1992 and was poised to capture the eastern half of the Jaffna Peninsula at the beginning of August 1992 in Operation Final Countdown. On August 8, 1992, however, military operations commander Major General Denzil Kobbekaduwa and eight other senior officiers were killed when their Land Rover drove over a land mine. The road had been previously used with no detonation, and an expert claimed that the explosion appeared to have been caused by a bomb attached to the vehicle. Suspicions were aroused because the LTTE uncharacteristically claimed responsibility and because Premadasa did not attend his funeral.

Kobbekaduwa was an extremely capable and popular commander, a relation of Sivímavo Bandaranaike, and in line to become army chief of staff. He could have been a strong presidential candidate, although his widow denied that he had any political ambitions. He had led the operation against the LTTE in Jaffna peninsula in 1987 before India intervened. Kobbekaduwa was commander of the northern armed forces, with headquarters in Anuradhapura in January 1990.

The government troops had lost many fighters in their attack on the Elephant Pass camp and had developed new tactics for this purpose. Many of the cadres that attacked Pooneryn in November 1993 were cadres from the east under the leadership of Karuna, and they suffered heavy casualties.

The LTTE shifted its strategy to all-out attacks on military bases. In July 1991 the LTTE tried to capture Elephant Pass, which cut Jaffna off from the rest of the island. It was resisted after a month-long seige at heavy cost by the army. The government used the camp to attack the LTTE, who had dug in nearby to prevent traffic from entering the peninsula there. In September 1993, Government troops began a major offensive against Tamil separatists in northern Sri Lanka but were ambushed in an attack that killed more than 150 soldiers and wounded many more. On November 11 the LTTE overran a base in Pooneryn in the fiercest fighting of the war. Many of the LTTE fighters were cadres from the east coast under the command of Karuna who personally took part in the operation. Later the east coast cadres were returned to the east to discourage the army from moving more troops from the east to the Jaffna peninsula.

NEGOTIATIONS, ASSASSINATIONS, AND ELECTIONS

Premadasa appeared willing in early 1992 to allow the merger of Northern and Eastern Provinces and to give real power to the provincial government. Sinhalese extremists mobilized so much opposition that the government dropped the proposal. The most hopeful development was the creation of a committee representing all parties in November 1991 to draft a peace proposal. This committee met until December 1992 and agreed to a federal solution for the devolution of power; it would have modified the thirteenth amendment to the constitution to give provincial councils substantial autonomy. They disagreed on the merger of the north and the east; Sinhalese and Muslim parties opposed the merger, whereas the Tamil parties insisted on it. It met again in March 1993 to complete its report without the Tamil parties. In June 1993 the committee proposed that a referendum be held on the unification of the north and east in those provinces but in July added that this should be postponed until conditions improved. By this time, politicians were looking ahead to the 1994 elections.

Sri Lanka was stripped of much of its leadership through assassination before the 1994 election. Although most of the evidence is circumstantial, it is difficult to avoid the conclusion that President Premadasa systematically had people who threatened his political power assassinated. These include Vijāya Kumaratunga, Lalith Athulathmudali, several other figures within the UNP, and police officers who were investigating their deaths. Given his autocratic methods and underworld connections, Premadasa was the only person who could have both ordered the assassinations and covered up the traces. The likelihood is so strong that many people also suspect his involvement in the deaths of General Kobbekaduwa and UNP Party Secretary (and Deputy Minister of Defense) Ranjan Wijeratne, a relative of the Senanayakes, in 1991.

The murder of Athulathmudali is the clearest case. He and Gamini Dissanayake and formed a new party, the Democratic United National Front (DUNF). Athulathmudali was elected party leader and campaigned around the country, gathering signatures on a petition calling for his resignation while building his following for the coming election. His well-attended meetings were harassed by thugs and deprived of police protection. He was shot dead by a hired killer while addressing a public meeting in Colombo in April 23, 1993. The police shot a Tamil man and identified his body the next day as an LTTE assassin, although eyewitnesses agreed that he was not the killer. At his cremation, the mourners were attacked by police.

President Premadasa died only eight days later. While mingling with a crowd of supporters on May Day, a youth approached him on a bicycle and exploded a bomb strapped to his body, in a similar manner to the assassination as Rajiv Gandhi in 1991. The bomber was a Tamil from LTTE territory who had ingratiated himself with a member of Premadasa's staff.

The transition to a new administration was remarkably smooth, possibly because the assassination seemed to many people to be a consequence of Premadasa's violent governing style. Prime Minister D. B. Wijetunge was sworn in as president, and Ranil Wickremasinghe, a loyal supporter of Premadasa related to J. R. Jayewardene, was appointed prime minister. Wijetunge quickly distanced himself from the autocratic methods of his predecessor and suggested that there might be a more open political process. The DUNF did poorly at the Provincial Council elections.

After parliament was dissolved in June 1994, the PA relied on Chandrika Bandaranaike Kumaratunga to lead its general election campaign. The PA won the election, but only by a majority of one seat. In August she assumed the office of prime minister and formed a government under President D.B. Wijetunga. Three months later she won the presidential election, polling over 62 percent of the total vote, the highest ever percentage polled by a single party or candidate in a national election in Sri Lanka.

Gamini Dissanayake was readmitted to the UNP in January 1994 and given back his Ministry of Mahaweli Development. After the UNP lost in the parliamentary election in August 1994, it selected him as the party leader over Ranil Wickremasinghe by a vote of 45 to 42 with 7 abstentions, and Dissanayake subsequently replaced Wijetunga as the UNP's presidential candidate. Just past midnight on November 24, 1994, as he was leaving a rally, a female suicide bomber stepped forward and detonated a bomb that killed Dissanayake and 53 others. Remains of a cyanide capsule of the type used by LTTE cadres were found.

The UNP had not recovered under Dissanayake's leadership; Thondaman's CWC was supporting the PA, and many party members had not forgiven his attacks on Premadasa. He was a strong presidential candidate, however, in part because his support for the accord with India countered Kumaratunga's peace campaign. His widow, Srima, was chosen to replace him as the party's presidential candidate instead of Ranil Wickremasinghe in hopes of a sympathy vote. She lost badly to Kumaratunga, winning only 36 percent of the votes cast.

After the UNP's loss in the 1994 elections, Ranil Wickremasinghe took control of the party as the last surviving leader. One of the few competitors for leadership was Anura Bandaranaike, who joined the party in 1994 after losing control of the SLFP to his sister. Kumaratunga's rivalry with Ranil Wickremasinghe was a continuation of the internecine battle between the two parties that had prevented a solution to ethnic differences since 1953. In this case, it was marked by deep personal hostility.

13

Searching for Peace

Chandrika Bandaranaike Kumaratunga, the daughter of two prime ministers and the widow of the assassinated Vijaya Kumaratunga, came to power in August 1994 at the head of a coalition, elected on a peace platform. Eleven years later she left office with peace as elusive as ever. She ruled through Eelam War III, frequent elections, a shaky truce that has been in effect since February 2002, and one of history's greatest natural disasters. In 2006, new President Mahinda Rajapakse faced the possibility of Eelam War IV.

ELECTORAL POLITICS

The SLFP returned to power in a coalition of most opposition parties called the People's Alliance (PA) in the parliamentary election of August 16, 1994. The UNP misjudged the mood of the time by taking a hard line against the LTTE at a time when Sinhalese voters were ready to attempt a negotiated settlement. It was also divided by factionalism, as followers of Premadasa opposed former members of the DUNF, who had now returned to the party. Kumaratunga's brother, Anura Bandaranaike, left the SLFP for the UNP.

The PA campaigned in favor of negotiations and against the corruption and political violence of the UNP era. In the end, the UNP resorted to personal attacks on Kumaratunga. The UNP won a substantial plurality of votes, but only 105 of the 225 seats, owing to the system of proportional representation.

With support from other parties, Kumaratunga was named prime minister, the first time the nation had a president and prime minister of different parties.

The great optimism that greeted Kumaratunga's election eroded quickly. She proved to be a poor manager and was unable to find a team to successfully implement her policies. She used her power to weaken the opposition at the cost of achieving national goals. This is most clear in her failure to abolish the executive presidency, which was promised by July 15, 1995, but was never done—the powers of the office were too useful to give up. There was opposition within the coalition to her policies and within the party to her politics, including the decision to make her 78-year-old mother prime minister instead of a more effective parliamentarian. The civil war resumed in April 1995, and a draft of her plans for devolution was not available until February 1996. The economy faltered as her goals of eliminating corruption, speeding up privatization, and controlling inflation were not met.

Provincial elections were held in January, April, and June of 1999, followed by a presidential election on December 21—more than a year before it was due. She called for an early election in hopes of breaking the stalemate on her proposals for the devolution of power. Kumaratunga defeated Wickremasinghe in the presidential elections with 51.1 percent to his 42.7 percent of the vote. She lost an eye in a terrorist attack on the last day of the election campaign, which may have produced a sympathy vote.

In the October 10, 2000, parliamentary election, the PA won 94 seats and the UNP, 77. Both parties lost votes and seats to the JVP, which had led the opposition to the devolution of power to regions. The PA vote fell from 50.7 percent to 45.2 percent, and the UNP from 44.0 percent to 40.1 percent. The JVP received 4.1 percent (and one seat) in 1994 and 6.0 percent (and eight seats) in 2000. All other candidates won 17 seats. Kumaratunga formed a government with a small majority by an alliance with a minority party, the Sri Lanka Muslim Congress (SLMC).

In the face of continuing warfare and economic decline, the government weakened. Seven members of the SLMC defected to the opposition, and Kumaratunga suspended Parliament on July 11, 2001, to avoid a vote of no confidence. She brought the JVP into the government, agreeing to reduce the size of her cabinet, to reduce wasteful expenditure, and to create (by the seventeenth amendment to the constitution) independent commissions to oversee the judiciary, police, public service, and elections. Others members of parliament left the party in opposition to the JVP's hard line on the Tamil minority.

As a result, Parliament was dissolved in October and elections were held in December 2001. The UNP-led coalition won control of Parliament under the name United National Front (UNF), with 109 seats and 45.6 percent of the vote to the PA's 37.3 percent and 77 seats. This resulted in a "cohabitation" government with Ranil Wickremasinghe as prime minister. Kumaratunga declined to create a "national government" but allowed him to form his own cabinet. It also continued the trend of success for fringe parties: The JVP won 16 seats and 9.1 percent of the vote; a coalition of Tamil parties, the Tamil National Alliance (TNA), won 15 seats.

The party positions on negotiations reversed after1994. Now Wickremasinghe pledged to start peace talks during the election campaign, and when the LTTE declared a month-long cease-fire beginning December 24, 2001, Wickremasinghe reciprocated. He and Prabhakaran signed a Memorandum of Understanding (MoU) on the Permanent Cessation of Hostilities, brokered by Norway, on February 22, 2002.

The UNF won 217 of the 222 local bodies for which elections were held in March 2002. These were seen as support for the UNF's initiatives to revive the economy and to end the civil war through unconditional negotiations. In November 2003 Kumaratunga precipitated a crisis by dismissing three key members of Wickremasinghe's cabinet while he was overseas and taking the ministries into her own hands. She suspended Parliament and briefly declared a state of emergency, accusing the UNF of making too many concessions to Tamil Tiger rebels, although she did not oppose the cease-fire. This led to another parliamentary election on April 2, 2004.

Her new alliance, the United People's Freedom Alliance —which included the JVP, CP, and LSSP—won 105 seats and 45.6 percent of the vote, compared with 82 seats and 37.8 percent of the vote for the UNP. Minority parties continued to strengthen as the TNA had 22 seats with 6.8 percent of the vote, and a Buddhist extremist party the Jathika Hela Urumaya (JHU) had 9 seats with 6 percent of the vote. In November 2005, Mahinda Rajapakse was elected president from the SLFP.

The frequent elections and shifting political alliances undermined the government's ability to implement policies. Both parties, for example, used the appointment of ministers as a form of patronage politics to win support of minorities, minor parties, non-*govigama* castes, and factions within the party. Kumaratunga promised before the 1994 election to limit the cabinet to 20 members. Instead, her first cabinet had 31 members; after the October 2000 elections, this was increased to 44 ministers. With 38 junior ministers, it was believed to be the largest cabinet of any country in the world. They were an extraordinary expense for the nation. Although their salaries were low, they were all entitled to free housing, fuel, and other perquisites that were estimated to cost about $4 million a month. It also meant that ministers were less likely to concern themselves with the business of the departments under them.

The political chaos of the Kumaratunga era was an important reason why her lofty goals in 1994 were never met. Nevertheless, political dissent was contained within a democratic framework, and even political extremists were brought into the mainstream. Neither a revolutionary nor an authoritarian alternative had much appeal. This is the one great success of her presidency.

EELAM WAR III

Eelam War III showed signs of being a stalemate from the beginning, but it took six years of bloody fighting for both sides to exhaust themselves before a cease-fire was possible. The LTTE lacked the numbers to hold the towns they captured, and the government forces were too small and undisciplined to occupy the countryside. Territory captured by the government was never secure enough to turn over to civilian control, which might have won support from the people.

In October 1994 the PA held four rounds of talks with the LTTE. The LTTE made four demands: lifting the embargo on nonmilitary goods to Jaffna, ending the ban on sea fishing, dismantling of the army base at Pooneryn, and allowing armed LTTE cadres to move freely in the Eastern Province. The government conceded the first two and agreed to review the last two, which it said could only occur after the cessation of hostilities. The LTTE accepted a cease-fire but at this point neither side was willing to risk peace for fear of losing power to their internal rivals. Talks began and ended abruptly in January and both sides began preparing for war.

The LTTE had built up its strength during the cease-fire and in 1995 was estimated to have between 14,000 and 18,000 cadres. They unilaterally ended the cease-fire when they withdrew from talks on April 19, 1995. They increased their attacks on the government while claiming to be ready to resume talks.

The LTTE suffered its biggest defeat in the war in July when the army repulsed a concerted attack on four bases in the Weli Oya region. Weli Oya is the largest settlement of Sinhalese colonists in the Eastern Province, in a region that divided the Eastern from the Northern Province, and thus a major target of LTTE attacks. In 1993 the LTTE had destroyed an army base in the area, when both the division commander and brigade commander had abandoned their posts. In 1995, the army was prepared and killed hundreds of LTTE guerrillas with little loss of life. The defender of the bases, Brigadier Janaka Perera, became a hero to militant Sinhalese nationalists.

In October 1995 the government undertook Operation Riviresa, a military offensive on Jaffna, over the objection of senior officers. Government troops entered Jaffna in November, after the LTTE had forced evacuation of most of the city's population and withdrew into the jungle. Holding the city tied down many of the undermanned government forces and weakened them elsewhere. Supplying the city became a logistical nightmare because the LTTE held the main road from the south; the civilian population and the troops had to be supplied by air and sea. Sinhalese euphoria over the victory ended when the LTTE retaliated with a suicide attack that destroyed the Central Bank in the center of Colombo. In April 1996 the army resumed its offensive and in two months controlled the remainder of the peninsula as the LTTE withdrew.

The government planned reconstruction and rehabilitation programs, but the peninsula remained under military control. When fighting resumed, the military occupation turned repressive, and the opportunity for winning support from the Tamil people for Kumaratunga's peace plan was lost.

The LTTE overran the Mullaitivu army camp on July 18, 1996. Despite warnings that the LTTE was concentrating forces in the area, the base was taken quickly and the army lost 1,344 men and military hardware worth more than $25 million. The LTTE lost 315 soldiers. The effect of the defeat was worsened by the government's attempts to minimize its importance. The Defense Ministry claimed for days after the defeat that troops were still holding part of the camp and that relief troops were fighting their way toward the camp. The government launched an attack on the town Kilinochchi, just outside the Jaffna Peninsula, and recaptured it in October.

The army gained control of the Mannar-Vavuniya Road in February, 1997, which allowed civilians to leave the territory, including deserters from the LTTE. In May the LTTE attacked their checkpoint. This LTTE provoked the army in to random firing, which destroyed the homes and fields of the local population.

After victory in the March 1997 local government elections, the PA government pushed forward their longest and most futile campaign. Operation Jaya Sikuru (Sure Victory) was intended to open a military supply route to the peninsula, 76 kilometers (47 miles) between the government-held towns of Vavuniya and Kilinochchi. If successful, the offensive would have split the LTTE forces in Mannar and the east coast and joined Jaffna to the rest of the island. It would strengthen the government's bargaining position both with the LTTE, who might be willing to accept Kumaratunga's peace plan, and Sinhalese extremists, whose resistance to the plan would weaken in view of the government's strength. It had little hope of success, however, and was opposed by military commanders. The IPKF had been unable to keep this road open with much stronger forces, and keeping the road open would have been a logistical nightmare.

Over 20,000 troops, supported by armor, artillery, and air cover moved north from Vavuniya and Weli Oya. Both divisions captured towns in the first week, but this opened them to LTTE counterattacks. In November the government launched what it called the final stage of the campaign, expecting only minor resistance. Instead, the government suffered heavy losses near Mankulam. The campaign dragged on for a total of 19 months, and ended only after the LTTE overran the army camp at northern Kilinochchi in September 1998, with another death toll of more than 1,000 soldiers. The government then captured the town of Mankulam, but Jaya Sikuru was quietly ended in December. In November 1999 the LTTE retook the towns that had been taken by the government during the campaign. Government soldiers reportedly refused to fight, and seven senior officers were ordered to retire.

The campaign created unimaginable hardship for the people of the region. Besides the casualties from the fighting, normal lives were disrupted, fields torn up, towns destroyed, and the number of refugees mounted. Tamil leaders in Colombo repeatedly called on the government to end the campaign.

In the meantime, LTTE terrorist attacks continued throughout Eelam War III. Although they do not claim responsibility for individual acts of violence, they honor 241 suicide people who have died, 30 to 40 percent of them women. Some suicide bombers have killed Tamil moderates, such as the two mayors of Jaffna, Sarojini Yogheswaran (May 1998) and P. Sivapalan (September 1998), and Sri Lanka's leading constitutional lawyer Neelan Tiruchelvam (July 29, 1999). Suicide bombers have been used against not only military targets but also civilian targets. On January 25, 1998, a truck bomb in Kandy killed and damaged the Temple of the Tooth. The low point in Eelam War III was a suicide assault on Sri Lanka's international airport and the adjoining air force base. On July 24, 2001, just 14 LTTE guerillas caused almost $1 billion worth of damage, destroying eight military planes and six commercial airliners before they blew themselves up to avoid capture.

Terrorism serves a number of purposes. It not only intimidates the Sinhalese, it provokes a military and civilian backlash against innocent Tamils, which helps drives Tamils into their hands. It helps to foster fanaticism in their followers. However, continued terrorism lost whatever international support there might have been for a separate state; the international community would not have recognized a separate state created by such means. Before the LTTE seized power, there was broad support for the redress of the legitimate grievances of Sri Lanka's Tamils.

The Sri Lankan military continued to grow in numbers and weaponry during Eelam War III but weakened in its will to fight. Its listed strength had declined in 1995 to about 112,000 but grew to almost 160,000 in 2002. The actual strength is impossible to determine, owing to the large numbers of desertions, estimated at as much as 20 percent of the forces.

Senior field officers have been rotated out of the highest positions in the military, and it is believed that Kumaratunga, like Jayewardene and Premadasa before her, feared that an individual or a faction might gain much power.

Desertion has been a persistent problem. Soldiers go on leave after a few months of service with a large amount of back pay. Some do not return until they have spent the money; many of these later try to rejoin their units during the many amnesties the military offers. (Amnesties have proved more successful than recruitment drives in recent years to build up the effective troop numbers.) Others use their military skills in the private security units created by politicians and other elites or turn to criminal gangs. A few have been arrested and sentenced by courts-martial. Up to the end of 2002, the army had 51,413 deserters; the navy, 4,833; and the air force 4,255. The number of army deserters actually increased after the cease-fire to 7,293 in 2002.

The civil war has been directly affected by the global offensive against terrorism. When the leading nations decided in July 1996 to enforce strong measures against terrorism, the LTTE's international activities were curtailed. Several countries, led by the United States, have declared the LTTE to be a terrorist organization and continue to do so. Their activities come under scrutiny of intelligence agencies, and the United Nations requires member countries to deny financial support to them and their networks. The resumption of U.S. anti-terrorist activities after September 11, 2001, put increased pressure on the LTTE. The international mood against terrorism contributed to the LTTE's willingness to negotiate, and a resumption of civil war would intensive global opposition. The United States has hinted at military support for the Government of Sri Lanka if this should happen.

DEVOLUTION

Kumaratunga's devolution proposals were announced in an Address to the Nation on August 3, 1995. A draft of the proposals was presented January 16, 1996. They require a new constitution that would give more powers to regional councils, including one in the northeast that would be administered by minority Tamils. The alternative, she said, was a continuation of the civil war indefinitely.

To avoid the politically charged alternatives of "Unitary state" and "Federalism," Kumaratunga described the political structure as a "Union of Regions." The country would be divided into eight or nine regions, in addition to a small Capital Territory. The regions would have independent judicial and police powers and autonomy in subjects devolved to them. They would be vested with the ownership of state lands with the right to alienate them. Their finances would also be independent subject to a National Finance Commission.

Even these modest proposals were subject to virulent attacks by Sinhalese-Buddhist nationalists. A self-appointed Sinhala Commission met in late 1996 and early 1997 to protest the draft proposals for the new constitution. It published a report on September 16, 1997, which called it "the biggest threat faced by Sri Lanka in its entire history of more than 2,500 years." It claimed that Sri Lanka had a "unitary character" for all this time and that the Sinhalese majority were "a disadvantaged section of the population." According to the Commission the central government would be "rendered almost totally impotent" by the devolution of power to the regions. The abolition of the Concurrent List would make the regions "almost independent states in so far as internal matters are concerned."

The draft of the proposed constitution that was prepared in November 1997 stood little chance in the face of Kumaratunga's unwillingness to stand up to such opposition. It was never formally presented to Parliament. The proposals suffered an irreparable blow with the assassination of Dr. Neelan Tiruchelvam in July 1999. Throughout 2000 Kumaratunga tried to rally a two-thirds majority for the constitution with only a one-vote majority. Wickremasinghe pledged support for the devolution proposals but wanted to confer with her over possible revisions. They met numerous times from March to July until a satisfactory draft was approved by both parties. The new draft proved unacceptable to minority parties, because they weakened the 1997 draft and did not go far enough, or to Sinhalese extremists, because they went too far. The latter staged many protest demonstrations and challenged the proposals in the courts. The draft was presented to a special session of parliament on August 3 but was withdrawn before a vote when it became clear that it could not get a two-thirds majority.

Eleven Tamil parties rejected the proposal on three grounds: It did not permanently merge the north and east; it placed too much power in the center; and it did not give the regions control over their land. The LTTE continued to insist on the Thimpu principles.

The proposal failed, however, not from differences on substantive issues (because no one had a better alternative), but from the open hostility between the president and Wickremasinghe. The government's devolution plan was similar to what the UNP had proposed earlier, but Wickremasinghe would not support it as long as it would be considered a political victory for Kumaratunga. It could only pass with UNP support, and this could have happed only if Kumaratunga would have found a way to share credit with the UNP. When it was proposed to Parliament, Wickremasinghe withdrew UNP support on the grounds that the president had not secured a consensus in favor of it.

CEASE-FIRE

Observers say battle fatigue had set in on both sides, and it was becoming increasingly difficult for the army and the rebels to find new recruits to fight a war that looked more and more unwinnable. The rebels and the government signed a cease-fire agreement in February 2002 and held peace talks until April 2003, when the LTTE withdrew. Since then a fragile truce has held.

The cease-fire has few concrete achievements other than getting the LTTE publicly to disavow their demand for a separate state. The government of Sri Lanka conceded the unification of the northern and eastern provinces under an LTTE government. There is opposition to these principles on both sides, but it remains a step forward. The great accomplishment is the reduction in the indiscriminate violence that characterized most of the previous two decades.

The cease-fire has had a number of other welcome benefits. Hundreds of thousands of internally displaced families have returned to their homes since.

(Although as of August 31, 2005, there were still 340,000 of an estimated 800,000 refugees who had not returned their homes.) Food and medical aid supplies were restored to the north and east. There has been rapid reconstruction of buildings, roads, and utilities on both sides of the border. Some land mines have been removed.

Six rounds of peace talks were held before the LTTE withdrew in April 2003 on the grounds that it was doing enough in reconstruction of the north and east. The first two rounds of talks were held in Thailand September 16–18 and October 31–November 3. Surprisingly, the LTTE agreed to accept regional autonomy rather than a separate state, and the Government of Sri Lanka agreed to share power with the LTTE. At the second meeting, security and development issues were discussed, and committees were set up to examine various needs, including a Subcommittee on De-escalation and Normalisation (SDN) to discuss the reduction of military forces. The third round was held in Oslo in December. Both sides agreed to share power within a federal system in which the Tamils would have autonomy in the north and east of the country.

At the fourth round of talks, the LTTE demanded a reduction in the size of army camps, and the army insisted the Tigers lay down their heavy weapons and disarm guerrillas in the northern peninsula of Jaffna at the same time. The LTTE adamantly refused and withdrew from the SDN in protest. The question of LTTE recruitment and abduction of child soldiers was brought up in the fifth round of peace talks in Berlin. The LTTE pledged that they would no longer recruit children, and both parties invited UNICEF to assist children affected by the war.

The sixth round of the Norwegian-brokered talks took place in the Japanese mountain spa resort of Hakone in March, where the Japanese envoy told the delegates that Sri Lanka risked losing huge amounts of international aid if peace negotiations failed to make progress. They could not agree on human rights issues. The LTTE chief negotiator, Anton Balasingham, denied reports that it was still recruiting children. That meeting was never held, as the LTTE suspended the talks. They cited the obstacles that the army presence in Jaffna presented for the resettlement of displaced persons was not allowed government, the lack of lack of financial support for resettlement and reconstruction, and an aid conference in Washington to which the LTTE was not invited. A seventh round was planned for April 2003, at which the LTTE was committed to make a declaration of human rights.

The LTTE demanded that they become an interim administration in the north and east, something that the UNF coalition had suggested in its December 2001 election campaign. This would legitimize the quasi-government it already had in place, however, and it would be politically impossible for any government to accept. The government responded with several proposals, such as offering the LTTE a Provincial Administrative Council with majority membership.

In June, a conference of aid donors in Tokyo pledged a total of $4.5 billion in aid, but this was contingent on progress toward peace and was never awarded. The LTTE said it refused to attend the conference because the government refused to agree to an interim administration but probably was unwilling to make further concessions to resolve differences.

Sri Lanka's Muslim population is increasingly distressed by the course of events. Muslims in the Eastern Province are angry at the failure of the ceasefire to protect them from LTTE persecution and have no wish to become part of state a dominated by the LTTE. They claim that more than half of the tsunami victims were Muslims, and they felt they should be consulted about aid distribution. In the 2005 presidential elections, many found it difficult to choose between Rajapakse, who seemed to be controlled by Sinhalese-Buddhist nationalists and Wickremasinghe, who seemed to be overly conciliatory toward the LTTE. Muslims have rioted, and some young Muslims are seeking a separate province, supported by extremist Muslim organizations outside the country.

TSUNAMI

Colombo received the first report of the earthquake from Indonesia at 7:05 A.M. Sunday morning, December 26, but did not respond. An hour and a half later the first wave hit the east coast; the west coast was not affected until 9:30 A.M. Forty minutes later the second, larger wave hit. The official death toll is 31,229 dead and 4,093 missing, according to the government's tsunami task force, although the Interior Ministry estimates the number of dead at 38,800. About one million people were displaced, and officially 98,525 homes were damaged. The total damage was estimated at $900,000,000 and replacement costs at $2.2 billion.

The disaster world-wide resulted in an unprecedented outpouring of government and private aid. Altogether, Sri Lanka received pledges of $3.2 billion. About 300 humanitarian agencies descended on the island and provided much needed emergency relief; they helped the Government of Sri Lanka to prevent further deaths from the lack of food, clean water, and sanitation.

Long-term reconstruction has been much less successful. A year after the catastrophe, only 20 percent of the homes have been rebuilt, and hundreds of thousands of people are in temporary shelters or living with relatives. Only 13 percent of the aid donated was spent. Many fingers have been pointed. Relief agencies competed with each other and sometimes did not cooperate with government. The agencies and government complained of the other's waste, corruption, and bureaucracy. Recipients complained of inequity in the distribution of benefits and of inappropriate or substandard goods or services.

The greatest problem was the distribution of benefits to victims in the territories controlled by the LTTE. The initial hope that the disaster would alleviate ethnic tensions was soon shattered. The LTTE response was swift and effective. Cadres immediately began evacuating survivors, moving the injured to hospitals, and recovering bodies. Bodies were photographed for later identification and cremated or buried. They insisted, however, that all aid be funneled through their Tamil Rehabilitation Organization (TRO). TRO is tainted by accusations that it raised money for weapons and used it for money laundering. In August, the British Charity Commission decided to remove the TRO from the list of registered charities. The LTTE in turn accused the military of harassing the TRO. LTTE propaganda did not acknowledge external aid. President Kumaratunga, at great political risk, agreed to sign a "joint mechanism" called the Post Tsunami Operational Management Structure (P-TOMS) for the administration of aid with the LTTE, but opposition from Sinhalese politicians almost toppled her government as the JVP withdrew its support.

One surprise was the resiliency of the tourist industry. One-fourth of 248 graded hotels were closed. Many of the large resorts were rebuilt and reopened for the 2005–2006 season, often with updated and expanded facilities. The government quickly launched a $320 million tourism drive, including a marketing campaign and priority to the restoration of tourism facilities. Tourist resorts were given exemption from the restriction on construction within 100 meters of the shore, and newer hotels replaced some budget accommodations and cafes. Many young entrepreneurs without insurance or capital were ruined, but new investors appeared. As a result, instead of the 10 to 15 percent decline in tourists, tourist numbers (which seem to include many relief workers) actually increased during the year until the renewal of ethnic conflict kept tourists away in the 2005–2006 season.

2005 ELECTIONS

Kumaratunga chose Prime Minister Mahinda Rajapakse as the SLFP candidate to succeed her in the November 17 elections. He defeated Wickremasinghe by 4.88 million votes, or 50.4 percent of the total 9.7 million votes cast, to 4.70 million, or 48.4 percent. The remainder of votes were scattered among 11 other candidates. Wickremasinghe shifted his policy from his peace program to economic issues, promising new subsidies, the creation of 3 million jobs, and doubling economic growth to 10 percent a year for a decade. He said increasing foreign investment to $1 billion a year would meet this growth target.

Wickremasinghe won support from CWC leader Arumugam Thondaman and Rauff Hakeem, the leader of the SLMC. They controlled large blocks of Tamil and Muslim votes, respectively. The decisive factor was the low turnout in Tamil districts, where the LTTE boycott the election and prevented Tamil voters from reaching the polls. In the Jaffna peninsula, for example, only 1,465 people voted out of 701,938 people eligible to vote. Those votes certainly would have tipped the election in Wickremasinghe's favor. After the polls, the LTTE murdered Muslim voters in the Eastern Province.

Rajapakse and his Prime Minister, 72-year-old Ratnasiri Wickremanayake, have been labeled "hawkish" and "hard-liners" for their close association with Sinhalese-Buddhist nationalists. Rajapakse made written agreements with both the JVP and the JHU. These included the revision of the cease-fire; abrogation of P-TOMS, and a peace solution within a "unitary" rather than federal state. The election manifesto did not contain these provisions, and Rajapakse may feel that he can amend them, particularly in light of his narrow victory.

Rajapakse has said that he would stop the privatization of state assets to overseas investors and would emphasize the development of agriculture, fisheries, construction, and industry. In order to help rural Lankans, some market-oriented policies might be restricted.

In his annual "Martyrs Day" speech on November 27, 2005, Prabhakaran said he thought that President Rajapakse had understood the fundamentals of the Tamil national question, but that he was considered a realist committed to pragmatic politics. He warned, however, that LTTE would "intensify" its struggle if the new Sri Lankan Government adopted a hard line position. Rajapakse immediately responded with an offer to reopen talks. Violence had escalated since the assassination of Foreign Minister Lakshman Kadirgamar on August 12 by suspected Tiger gunmen. The killing produced a strong international reaction, including a ban on LTTE travel in the European Union. Kadirgamar, a Tamil, had been an internationally known lawyer. In December and January there was a spate of killing of government security forces and anti-LTTE Tamil leaders. Although it has been called an "undeclared war," the response of the Government of Sri Lanka was restrained. The resumption of a civil war neither could handle would have disastrous consequences for both sides.

The Sri Lanka Monitoring Mission (SLMM) has been working hard to keep the cease-fire going, overlooking violations in order not to trigger a war. The government has now recorded more than 1,000 cease-fire violations by the LTTE, and the government itself continues to ignore their promises to withdraw troops and restrain the STF. Many Lankans believe that they are pro-LTTE because they do not treat them simply as terrorists, and there is a movement, supported by President Rajapakse, to enlist the support of India to guarantee the unity of the island.

The LTTE initially made considerable gains during the cease-fire. They were able to recruit fighters, propagandize Tamils, and carry out espionage in government-controlled territory; to fortify defenses, murder opponents and strengthen administration in Mullaitivu and Kilinochchi Districts (where the mou did not apply); and to attempt to reshape its image from that of a terrorist organization to that of a legitimate government. They have had a number of setbacks, however, that suggest they were weaker in 2006 than they had been for many years. In March 2004, Vinayagamurthy Muralitharan, known as Colonel Karuna, broke away and is suspected of commanding a force of 200 to 300 soldiers who have attacked the LTTE. Karuna has renounced separatism and is believed to be supported by government security forces. The tsunami is believed to have damaged much of their equipment.

Most of all, it has lost much of its international support. The European Union banned the LTTE, and nations in which the LTTE has collected funds from expatriates have moved to prevent such fund collection. Most important in this regard in Canada, where there are 160,000 Tamil Canadians. In April 2006, the newly-elected conservative government banned the LTTE and began surprising its front organizations. There was an abrupt reduction in cease-five violations on January 25, 2006, when the two parties agreed to meet in Geneva. They met on February 22 and 23, but follow up meetings on April 19–21 were cancelled, and the LTTE refused to meet with the government when both came to Oslo June 9. The government wanted to renegotiate the cease-fire agreement on the grounds that sections of the agreement violated the constitution. The LTTE wanted the government to restrain Karuna.

Neither happened, and cease-fire violations escalated to low-intensity warfare by July. Karuna refused to give up his weapons and continues to attack the LTTE. On April 25 a Tamil suicide detonated a bomb at Army headquaters, killing 11 people and wounding 26, including Army Chief of Staff Lt. Gen. Sarath Fonseka. In June bombs killed 64 people on a bus, and another suicide bomber killed Deputy Chief of Staff Lt. Gen. Parami Kulatunga on June 26. The government retaliated to these by air strikes on LTTE territory near Trincomalee and Kilinochchi.

As Sri Lanka headed toward Eelam War IV, diplomatic initiatives were underway by many countries, including the United States and India, to prevent a resumption of all-out war and to encourage steps toward a peaceful resolution.

A SINHALESE-BUDDHIST STATE

Sri Lanka has taken steps toward creating a Sinhalese-Buddhist state. It is possible that the nation will reassert its secular character after the civil war has ended, but for the time being, minorities are second-class citizens. Tamils are required to carry multiple forms of identification and are subject to searches and interrogation at any time. Non-Sinhalese-Buddhist areas under government control are under the occupation of Sinhalese troops. Government business is almost exclusively in Sinhala. Sinhalese-Buddhist nationalists clamor for increased privileges for the majority and have put pressure on Rajapakse to implement them, since he was elected by a solid Sinhalese-Buddhist majority.

The mood of the times can be gauged by reaction of Sinhalese-Buddhist nationalists to the growing conversions to Evangelical Christianity. Their numbers are not large, but the converts are highly visible, and some Buddhists (as well as some Hindus and Christians) have protested. Pentecostalism began in Sri Lanka in 1923, and the Ceylon Pentecostal Mission became the largest mission in the colony. The Assemblies of God is the largest Protestant church, even though the American Assemblies of God missionaries withdrew in 1963. Since the 1980s there have been waves of conversion, most often following the tsunami. Depending on one's point of view, Evangelical Christianity either is giving the converts something their previous faith did not or it is exploiting the people in a time of weakness.

Although Sinhalese-Buddhist nationalists have been proud of the conversion of Christians to Buddhism (e.g. A. E. Buultjens in the nineteenth century, S.W.R.D. Bandaranaike, Egerton C. Baptist, and Alec Robertson), some now argue that proselytization itself is immoral and compare the situation to the nineteenth century, when the government openly supported Christian missionaries. The Evangelicals themselves are well-funded, highly organized, and aggressive. They tend to use agricultural metaphors—"planting" churches and using "high-yield" methods to "harvest" Christians. Often converts are trained to open churches and to recruit new Christians.

The opposition to the Evangelicals is centered in Sinhalese-Buddhist nationalists, who seem to see the conversions as a global conspiracy to destroy Buddhism and Sinhalese culture. It is sometimes treated as an American plot—and the Web sites of the churches and George W. Bush are quoted to support this. There have been sporadic acts of mob violence in Buddhist-majority areas against Christian churches, but the main effort has been to pass a bill to prevent what they consider "forcible conversion." Although the right to convert is protected by the Constitution, the JHU introduced a bill in Parliament to prevent conversion "by the use of force or by allurement or by any fraudulent means." The Supreme Court ruled that at least some provisions of the bill would be constitutional, but it has little chance of success. Most top leaders oppose it, and foreign aid would probably suffer if even a watered-down bill passed.

Even if a resumption of war is avoided and steps toward peace are taken, the problems ahead for Sri Lanka are vast. Tsunami reconstruction will continue for years. Hundreds of thousands of Lankans are homeless, and hundreds of thousands are overseas contemplating whether to return. There are 1 million–1.5 million land mines in the north and east. They have injured or killed more than 1,000 people since 1995, including 153 deaths (not counting more than 2,500 military causalities). There continue to be 4–7 incidents a month (compared with 15 to 20 a month before the cease-fire). There are hundreds of cases of human rights violations by security forces personnel on which little progress has been made, and many charges that could be filed.

Many Tamil and Muslim parties have formed, and they want to be heard, both in regard to the government of then north and east and in such matters as discrimination in government employment. Economic liberalization may slow, but appears likely to continue, but its ability to lead to self-sustaining growth is still in question.

Notable People in the History of Sri Lanka

This biographical dictionary omits the governors, prime ministers, and presidents of Sri Lanka, who are listed in the Appendix.

Abdul Cader, Noordeen Hadjiar Mohamed (1879–1938). An MLC from 1913 to 1936, elected 1924–1930 and nominated the other years. President of the All-Ceylon Muslim league and Maradana Mosque, and manager of Zahira College. He wanted votes for Muslim women. Younger brother of gem dealer N.H.D. Abdul Gaffoor. Owned New Olympia Theater in Maradana.

Abdul Rahman, Wapachcha Marikar (1868–1933). Wealthy business contractor whose father (A. M. Wapachcha Marikar) had built the Colombo Museum in 1877. He was a nominated MLC from 1900 to 1930. He opposed the election of MLC and supported S.W.R.D. Bandaranaike.

Akbar, Mass Thajoon (1880–1944). Eldest son of a wealthy Malay coconut planter, who won a University Scholarship to Cambridge. As a leader of Muslims in the Legislative Council, he successfully lobbied to have *Mohammedan* replaced by *Muslim* in official records. He proposed building a University Campus in Kandy and making it a center of learning for all Asia. Served as Crown Council, Solicitor General, and acting Attorney General.

Alwis, James (1823–1878). Sinhalese intellectual leader of the mid-nineteenth century. Educated in English, he studied Sinhala, Pāli, and Sanskrit and published a translation of *sidat sangar_va,* a thirteenth-century Sinhala grammar, and a history of Sinhalese literature. He was a lawyer and Member of the Colombo Municipal Council, 1866–1878, and an MLC in 1864 and 1876–1878.

Amirthalingam, Appapillai (1927–1989). Lawyer who joined the FP in 1952 and became leader of the TULF until the LTTE assassinated him. He was an MP 1956–1970 and 1977–1983. As leader of the opposition, he negotiated with the UNP on the creation of District Development Councils. After he was forced out of Parliament he spent much time in Madras.

Arunachalam, Ponnambalam (1853–1924). A brilliant civil servant, he was prevented by racial discrimination from deserved promotions, but excelled at the appointments he did hold, such as Registrar-General and Fiscal of Western Province and director of the 1901 census—over the objections of English civil servants. After his retirement in 1913, he was knighted. He founded the Ceylon Social Service League (1915), Ceylon Reform League (1917), and Ceylon National Congress (1919). He was unanimously elected first president of the Ceylon National Congress.

Athulathmudali, Lalith (1936–1993). He was president of the Oxford Union in 1958 and taught law in Singapore before coming back to Sri Lanka in 1964 to practice law and, in 1977, enter politics. He was a leading figure in the writing of 1978 constitution, and he directed government actions in the civil war as Minister of National Security from 1984 to 1989. He supported Premadasa for president in 1988 but broke with him in 1991. He was assassinated in 1993.

Buddhaghosa (fl. fifth century). A Brahmin who came to Sri Lanka to translate Buddhist commentaries in Sinhala into Pāli. He based his *Visuddhimagga* (The Path of Purification), an encyclopedic compilation of Theravada Buddhist doctrine and meditation, on Sinhala sources.

Chelvanayakam, Samuel James Velupillai (1898–1977). A prominent lawyer who joined the TC when it was formed in 1944 but left it when its leader, G. G. Ponnambalam, joined the UNP government. He helped found the ITAK and remained the leader of the Tamils until his death, despite having Parkinson's disease, which debilitated him and impaired his speech.

Coomaraswamy, Ananda Kentish (1877–1947). Son of Sir Muthu Coomaraswamy (1833–79), the first Asian called to English Bar and Tamil MLC 1861–1879. After three years, he decided to dedicate himself to the history of art, and his *Medieval Sinhalese Art* (1908) gave him an international reputation. He founded the Ceylon Social Reform Society and the journal *Ceylon National Review.* In 1917 he became a research fellow of the Museum of Fine Arts in

Boston. He was made curator of the Asian Collection and remained there the rest of his life.

Corea, Gamini (b. 1925). A distinguished Sri Lankan economist who was a senior official in the Central Bank and chief economic adviser to the UNP administration of 1960–1965. He was Secretary-General of the UN Conference on Trade and Development (UNCTAD) from 1973 to 1984. After returning to Sri Lanka, he was President of the National Academy of Sciences 1994–1997 and active in the South Commission, serving as chairman in 2002–2003.

de Sampayo, Thomas Edward (1855–1927). A Roman Catholic who was son of a leading family of the *navandannō* caste. He won the university scholarship in 1877 and became a leading lawyer and judge, despite discrimination on the basis of caste. He was acting Chief Justice in 1923 and knighted in 1924.

de Silva, Colvin Reginald (1907–1983). A lawyer and founding member of the LSSP and the BLP, he also wrote the definitive history of early British Sri Lanka. He was Minister for Constitutional Affairs in the UF and was a key figure in the writing of the 1972 constitution.

de Soysa, Charles Henry (1836–1890). Son of *karāva* arrack renter and landowner Joronis de Soysa and also heir to his uncle Susew de Soysa's fortune. He devoted his efforts to agricultural development and philanthropy and was leader of the Ceylon Agricultural Association. He and his wife, Catherine, an heiress, had eight sons and seven daughters; their descendants and sons-in-law became some of the most important leaders of twentieth-century Sri Lanka.

Dharmapāla, Anagārika (1864–1933). Born Don David Hewavitarane, the son of a prosperous furniture merchant in Colombo, he took the name Dharmapala and the title *anag_rika* ("ascetic layman") when he devoted himself full-time to Sinhalese Buddhist revival. He denounced Europeans and non-Sinhalese Lankans for corrupting Sinhalese Buddhist society in his newspaper, *Sinhala Bauddhaya.* He founded the Mahā Bodhi society to remove the Bodhi tree in India (under which the Buddha is believed to have achieved enlightenment) from Hindu control.

Dias, Sir Henry (1822–1901). Sir Henry (Harry) Dias was educated by his elder brother, Rev. Samuel William Dias (1807–1883), in London. He was admitted to the English bar in London. He succeeded his other brother, John Charles Dias (1810–1877), as Sinhalese MLC 1861–1864. He was Puisne Judge of the Supreme Court in 1875 and 1879–1892. He acted as Chief Justice in 1879 and 1888 and was the first Sinhalese to be knighted in 1893.

Dias Bandaranaike, Felix Reginald (1931–1985). A kinsman of S. W. D. Bandaranaike and a descendant of James Alwis, he was a close adviser to

Sirimavo Bandaranaike. He served as Minister of Finance in 1960–1962 and 1975–1977 and was Minister of Justice in 1970–1975. His use of his office against UNP politicians led to commission of enquiry after he was defeated in 1977. He lost his civic rights for six years when he was found guilty of abuse of power.

Dissanayake, Lionel Gamini (1942–1994). One of the few successful UNP candidates in 1970, he helped rebuild the party. He became Minister of Lands and Mahaweli Development in 1977 and directed the AMP. He was expelled from the UNP after unsuccessfully attempting to impeach President Premadasa but was invited back after Premadasa's death. He was assassinated while campaigning for the presidency.

Goonesingha, Alexander Ekanayaka (1891–1967). As a pioneer labor leader, he founded the radical Young Lanka League in 1915 and was imprisoned by the British in 1915. He created the Ceylon Labour Union and became the leader of Sinhalese workers. He was an advocate of universal franchise during the meetings of the Donoughmore Commission. In 1947 he joined the UNP government.

Goonetilleke, Oliver Ernest (1892–1978). Civil servant who was Civil Defense and Food Commissioner and eventually Financial Secretary during World War II. As D. S. Senanayake's representative, he was High Commissioner for Sri Lanka in London, and he became the first Lankan Governor-General.

Guṇānanda, *bhikkhu* Mohoṭṭivattē (1824–1891). He learned English and studied Christianity at a mission school. While a *bhikkhu* at the Kotahena temple in Colombo, he became a skillful orator and a debater against Christianity in a series of debates from 1865 to 1873. He also made thousands of speeches and published many pamphlets

Jayah, Tuan Branudeen (1890–1960). Principal of Zahira College and one of the few Muslim leaders not from the wealthy entrepreneurial elite. The Maradana Mosque subsidized his salary to enable him to remain active in politics. He was elected the second Muslim MLC in 1924 but lost his seat in 1931. He supported the Sinhalese leaders before independence and was appointed Minister of Labour and Social Services in 1947.

Jayatilaka, Don Baron (1868–1944). Buddhist educator and temperance worker who became the leader of the State Council. After earning degrees from Oxford University, he was elected MLC in 1924. In the State Council, he was Minister of Home Affairs and Deputy Chairman of the Board of Ministers until 1942. He was editor-in-chief of the *Sinhala Dictionary* and also edited other Sinhala works.

Kannangara, Christopher William Wijeyekoon (1884–1969). He was an elected MLC from 1924 to 1931. In the State Council as Minister of Education from 1931 to 1947, he was a tireless advocate for universal free education.

Lorenz, Charles Ambrose (1829–1871). A leading lawyer in mid-nineteenth-century Sri Lanka. He represented Burghers in the Legislative Council. He founded the journal *Young Lanka* and made the *Examiner* the first Lankan-owned English newspaper in the island. He coined the word *Ceylonese* and advocated a nationalism beyond ethnic identities.

Macan Markar, Hadji Mohamed (1879–1952). Son of wealthy jeweler Oduma Lebbe Marikar of Galle. He was elected MLC in 1924. Elected in 1931 from Batticaloa to State Council, but lost in 1936. He openly supported the establishment of a Sinhalese majority government.

Mahanama (fl 500–520). He is identified in the first section of the Mahāvamsa as its author. He was *bhikkhu* from the Mahāvihāra named Mahanama. There are two other Pāli scholars named Mahanama at about the same time, and it is not certain if they refer to the same person.

Morgan, Sir Richard Francis (1821–1876). Although of Welsh and Indian ancestry as well as Burgher, he became a leader of the Burghers and very influential as an MLC. He had been one of the first students of the Colombo Academy and became the most successful lawyer in the colony. He was attorney-general and acting Chief Justice of the Supreme Court, but the governor knighted him in 1874 rather than make the latter appointment permanent.

Nāvalar, Ārumuga (1822–1879). Leader of the nineteenth-century revival of Hinduism in Jaffna who published anti-missionary literature along with scholarly books on Saivite Hinduism. He opposed social reform, however, and his commitment to preserving the power and status of the *veḷḷāḷa* caste weakened his appeal.

Péiris, Sir James (1856–1930). Son of a prominent *karāva* family. His father had lost a fortune as an arrack renter and he was sponsored by wealthy relatives. He won the University Scholarship in 1877 and was called to the English bar in 1881. In 1883 he returned to Ceylon. He became the spokesman for Sinhalese reformers in the early twentieth century.

Perera, Nanayakkarage Martin (1905–1979). Student of Harold Laski at the London School of Economics who left his position on the faculty of the University College to found the LSSP and win election to the State Council in 1936. In the early 1940s, the British proscribed the party and jailed him. He was mayor of Colombo from 1954 to 1956 and leader of the opposition in parliament from 1956 to 1960. He was Minister of Finance in 1964–1965 and 1970–1975.

Ponnambalam, Ganapathipillai Gangasar (1902–1977). A leading criminal lawyer, he was elected to the State Council in 1934. He founded the Tamil Congress and joined the first UNP government as Minister of Industries. In early 1938 he proposed the "50:50" formula, whereby the Sinhalese would have half of the seats in the legislature and the minorities half. After independence he was accused of sacrificing Tamil interests to his self-interest because he did not resist the disenfranchisement of the Plantation Tamils and did press for implementation of the BC Pact. At the end of his career he joined the TULF.

Prabakaran, Velupillai (b. 1954). From the *karaiyar* village of Velvettiturai, noted historically for its trade, legal and illegal, with India, he founded the LTTE in 1976 and used it to eliminate other Tamil leaders and separatist groups while fighting the Sri Lankan government. He remains the chief leader of the LTTE and dictator of the territories they control.

Ramanathan, Ponnambalam (1851–1930). A lawyer is best known for editing the official Law Reports. He served as Solicitor General from 1892 to 1908 and was appointed a King's Counsel in 1903. He was elected MLC in 1911, but, unlike his brother, he was socially and religiously reactionary. He alienated Muslims, first by saying in 1885 that they should be considered ethnically Tamils and then by his efforts to secure justice for Sinhalese after the 1915 riots. He opposed the Donoughmore reforms.

Saranankara, *bhikkhu* Väliviti (1698–1778). He established his reputation as a scholar and carried out reforms of the Sangha, particularly under Kirti Sri Rajasingha, who had him ordained Sangharaja, or head of the *sangha*. The *upasampada* (higher ordination) was restored in 1753; with the assistance of *bhikkhus* from Siam the Siyam Nikāya was founded.

Śrī Sumaṅgala, *bhikkhu* Hikkaḍuvē (1827–1911). Buddhist scholar and teacher whose influence spans the period from the revival of Kandyan Buddhist to modern Sinhalese-Buddhist nationalism. In 1865 he presided over a Buddhist council in imitation of the historical ones. He took part in Buddhist-Christian controversies without losing the respect of British officials. He founded Vidyodaya Pirivena in 1873 and was editor of the Theosophical Society's newspaper *Sarasavi Sandarasa* (1880).

Sundaram, Periannan (1890–1957). The son of a *kangāni* who became a lawyer and spokesman for Plantation Tamils. He founded the Ceylon Workers' Federation and was lecturer the Ceylon Law College. He was elected to the first State Council and was Minister of Labour 1931–1936, during which time he led labor legislation through the State Council and negotiated with the pro-planter Commissioner of Labour. He was the first president of the CIC and worked with S. Thondaman for Plantation Tamil rights.

Thondaman, Wana Ena Kana Runa Saumiya moorty (1913–1999). The leader of the CWC, he became a valuable ally to the Sinhalese parties because he could bring Plantation Tamil support to their governments. He was first elected to Parliament in 1947 and was appointed to Parliament in 1960. He served as a Minister continuously from 1977 until his death. His efforts contributed to the government belatedly giving citizenship to Plantation Tamils.

Wickramasinghe, Martin (1891–1976). Influential editor and author. He wrote his first novel in 1914 and became editor of the two Sinhala publications of the Lake House group of newspapers, *Silumina* (weekly) and *Dinamina* (daily). He wrote eighteen novels, several collections of short stories, and works on literary history and literary appreciation, society, and culture of the Sinhalese, which in translation influenced the English-educated population.

Wijeweera, Rohana (1943–1989). Leader of the JVP, he founded the party on his return from the Soviet Union in the late 1960s. He was convicted and imprisoned for his role in the abortive insurrection of the JVP in 1971. On his release from prison in 1978, he reorganized the JVP and entered mainstream politics. He was believed to have led the JVP terror campaign of 1988–1989 hat virtually paralyzed the normal life of the country outside the northeast.

Appendix: Sri Lankan Sovereigns, Dutch and British Governors, Prime Ministers, and Presidents

NOTABLE KINGS AND QUEENS

B.C.E.

Devānampiya Tissa	250–210
Elāra	205–161
Duṭṭhagāmani	161–137
Vaṭṭagāmani Abhaya	103, 89–77
Queen Anuḷā	44–22

C.E.

Vasabha	67–111
Gajabāhu I	114–136
Mahāsena	274–301
Dhātusena	455–473
Kasyapa I	477

Mānavarma	684–718
Sena I	831–851
Sena II	853–887
Vijayabāhu I	1055–1110
Parākramabāhu I	1153–1186
Nissanka Malla	1232–1236
Queen Lilāwatī	1197–1200, 1209–1210, 1211–1212
Kaliga Māgha	1214–1256
Vihayabāhu III (Gampola)	1232–1236
Parākramabāhu II	1236–1270
Vijayabāhu IV	1270–1272
Bhuvanekabāhu I	1272–1284
Parākramabāhu III	1287–1293
Bhuvanekabāhu II	1293–1302
Parākramabāhu IV	1302–1326
Varōtaya Cikaiyāriyan (Jaffna)	1310–1323
Bhuvanekabāhu IV	1341–1351
Parākramabāhu V	1344–1359
Vikramabāhu III	1356–1374
Bhuvanekabāhu V (Gampola and Koṭṭē)	1371–1408
Parākramabāhu VI (Koṭṭē)	1411–1467
Pararājāsekara (Jaffna)	1478–1519
Dharma Parākramabāhu	1498–1527
Cakili I (Jaffna)	1519–1561
Bhuvanekabāhu VII	1521–1551
Māyadunnē (Sītāwaka)	1521–1581
Vijayabāhu VII	1527–1534

Dharmapāla (Koṭṭē)	1551–1597
Rājasingha I	1581–1593
Vimaladharmasūriya	1592–1604
Senerat	1604–1635
Rājasingha II	1635–1687
Vimaladharmasūriya II	1687–1707
Śrīvijayarājasingha	1739–1747
Kirtīśrīrājasingha	1747–1782
Rājadirājasingha	1782–1798
Śrīwikremarājasingha	1798–1815

DUTCH GOVERNORS

Willem Jacobsz Coster	1640
Jan Thijssen	1640–1646
Joan Maetsuycker	1646–1650
Jacob Van Kittensteyn	1650–1653
Adriaan Van Der Meijden	1653–1662
Rijcklof Van Goens	1662–1663
Jacob Hustaert	1663–1664
Rijcklof Van Goens	1665–1675
Rijcklof Van Goens Junior	1675–1679
Laurens Pijl	1679–1692
Thomas Van Rhee	1692–1697
Gerrit De Heere	1697–1702
Cornelis Jan Simonsz	1703–1707
Hendrik Bekker	1707–1716
Isaac Augustijn Rumf	1716–1723
Johannes Hertenberg	1723–1725
Johan Paul Schagen	1725–1726
Pieter Vuyst	1726–1729

Stephanus Versluys	1729–1732
Jacob Christiaan Pielat	1732–1733
Diederik Van Domburch	1733–1736
Gustaaf Willem Baron Van Imhoff	1736–1740
Willelm Maurits Bruininck	1740–1742
Daniel Overbeek	1742–1743
Julius Valentijn Steijn Van Gollonesse	1743–1751
Gerard Joan Vreelandt	1751–1752
Joan Gideon Loten	1752–1757
Jan Schreuder	1757–1762
Lubbert Jan Baron Van Eck	1762–1765
Iman Wilhelm Falck	1765–1785
Willelm Jacob Van De Graaff	1785–1794
Johan Gerard Van Angelbeek	1794–1796

BRITISH GOVERNORS

Frederick North	1798–1805
Sir Thomas Maitland	1805–1811
Sir Robert Brownrigg	1812–1820
Sir Edward Paget	1822–1823
Sir Edward Barnes	1824–1831
Sir Robert Wilmot Horton	1831–1837
J. A. Stewart Mackenzie	1837–1841
Sir Colin Campbell	1841–1847
Lord Torrington	1847–1850
Sir George Anderson	1850–1855
Sir Henry Ward	1855–1860
Sir Charles MacCarthy	1860–1863
Sir Hercules Robinson	1865–1872

Sir William Gregory	1872–1877
Sir James Longden	1877–1883
Sir Arthur Hamilton Gordon	1883–1890
Sir Arthur Havelock	1890–1895
Sir Joseph West Ridgeway	1895–1903
Sir Henry Blake	1903–1907
Sir Henry McCallum	1907–1913
Sir Robert Chalmers	1913–1916
Sir John Anderson	1916–1918
Sir William Manning	1918–1925
Sir Hugh Clifford	1925–1927
Sir Herbert Stanley	1927–1931
Sir Graeme Thomson	1931–1933
Sir Reginald Edward Stubbs	1933–1937
Sir Andrew Caldecott	1937–1944

GOVERNORS-GENERAL

Sir Henry Monck-Mason-Moore	1948–1949
Viscount Soulbury	1949–1954
Sir Oliver Ernest Goonetilleke	1954–1962
William Gopallawa	1962–1972

PRESIDENT

William Gopallawa	1972–1978

EXECUTIVE PRESIDENTS

Junius Richard Jayewardene	Feb. 1978–Jan. 1990
Ranasinghe Premadasa	Jan. 1990–May 1993
D. B. Wijetunge	May 1993–Nov. 1994

Chandrika Bandaranaike Kumaratunga	Nov. 1994–Nov. 2005
Mahinda Rajapakse	Nov. 2005–present

PRIME MINISTERS

Don Stephen Senanayake	Sep. 1947–Mar. 1952
Dudley Shelton Senanayake	Mar. 1952–Oct. 1, 1953
Sir John Kotelawala	Oct. 1953–Apr. 1956
Solomon West Ridgeway Dias Bandaranaike	Apr. 1956–Sep. 1959
Wijayananda Dahanayake	Sep. 1959–Mar. 1960
Dudley Shelton Senanayake	Mar. 1960–Jul. 1960
Sirimavo Ratwatte Dias Bandaranaike	Jul. 1960–Mar. 1965
Dudley Shelton Senanayake	Mar. 1965–May 1970
Sirimavo Ratwatte Dias Bandaranaike	May 1970–Jul. 1977
Junius Richard Jayewardene	Jul. 1977–Feb. 1978
Ranasinghe Premadasa	Feb. 1978–Jan. 1990
D. B. Wijetunge	Jan. 1990–May 1993
Ranil Wickremasinghe	May 1993–Aug. 1994
Chandrika Bandaranaike Kumaratunga	Aug. 1994–Nov. 1994
Sirimavo Ratwatte Dias Bandaranaike	Nov. 1994–Aug. 2000
Ratnasiri Wickramanayake	Aug. 2000–Dec. 2001
Ranil Wickremasinghe	Dec. 2001–Apr. 2004
Mahinda Rajapakse	Apr. 2004–Nov. 2005
Ratnasiri Wickramanayake	Nov. 2005–present

Glossary

Accelerated Mahaweli Program: A 1960s irrigation and hydroelectric project "accelerated" in the 1980s by implementing four large dam projects.

***adigār*:** One of two principal ministers of the Kandyan kingdom.

***āracci*:** Village level officer, generally below a *k_rala* [Kandyan] or *muhandiram* [colonial southwest]; noncommissioned officer in *lascarin* force.

arrack: fermented toddy collected from the flowers of palms.

***aṭimai*:** Untouchable castes who were hereditary dependents of *veḷḷāla*.

***ayurvēda*:** Indigenous system of medicine. Now ayurvedic doctors, hospitals, and colleges are recognized by the government.

***badda*:** Department of caste-based service providers in the Kandyan Kingdom; a tax.

***batgama*:** Large Kandyan Sinhalese caste considered low status.

***bhikkhu*:** A member of the *sangha* , the Buddhist order.

***bisōkoṭuwa*:** Valve pit which controlled the flow out of ancient reservoirs.

***bodhisattva*:** Buddha-to-be.

***caṇḍalā*:** Untouchable caste among the ancient Sinhalese.

***chēna* also *hēna*:** Forest burnt and cultivated at intervals; generally sown with fine grains and vegetables until its productivity falls.

***cheṭṭi*:** South Indian merchant caste.

Crown Land: Public lands, claimed as state property by the British, equivalent to federal public lands in the United States.

***dāgäba*:** Also *cetiya;* dome-shaped monument built over relics of the Buddha.

***daladā*:** Relic representing a tooth of the Buddha.

***Daladā Māligāva*:** Temple of the Tooth at Kandy.

***disāva*:** Administrator of a province (*disāvani*) in the Kandyan Kingdom; also used by the VOC; the title was used by the British in Kandyan territoríes.

Dravidian: Family of languages spoken in India and Sri Lanka, used as the basis of ethnic identity.

Dry Zone: Area in the north and east of Sri Lanka that has a longer dry season and lower total rainfall.

***durāva*:** The third of the higher-status coastal castes; identified with "toddy-tapping" and often considered of lower rank than the *karāva* and *salāgama.*

Eelam: Tamil name for Sri Lanka; name given to proposed Tamil state.

***fidalgos*:** Portuguese noblemen.

***gamasabhāva*:** Village council or tribunal.

***gam udawa*:** "Village awakening."

***gaṇinānse*:** Members of the monastic community in the sixteenth to eighteenth centuries in Kandyan kingdom not admitted to the order as a *s_manera.*

***Gate Mudaliyar, Gate Muhandiram*:** Ranks given by British to mudaliyārs serving the governor.

***giri durga*:** Fortress in a high rock formation.

***goḍayā*:** Uncultured rural person; country bumpkin.

***govigama* (also *goyigama, govivanse, goyivanse*):** The most numerous Sinhalese caste, usually considered the highest in social status.

***hēna*:** See *chēna.*

***hēvāpannā*:** *Lascarin* grade of the *salāgama* caste.

***hēvāvasam*:** *Lascarin* grade.

***hinnāva*:** Low Country Sinhalese caste associated with washing for *salāgama.*

Indian Tamils: Identity assigned to Lankans whose ancestors came to Sri Lanka to work in coffee and tea plantations.

***Janasaviya*:** UNP welfare program.

***jātiya*:** "Kind" Sinhala term that can mean race, nation, caste, or kindred.

***kachcheri*:** Office of a Government Agent.

***kaduva*:** Lit. sword; used to refer to language as a weapon of the English-educated elite.

***kanakapilai*:** Tamil accountant.

***kangāni*:** Headman selected from among themselves or appointed by the employer of gangs of Indian immigrant labor in the plantation sector.

karaiyar: Caste below the *veḷḷāla* in the Tamil caste system, but still a high caste; called "fishers."

karāva: Caste below the govigama in the Sinhalese caste system, but still a high caste; called "fishers."

kōrāla: Chief of territorial unit known as *kōralē.*

kōralē: Unit of administration, generally part of a *disāva* or *disāvany.*

kōralē vidāna: See *kōrāla.*

kurudukāra: Cinnamon peelers, the section of the *salāgama* caste with that occupation.

kutimai: Tamil service and artisan castes.

lascarin: Indigenous militia. The term was first used by the Portuguese and continued by the Dutch.

mahā: Principal paddy harvest of the year, sown between August and October.

mudalāli: Sinhalese merchant or entrepreneur.

mudaliyār: Military officer of the *lascarin* force until the eighteenth century; representative of the Government Agent in a *kōralē* in British times.

muhandiram: Revenue officer in the Kandyan Kingdom; officer of the *lascarin* force below the rank of *mudaliyār*; used for assistant to *mudaliyār* by the British.

***nibbāna* (Skt. *nirvāṇa*)**: Ultimate goal of Buddhist practice.

nikāya: Lit. group, collection; a collection of *pāli* canonical texts, or a group of monasteries under the same leadership.

nirvāṇa: See *nibbāna.*

paddy: Milled rice.

Pāli: Canonical language of Sinhalese Buddhism.

paṭṭu: Subdivision of a *korale.*

pirivena: Seminary attached to a temple for the higher education of *bhikkhus.*

radaḷa: Pertaining to chiefs or nobles; highest sub-caste of the *govigama.*

Rājakāriya: Compulsory service owed to the king; any service to the king, a chief, or *vihara;* compulsory service to the state under the British.

rājaraṭa: The ancient heartland in the Dry Zone.

raṭē mahatmaya: Chief of a raṭa *in Kandyan territory* or district.

roḍiya: Sinhalese untouchable caste.

Rohaṇa: Southern Sri Lanka in ancient times.

rupee: Monetary unit of Sri Lanka since the late nineteenth century.

salāgama: Sinhalese caste identified with cinnamon peeling.

sangha: Buddhist monastic community.

sangharāja: Leader of the Buddhist monastic community, highest position in the monastic hierarchy created in 1753.

sāsana: Teachings and institutions of Buddhism.

Sinhala: Majority language of Sri Lanka, derived from a Prakrit, or dialectical, form of Sanskrit with substantial borrowing from Tamil.

Tamil: Dravidian language spoken in south India and Sri Lanka; named also given to an ethnic group that speaks Tamil.

***Theravāda*:** Lit. way (or doctrine) of the elders; Buddhist tradition that considers Buddha to be a man who achieved enlightenment and developed monks as to follow his teachings—not a deity.

***upasampadā*:** Higher ordination of *bhikkhus*.

***väddā* :** Rural people popularly believed to be descendants of the ancient inhabitants of the island.

***vanni*:** Region between Portuguese and Dutch territories in the north and northeast and the Sinhalese kingdom.

***veḷḷāḷa*:** Highest Tamil caste, which comprises more than half of the Tamil population.

***vihāra*:** Buddhist temple.

Wet Zone: Southwest region of Sri Lanka receiving an average of 250 centimeters of rain per year.

***yala*:** The secondary growing season for paddy; sowing occurs between April and May.

Bibliographic Essay

The best general history of Sri Lanka is Chandra R. De Silva's work, *Sri Lanka, a History*, 2nd ed. (New Delhi, 1997). K. M. de Silva's *A History of Sri Lanka* (London, 1981) emphasizes the history of the British colonial era. Some older general histories are useful: S. Arasaratnam, *Ceylon* (Englewood Cliffs, NJ, 1964); E.F.C. Ludowyk, *The Modern History of Ceylon* (London, 1966) and *A Short History of Ceylon* (New York, 1967); S. A. Pakeman, *Ceylon* (London, 1964); Zeylanicus, *Ceylon: Between Orient and Occident* (London, 1970); and K. M. de Silva, Ed. *Sri Lanka: A Survey* (Honolulu, 1979). The latest work on modern Sri Lanka history is Nira Wickramasinghe, *Sri Lanka in the Modern Age* (Honolulu, 2006).

The University of Peradeniya (previously University of Ceylon) is slowly producing a history of Sri Lanka. H. C. Ray's edited work *History of Ceylon. I, Part 1* (Colombo, 1959) and S. Paranavitana edited work *History of Ceylon. I, Part 2* (Colombo, 1960) appeared first. An abridged edition—C. W. Nicholas and S. Paranavitana, *A Concise History of Ceylon* (Colombo, 1961)—followed. K. M. de Silva edited the *University of Ceylon. History of Ceylon. Vol. III. From the Beginning of the Nineteenth Century to 1948* (Peradeniya, 1973) and *University of Peradeniya History of Sri Lanka, Vol. II: C. 1500 to C. 1800* (Peradeniya, 1995). All these volumes are collections of essays on major topics.

H.A.I. Goonetileke's *A Bibliography of Ceylon* (5 vols; Zug Switzerland, 1970–1983), is an exhaustive bibliography with many careful annotations. D. and C. R. de Silva, *Sri Lanka since Independence: A Reference Guide to the Literature* (New Delhi, 1992) is an excellent bibliography on independent Sri Lanka.

C. A. Gunawardana's *Encyclopedia of Sri Lanka* (New Delhi, 2003) is a personal view of many topics. S.W.R. de A. and V. Samarasinghe's *Historical Dictionary of Sri Lanka* (Metuchen, NJ, 1998), emphasizes recent economic history. P. Peebles's *Sri Lanka: A Handbook of Historical Statistics* (Boston, 1982) is outdated but contains historical series on many topics.

Ancient and Medieval History

The ancient history of Sri Lanka is slowly being pieced together. W. I. Siriweera's *History of Sri Lanka from the Earliest Times up to the Sixteenth Century* (Colombo, 2002) emphasizes economic history. Some landmarks of scholarship are S. U. Deraniyagala's "A Theoretical Framework for the Study of Sri Lanka's Prehistory" (*Ancient Ceylon* 5 [1984]:81–104) and *The Prehistory of Sri Lanka: An Ecological Perspective* (Colombo, 1992); S. Karunaratne's edited work *Brahmi Inscriptions of Ceylon* (Colombo, 1984); R.A.L.H. Gunawardana's *The People of the Lion* (London, 1990); R.A.E. Coningham's "Monks, Caves and Kings: A Reassessment of the Nature of Early Buddhism in Sri Lanka" (*World Archaeology*, 27 [1995]: 222–42); M. Ismail's *Early Settlements in Northern Sri Lanka* (New Delhi, 1995); and R.A.E. Coningham and N. Lewer's "The Vijayan Colonization and the Archaelogy of Identity in Sri Lanka" (*Antiquity* 2000) 74: 707–12. Collections of essays include those edited by K. M. de Silva, et al. (*Asian Panorama*, New Delhi, 1990), and R.A.L.H. Gunawardana et al. (*Reflections on a Heritage*, Colombo, 2000).

G. C. Mendis's *The Pali Chronicles of Sri Lanka* (Colombo, 1996) and L. S. Perera's *The Institutions of Ancient Ceylon from Inscriptions* (Kandy, 2001) deserve special mention as the published dissertations of two of Sri Lanka's leading teachers. Specialized studies include W. Rahula's *The History of Buddhism in Ceylon* (Colombo, 1956), T. Hettiaratchy's *History of Kingship in Ceylon up to the Fourth Century AD* (Colombo, 1972), and R. L. Brohier's *Ancient Irrigation Works in Ceylon* (Colombo, 1934).

Monographs on medieval Sri Lanka include P.A.T. Gunasinghe's *The Political History of the Kingdoms of Yapahuva, Kurunagala, and Gampala, 1270–1400* (Colombo, 1987), A. Liyanagamage's *The Decline of Polonnaruwa and the Rise of Dambadeniya* (Colombo, 1968), S. C. Berkwitz's *Buddhist History in the Vernacular* (Boston and Leiden, 2004), H.M.B. Ilangasinha's *Buddhism in Medieval Sri Lanka* (Delhi, 1992), S. Pathmananthan's *The Kingdom of Jaffna* (Colombo, 1978), M. B. Ariyapala's *Society in Mediaeval Ceylon* (Colombo, 1956), and G. Obeyesekere's *The Cult of the Goddess Pattini* (Chicago, 1984).

The Kandyan Kingdom is discussed in L. S. Dewaraja's *A Study of the Political, Administrative, and Social Structure of the Kandyan Kingdom of Ceylon, 1707–1760* (Colombo, 1972); A. H. Mirando's *Buddhism in Sri Lanka in the 17th and 18th Centuries* (Dehiwala, 1985); J. Holt's *The Religious World of Kirti Sri* (New York, 1996); M. W. Roberts's *Sinhala Consciousness in the Kandyan Period 1590s to 1815* (Colombo, 2004); and C. Wickremesekera's *Kandy at War* (Colombo and New Delhi, 2004).

Colonial Era to 1833

For the Portuguese and Dutch era, there are very readable firsthand accounts: P. Baldaeus's *A True and Exact Description of the Great Island of Ceylon* (1672), R. Knox's *An Historical Relation of the Island Ceylon* (1681), J. Ribeiro's *The Historic Tragedy of the Island of Ceilao* (1685), and F. Valentijn, *Old and New East India* (1724–1727). Many Dutch records of the colony have been translated into English.

Important monographs are P. E. Pieris's *Ceylon: The Portuguese Era* (Colombo, 1913–1914) and *Ceylon and the Portuguese 1505–1658* (Tellippalai, Ceylon, 1920); T. Abeyasinghe's *Jaffna under the Portuguese* (Colombo, 1986); K. W. Goonewardena's *The Foundation of Dutch Power in Ceylon, 1638–1658* (Amsterdam, 1958); S. Arasaratnam's *Dutch Power in Ceylon, 1658–1687* (Amsterdam, 1968); P. E. Pieris's *Ceylon and the Hollanders, 1658–1796* (Tellippalai, 1920); W. A. Nelson's *The Dutch Forts of Sri Lanka* (Edinburgh, 1984); G. D. Winius's *The Fatal History of Portuguese Ceylon* (Cambridge, 1971); and J. van Goor's *Jan Kompenie as Schoolmaster* (Groningen, 1978). S. Arasaratnam's *Ceylon and the Dutch, 1600–1800* (Aldershot, 1996) is a reprint of nineteen articles by the leading historian for the period.

Notable scholarly studies are Colvin R. de Silva's *Ceylon under the British Occupation, 1795–1833* (Colombo, 1953); P. E. Pieris's *Sinhale and the Patriots 1815–1818* (Colombo, 1950); B. and Y. Gooneratne's *This Inscrutable Englishman: Sir John D'oyly, Baronet, 1774–1824* (London, 1999); U. C. Wickremeratne's *The Conservative Nature of the British Rule of Sri Lanka* (New Delhi, 1996); T. R. Ruberu's *Education in Colonial Ceylon* (Kandy, 1962), and G. C. Mendis's edited work *The Colebrooke-Cameron Papers* (London, 1956).

Nineteenth Century

Scholarship on nineteenth-century Sri Lanka has never recovered from the decline of the humanities in the universities in the 1970s; much of the work under way then has never been published. Important works are L. A. Mills's *Ceylon under British Rule 1795–1932* (London, 1933); K. M. de Silva's *Social Policy and Missionary Organizations in Ceylon, 1840–1855* (London, 1965); K. Malalgoda's *Buddhism in Sinhalese Society 1750–1900* (Berkeley, 1976); H. Chattopadhyaya's *Indians in Sri Lanka* (Calcutta, 1979); M. W. Roberts's *Caste Conflict and Elite Formation* (Cambridge, 1982); J. D. Rogers's *Crime, Justice, and Society in Colonial Sri Lanka* (London, 1987); K.N.O. Dharmadasa's *Language, Religion, and Ethnic Assertiveness* (Ann Arbor, 1993); E. J. Harris's *The Gaze of the Coloniser* (Colombo, 1994); L. A. Wickremeratne's *The Roots of Nationalism: Sri Lanka* (Colombo, 1995); P. Peebles's *Social Change in Nineteenth Century Ceylon* (New Delhi, 1995) and *The Plantation Tamils of Ceylon* (London, 2001); J.L.A. Webb's *Tropical Pioneers* (Athens, 2002); K. Jayawardena's *Nobodies to Somebodies* (New York, 2002); R. F. Young's *Vain Debates: The Buddhist-Christian Controversies of Nineteenth-Century Ceylon* (Vienna, 1996); and R. F. Young and

S. Jebanesan's *The Bible Trembled: The Hindu-Christian Controversies of Nineteenth-Century Ceylon* (Vienna, 1995).

Sinhalese and Tamil Nationalism

Much of the history of the twentieth century is covered only in articles and survey texts. N. Wickramasinghe's *Ethnic Politics in Colonial Sri Lanka, 1927-1947* (New Delhi, 1995) is an important exception. A. J. Wilson's *Sri Lankan Tamil Nationalism* (Vancouver, 2000) is the personal perspective of a scholar and participant. A. Richardson's edited work *Blows against the Empire* (London, 1997) contains essays on Trotskyism. Major document collections are M. W. Roberts's edited work *Documents of the Ceylon National Congress and Nationalist Politics in Ceylon 1929–50* (4 volumes, Colombo, 1979) and K. M. de Silva's edited work *Sri Lanka: British Documents on the End of Empire* (2 volumes, London, 1997). Biographical (and literary) studies are M. Ondaatje's *Running in the Family* (Toronto, 1982) and Y. Gooneratne's *Relative Merits* (New York, 1986).

Economic and Social Change

There is a massive literature on Sri Lanka's economy, particularly since the economic changes in 1977. W. D. Lakshman and C. A. Tisdell's edited work *Sri Lanka's Development since Independence: Socio-Economic Perspectives and Analyses* (Huntington, NY, 2000) is a good introduction, as is S. H. Hasbullah and B. M. Morrison's *Sri Lankan Society in an Era of Globalization* (New Delhi, 2004) from a very different perspective. D. Winslow and M. D. Woost's edited work *Economy, Culture, and Civil War in Sri Lanka* (Bloomington, IN, 2004) is a collection of essays on how Sinhalese society has changed.

There is a substantial literature on women in Sri Lanka. Some of the most notable are B. S. Siriwardena's *The Life of Ceylon Women* (Paris, 1965); R. Coomaraswamy's *Women, the Law and Social Justice* (Colombo, 1983); S. Kiribamune and V. Samarasinghe's edited work *Women at the Crossroads* (Kandy, 1985); L. Wanasundera's *Women of Sri Lanka: An Annotated Bibliography* (Colombo, 1986); R. De Silva's *Women and Violence: A Socio Legal Study* (Colombo, 1993); C. Wijesekera's *Women in Our Legislature* (Ratmalana, 1995); S. Kiribamune's edited work *Women and Politics in Sri Lanka* (Kandy, 1999); N. De Mel's *Women & the Nation's Narrative* (Lanham, MD, 2001); S. Jayaweera's edited work *Women in Post-Independence Sri Lanka* (New Delhi, 2002).

Among the studies of how modern changes have affect village life are J. Brow's *Demons and Development* (Tucson, 1996); M. R. Gamburd's *The Kitchen Spoon's Handle* (New Delhi, 2002); J. Spencer's *A Sinhala Village in a Time of Trouble* (Delhi, 1990); and R. L. Stirrat's *Power and Religiosity in a Post-Colonial Setting* (Cambridge, 1992).

Some biographies of political leaders are H.A.J. Hulugalle's *The Life and Times of Don Stephen Senanayake* (Colombo, 1975); M. Seneviratne's *Sirimavo Bandaranaike, the World's First Woman Prime Minister* (Colombo, 1975); G. Dissanayake's *D.S., Man of Great Vision* (Colombo, 1984); K. M. de Silva and

W. H. Wriggins's *J. R. Jayewardene of Sri Lanka* (London, 1988, 1994); J. Manor's *The Expedient Utopian* (Cambridge, 1989); B. Weerakoon's *Premadasa of Sri Lanka* (New Delhi, 1992); A. J. Wilson's *S. J. V. Chelvanayakam and the Crisis of Sri Lankan Tamil Nationalism, 1947–1977* (London, 1994); L. D. Bandaranaike's *FDB* (Colombo, 1994); T. E. Gooneratne's *S.W.R.D. Bandaranaike, Prime Minister of Ceylon* (London, 1995). P. Liyanage's *VIVI: A Biography of Vivienne Goonewardena* (Colombo, 1998).

Language and Literature

Sri Lanka's historical literature is discussed in G. P. Malalesekera's *The Pali Literature of Ceylon* (Colombo, 1958); E. R. de S. Sarathchandra's *The Sinhalese Novel* (Colombo, 1950); M. Y. Gooneratne's *English Literature in Ceylon 1815–1878* (Dehiwala, 1968); C. E. Godakumbura's *Sinhalese Literature* (Colombo, 1955); and S. Ambikaipakan's *Some Landmarks in the History of Tamil Literature in Ceylon* (Mallakam, 1974).

Recent authors include J. Arasanayagam, who wrote *All Is Burning* (New Delhi, 1995), *Peacocks and Dreams* (New Delhi, 1996), and *Inheritance* (Colombo, 2001); D. de Silva, who wrote *Fading Traditions* (Sri Lanka, 1997); Y. Gooneratne, who wrote *A Change of Skies* (New Delhi, 1991) and *The Pleasures of Conquest* (New Delhi, 1995); R. Gunesekera, who wrote *Reef* (New York, 1994), *Monkfish Moon* (New York, 1996), and *The Sandglass* (New York, 1998); G. Liyanage, who wrote *Dona Kamalawathie* (Colombo, 1977); C. Muller, who wrote *The Jam Fruit Tree* (New Delhi 1993), *Yakada Yaka* (New Delhi, 1994), *Colombo: A Novel* (New Delhi, 1995), *Once Upon a Tender Time* (New Delhi, 1995), and *Children of the Lion* (New Delhi, 1997); M. Ondaatje, who wrote *Anil's Ghost* (New York, 2000); S. Selvadurai, who wrote *Funny Boy* (San Diego, 1997) and *Cinnamon Gardens* (London, 2000); K. Roberts, who wrote *The Flower Boy* (New Delhi, 1999) and *July* (London, 2001); A. Sivanandan, who wrote *When Memory Dies* (London, 1997); and P. Wijenaike, who wrote *The Third Woman and Other Stories* (Maharagama, 1963) and *The Waiting Earth* (Colombo, 1966).

Religion

Books about Buddhism in contemporary Sri Lanka abound. Some of the most notable are T. J. Bartholomeusz's *Women under the Bo Tree: Buddhist Nuns in Sri Lanka* (Cambridge, 1994); T. J. Bartholomeusz and C. R. de Silva's *Buddhist Fundamentalism and Minority Identities in Sri Lanka* (Albany, NY, 1998); G. D. Bond's *The Buddhist Revival in Sri Lanka* (Columbia, SC, 1988) and *Buddhism at Work* (Bloomfield, CT, 2003); R. F. Gombrich and G. Obeyesekere's *Buddhism Transformed: Religious Change in Sri Lanka* (Princeton, NJ, 1988); S. Kemper's *The Presence of the Past. Chronicles, Politics and Culture in Sinhala Life* (Ithaca, 1991); and H. L. Seneviratne's *The Work of Kings* (Chicago, 2000).

Contemporary Sri Lanka

The most thorough analysis of the political causes of the civil war is John Richardson's magisterial *Paradise Poisoned. Learning about Terrorism and*

Development from Sri Lanka's Civil Wars (Kandy, Sri Lanka, 2005). The latest word on politics is Neil Devotta and P. Sahadevan, *Politics of Confict and Peace in Sri Lanka* (New Delhi, 2006). Other works that place the contemporary situation in a historical context.

Some of the works on recent history that might stand up as historical studies are E. V. Daniel's *Charred Lullabies* (Princeton, NJ, 1996); M. R. Narayan Swamy's *Tigers of Lanka: From Boys to Guerrillas* (Delhi, 2002); A. J. Wilson's *The Break-up of Sri Lanka* (Honolulu, 1988); L. N. DeVotta's *Blowback* (Stanford CA, 2004); S. D. Muni's *Pangs of Proximity* (Newbury Park, CA, 1993); R. I. Rotberg's edited work *Creating Peace in Sri Lanka* (Cambridge, MA, 1999); R. Siriwardene's edited work *The Devolution Debate* (Colombo, 1996); J. Spencer's edited work *Sri Lanka: History and the Roots of Conflict* (London, 1990); and S. Gamage and I. B. Watson's edited work *Conflict and Community in Contemporary Sri Lanka* (New Delhi, 1997).

R. Gunaratna's books—*War and Peace in Sri Lanka* (Kandy, 1987), *Sri Lanka: A Lost Revolution? The Inside Story of the* JVP (Colombo, 1990), and *Indian Intervention in Sri Lanka: The Role of India's Intelligence Agencies* (Colombo, 1993)—chronicle the early years of the civil war.

The best source of information about contemporary Sri Lanka is the Web, although is it also the source of vastly more fanatical nonsense. Some of the best sites are The Lanka Academic (http://www .theacademic.org/), National Peace Council of Sri Lanka (http://www.peace-srilanka.org/main.html), Embassy of Sri Lanka (http://www.slembassyusa.org/), Department of Census and Statistics (http://www.statistics.gov.lk/index.asp), Central Bank of Sri Lanka (http://www.lanka.net/centralbank/), Art of Sri Lanka (http://www.artsrilanka.org/homeskip.html), CIA Fact book for Sri Lanka (http://www.cia.gov/cia/publications/factbook/geos/ce.html), Reuters Alertnet for Sri Lanka (http://www.alertnet.org/thenews/emergency/LK_CON.htm).

Index

About the Author

PATRICK PEEBLES is Professor of History at the University of Missouri, Kansas City.

Other Titles in the Greenwood Histories of the Modern Nations
Frank W. Thackeray and John E. Findling, Series Editors

The History of Argentina
Daniel K. Lewis

The History of Australia
Frank G. Clarke

The History of the Baltic States
Kevin O'Connor

The History of Brazil
Robert M. Levine

The History of Canada
Scott W. See

The History of Central America
Thomas Pearcy

The History of Chile
John L. Rector

The History of China
David C. Wright

The History of Congo
Didier Gondola

The History of Cuba
Clifford L. Staten

The History of Egypt
Glenn E. Perry

The History of France
W. Scott Haine

The History of Germany
Eleanor L. Turk

The History of Ghana
Roger S. Gocking

The History of Great Britain
Anne Baltz Rodrick

The History of Holland
Mark T. Hooker

The History of India
John McLeod

The History of Indonesia
Steven Drakeley

The History of Iran
Elton L. Daniel

The History of Iraq
Courtney Hunt

The History of Ireland
Daniel Webster Hollis III

The History of Israel
Arnold Blumberg

The History of Italy
Charles L. Killinger

The History of Japan
Louis G. Perez

The History of Korea
Djun Kil Kim

The History of Mexico
Burton Kirkwood

The History of New Zealand
Tom Brooking

The History of Nigeria
Toyin Falola

The History of Panama
Robert C. Harding

The History of Poland
M.B. Biskupski

The History of Portugal
James M. Anderson

The History of Russia
Charles E. Ziegler

The History of Serbia
John K. Cox

The History of South Africa
Roger B. Beck

The History of Spain
Peter Pierson

The History of Sweden
Byron J. Nordstrom

The History of Turkey
Douglas A. Howard

The History of Venezuela
H. Micheal Tarver and Julia C. Frederick